are we
there
yet?

are we there yet?

to indignity . . .
and beyond!

emily atack

SEVEN DIALS

First published in Great Britain in 2019 by Seven Dials
an imprint of The Orion Publishing Group Ltd
Carmelite House, 50 Victoria Embankment
London EC4Y 0DZ

An Hachette UK Company

1 3 5 7 9 10 8 6 4 2

A CIP catalogue record for this book is
available from the British Library.

ISBN (Hardback) 978 1 8418 8368 7
ISBN (eBook) 978 1 8418 8370 0

Printed and bound in Great Britain by Clays Ltd, Elcograf S.p.A.

www.orionbooks.co.uk

Contents

For my Uncle, Simon Barnes

Prologue

Hiya. This is weird. I'm sat on the 16.40 train from London Euston to Manchester. That's not the weird part. The weird part is that I'm typing on my own laptop for the first time ever. That is honestly no exaggeration. THE FIRST TIME EVER. I've obviously typed on a computer before as a kid – at school in those shabby little computer rooms that smelt like farts, where it was apparently just the perfect time to flirt with the boy you fancied. Swinging around on your chair and saying things to him like, 'I might get plastic surgery when I'm older', for attention. Or on MSN, or secretly trying to look at minger.com with my mates after school (still feel guilty about that). And there was, of course, Myspace, Bebo, Facebook etc. as I became a teen. But this is genuinely the first time I have ever typed on a laptop that I own. I'm 29, and I thought maybe that was a step I should tick off as an adult. So here we are.

It's Wednesday 16 January 2019, and I can honestly say the last year, and especially the last few months, have been the most interesting, insanely challenging, eye-opening and wonderfully life-changing months of my life. I decided to make some very bold decisions and changes, both in my personal wellbeing and in my career. Both of which, over the years, have been at times utterly joyous, and at other times really, REALLY shite. Whose twenties aren't sometimes? But by 2018, I had got to a point where things were at a bit of a standstill and I felt unhappy. Don't get me wrong – I have been blessed with a great life and so many wonderful things have happened to me that I will be forever grateful for. But ... I have also found that some of life's struggles have really got the better of me at times. And as the last year of my twenties was creeping closer, I decided to try to take control of my life, whatever that means.

This book is part of that. I'm trying to under-stand myself more, to work out what I want and to accept that I'm an all right human being, really, just how I am. Doing that properly means looking back and reflecting on how I got to this point: all the highs, the lows, the hangovers, the relationships, the lucky breaks – and breaks I worked my arse off for – that have got me to the here and now. Standing on this exciting but sometimes-bloody-scary precipice of 30, working out how I feel about it and which road I want to go down now. Basically, I hope you're sitting comfortably because you're all my therapists for the next couple of hundred pages. Think of me as that drunk friend who is waffling on in the back of the cab while you scoff your kebab at the end of the long night.

Some of you might know who I am from *The Inbetweeners*, some of you might only know about me from *I'm a Celeb* ..., some of you might have watched me in both. A very small (and I mean a teeny tiny amount of you) may have caught me in the odd film or two, on a random channel, on a Sunday night, when you should probably be asleep and there was nothing else on. But none of you will really know the blurry bits and bumpy moments in between. So, I guess this is a book that fills in those blanks. If you're on the tube to work, I hope you have a nice day. If you're in your bedroom, well done for not being on your phone! Light a scented candle, pretend you're an Instagram influencer (probably take a photo to show off) and get cosy.

are we there yet?

I've got my packet of crisps, miniature white wine and my shiny-new-totally-unfancy laptop (I've accidentally bought one that is absolutely massive. It's certainly not very portable and it's actually too big for my lap despite its name, oh and it's definitely NOT a Mac), so I'm good to make a start.

The 'Gang'

My earliest memory is when my sister Martha was being born. Nobody believes me, and you won't either, but I was 20 months old and sat in the back of a car with my dad's mum, Grandma Doris. (Yes, she's called Doris, ledge.) I remember being sat next to her, when my dad pulled over to have a massive row with a man who had a huge moustache. That's all I remember. Years later I told my mum that and she said that was when Martha was being born. I swear to God, to this day I remember that. I thought my dad was a hero because he shouted at the big hairy tash man who was scaring me and Grandma. (Although Doris would have absolutely obliterated him if push came to shove. She once grabbed two blokes by the scruff of their necks who broke into her home, whacked them with her gold walking stick and locked them in the bathroom. She's from Pontefract. Don't worry about it.)

My brother George soon came along, a year after that. I don't remember him being born, but story has it he was so massive that he had to be seriously sucked out by his head, which makes sense because his head is honestly the biggest head you will ever see on a human being.

So, there were three of us. Emily, Martha and George. We sound like a load of Victorian orphans. Martha is very organised, insanely smart, and utterly hilarious. She is extremely compelling, and strong-willed. Anybody who meets her never forgets her. She's powerful, yet really warm – I think it's quite special to have a solid balance of the two. People call it 'middle child syndrome' because the middle one is often left to fend for themselves slightly more than if they were born first or last, and I think that has always worked in Martha's favour. Since we were kids, she has always been getting me out of the shit. (She now happens to be my agent, so definitely still getting me out of the shit. But at least I can finally pay her to do it.)

In case I haven't made it clear enough yet, I bloody love her. She's my twin soul. You know the way twins say they can feel it if the other one has hurt themselves, or they get a strange feeling when one of them is in trouble or upset by something? We're convinced we can do that. Martha has called me some mornings knowing that I've had a rough night's sleep, or that something's troubling me: 'I'm getting a twin vibe … what's wrong?' It's bizarre!

Then there's George. He's a six-foot-one, very hairy, guitar-playing veggie who loves to travel and cook and garden. His phone is always smashed to pieces and he loses his bank card every weekend but he will give you the Black Sabbath t-shirt off his back and make you howl with laughter at any given opportunity. Everybody adores being in George's company because he has that skill of making you feel like you're the only person in the room when he's talking to you. He's like a hungover Jesus. It took him a while to find his feet in life, and he certainly had his struggles. Put it this way … the police used to describe him as 'a joy to arrest'. George was always, ALWAYS in trouble. But his charm and kindness have always won people over in the end.

Being three siblings born within a few years of each other meant an unbreakable closeness; despite the variety of head sizes we were like triplets. We shared a bedroom (Martha and George in a bunk and me in the corner in a very over-the-top double bed like a diva). We played nicely together, we got bollocked together. A trio of different personalities united by our sense of humour – and god, we were loved. Our parents smothered us with love.

Mum and Dad. Wow, where to even begin. Let's start with Mum.

My mum, Kate, raised on the Wirral, now queen of jazz bars in Soho, was once described as 'one hell of a woman' by a fan who came over to her at one of her shows. I was about nine at the time, and I remember thinking that was a perfect way to describe her. Mum's first big break in showbusiness was writing the song 'Surprise, Surprise' for Cilla Black. Later, her hit 'More Than In Love' got to number two in the charts. She went on to become an actress, impressionist, comedian, the lot. She's even represented the UK in Eurovision (they came third, smashed it). Her talents know no bounds and she's the most beautiful woman in the whole wide world. Okay, I know I'm biased, but seriously – she's utterly, wonderfully bonkers. (The anagram of Kate Robbins is 'a bit bonkers'.)

Dad. Keith – 'Keefy boy' as my mates call him. Born and raised in Pontefract, Yorkshire. A musician, a guitarist – a bit of a legend. My dad has been called handsome his entire life. As a kid, everyone would say to me he looked like Brad Pitt. Dad was part of the pop scene in the eighties; with his twin brother Tim they had a band called Child, and their biggest hit got to number ten in the charts. Not as good as Mum's number two, but what you gonna do? I'm just joking. Same as mum, my dad is an extremely talented musician. The guitar being his first love, but don't knock his piano playing – unreal.

Great for house parties. He has played in bands all around the world, and was Bonnie Tyler's guitarist for 25 years. I'll never forget going to watch him in this amazing tribute band for the Eagles and falling in love with their songs. (The Illegal Eagles. What a name!)

And that's the number one squad. The OGs. We called ourselves the 'Gang'. The five of us.

But really, we're a clan. Or as many a newspaper column has called us 'a showbiz dynasty' (lols). My life is blessed and cluttered with aunts, uncles and cousins. We are and have always been the closest family you could imagine, and, while I'm well aware that this is blowing my own horn here, I can promise you that you haven't truly lived until you've been to one of our parties. The good news is there's plenty of them to choose from – a Sunday roast can soon turn into a singing Sunday service like at Kim & Kanye's house – without the mansion. Our Boxing Day parties were particularly legendary growing up: hundreds of people would pile into our house, around the piano. My uncle Simon was a professional dancer and I remember him twirling all my aunts around the living room, winking at me and calling me Claudia – he'd tease me that I looked like Claudia Schiffer. Every year he'd line us up and choreograph dance routines for each of us. Just total joy. You have to come fully prepared for the tidal wave of booze, though. I'd advise milkthistle, alka-seltzer and the Monday off work. Famously, my aunt Lynne once slipped down the stairs on the balls of her feet carrying a drink in each hand and didn't spill a drop of either. That's a real Scouser for you.

Nowadays we sit in my aunty Amy's kitchen most weekends and have a laugh over a massive bowl of pasta and gallons of wine. My cousins are like siblings to me, and are the funniest people on the planet. Our family WhatsApp group is popping off every single day. We go from chatting about weekend away trips, to who we think would have the worst breath out of the *X Factor* judges.

And, okay, fair enough since you've asked, yes I *am* related to Paul McCartney. I'm sure he goes around bragging to all his friends about me (cough, cough). He's my grandma Betty's first cousin, second cousin to my mum. I have extremely fond, loving memories of Paul and his presence within the family growing up. He was very close to my grandma as she was there for him a lot when his mum, Mary, died. My grandma was a bit older and so really took him under her wing. She taught him how to play the ukulele. It was her and my grandad Mike Robbins who suggested Paul and his friend John (Lennon) play in their pub, the Fox and Hounds during a busy lunch time. They called themselves the Nerk Twins. And it all pretty much took off from there! They would rehearse in my grandparents' garage, and play with my mum, her brother and three sisters and sort of babysit them while my grandparents worked in their pub downstairs.

We spent weekends at Paul's house in Sussex when we were young. I remember acres and acres and ACRES of land with horses. Linda took us out riding when she was alive; I only have very vague memories of Linda as I was so young, but I remember her passing away, I actually seem to recall it was probably the first death in the family I was aware of.

Paul is so warm and chilled and loving. He once had Martha on his knee singing 'Martha My Dear' to her, a song that Mum and Dad used to always sing to her too. She turned and said to him, 'Oh, you know that song too!' To which he replied, 'Know it? I wrote it!'

I remember how lovely his kids were to us as well. I have particular memories of Stella, Mary and

James. Apparently, I used to watch James shaving in the bathroom like a little weirdo. He told me a few years ago at a party that I used to do that. How embarrassing.

My grandma Betty, my mum's mum, was one of the most beautiful women ever to grace this earth. She and my grandad Mike met at Butlins in the early 1950s, when my grandad was working as a Redcoat. He instantly fell in love with Grandma. He made her enter beauty competitions and she won every time. 'Miss Holiday' was her last title, I believe! I'd love to say I was also awarded a similar title in Ibiza but it's a book and they'll fact check it, so I can't lie.

Grandma was the funniest woman I've ever known. Her toilet humour ensured she would howl with laughter every time someone mentioned anything to do with farting. Together we'd gawp at gorgeous Spanish men on holiday and giggle in the corner, while she sipped gin and tonics and reapplied her lipstick. You would never see Grandma without her face on, ever. It was part of her routine every single morning. I often think of her doing her mascara, holding her mirror in one hand and the wand in the other, with a pouting concentration face as she applied it. Her skin was so soft and she always smelt of lavender. I can still smell her. Always laughing, always joyous, and just the kindest, most softly spoken and non-judgemental woman ever. She was a Samaritan for a long time, so she was perfect to talk to about any problem you had. I, of course, always spoke to her about boys.

She sadly got very poorly and deteriorated quite quickly in 2007. We sat around her bed in my aunty Amy's house and said our goodbyes, all of us together, as she passed. I remember clutching onto her body when she'd gone. I couldn't bear the thought that it was the last time I was going to see her and tell her how much I loved her.

My grandad Mike … what a man he was! The funniest man in the world. Utterly hilarious. An original Butlins Redcoat, he was a die-hard Wrexham supporter, and he adored Grandma. They called each other 'Percy' – no idea why. My grandad would be in the kitchen and he'd call to her in the next room, as she sat doing a crossword, 'Can I get you anything Percy?'

They both took great delight in watching all their grandkids grow up and were intrigued to see what happened for us, as they had such eventful times with their own kids.

Sadly, a year to the day that my grandma had passed away, grandad died. It was an unusual day, everything happened so quickly. I'm sure our mum knows what happened to him physically but it was never discussed at great lengths. I realise now that because our lives are so full of love, when somebody passes, we grieve and we take our time to do so but the crux of that person's death isn't ever discussed in detail (I suppose, why would you?). He fell out of bed, and as a result of the fall became very unwell over a period of a few hours. He had laid on his bedroom floor for a while, unable to get himself up, an ambulance was called (I don't know by who) and he was taken to hospital. I remember some family were in the area but my aunt and uncle who he lived with were away. Martha and I were around (we still lived near home then) and were called by Aunty Amy to go and see if he was okay. We got to the hospital expecting him to maybe have a broken wrist, but the doctors said he only had a few hours to live and that we should get all the family there. They were some of the hardest hours I've ever been through in my life – making those phone calls to everyone. To my mum, aunts and uncles, telling them their perfectly healthy dad was about to die, and that they all had to get there as soon as possible. Grandad was still conscious when Martha and I were there, and I'm so lucky, but feel so guilty, that I got to hear his last words. The football had been on that day and he said to me, 'Did Wrexham win?' They hadn't, but I told him they had.

Not long after that he slipped into a coma-like state and Martha and I just sat there, holding his hands and stroking them and saying our good-byes. Everyone else made it in time, rushing back from where they were just before his heart stopped beating at exactly midnight, apart from my aunty Amy. My heart broke for her as she rushed in pleading, begging not to have missed him. He'd been gone for just a couple of minutes. Watching her sobbing and saying sorry over and over to him was utterly devastating. A wonderfully kind nurse looked at her and said, 'Your mother was calling to him.' I truly believe she was. A year to the day, just, a few minutes past midnight.

Out of everything that's happened so far in my life, I truly believe that the thing I'm luckiest for is my family. I like to think I have a little piece of all of them in me, but I worry that saying that sounds big-headed because then I would be describing myself as the best person on earth. But I really hope I've picked up some of their kindness and generosity.

Together we've been through the most incredible times, but there's also been tragedy. We've lost people along the way, some sooner than expected, but our strength as a family knows no bounds. We'd go to the ends of the earth for each other, and always find a smile, glass of wine, and a party at the root of anything, whether it be for happy or sad reasons. Being together has always got us through anything.

My parents got divorced when I was 16. It was hell, but they're still very much together now. Not in terms of a romantic relationship or anything – my dad is happily settled with his girlfriend Claire, who my mum also loves. And they have a beautiful little girl, Nancy, our half-sister, who is the absolute best and very much involved in our lives. But they are together as friends, together as respectful humans who raised three children and gave us the lives we had, and now have. They are best friends. And they are a wonderful example of how it can be even after a messy and sad divorce. If you can let go of anger, bitterness, guilt and regret, and just cherish the good times; let go of grudges and look at the bigger picture. Was my mum and dad's marriage a successful one? Hell, yes it was. Divorce doesn't make it unsuccessful. Their marriage was just a part of my parents' 'journeys' that had come to an end. But everything else carries on; they will be our parents forever. That love will never die.

Growing Up

I guess you could say our childhood wasn't like other people's. My parents were off touring a lot of the time. Touring, working, filming. Sometimes we got to go with them which was really fun – before the days when parents were fined for taking their kids out of school, we'd often be found watching Dad from the side of the stage at a Bonnie Tyler gig. I remember thinking once, 'Wow … I can't believe all these people are here to watch my dad!'

I remember Mum being away more – not because she actually was, I just remember the feeling of it. I missed her! She worked her arse off to put a huge gorgeous roof over our heads and I would never make her feel bad for that. But I did miss her a lot, and I clung onto the moments of being with her when she was around. I think when you're little those things seem more extreme and you are way more sensitive to them, so she probably felt she was around enough. When she was away, we were very lucky to have a wonderful nanny, or child minder as my mates called her: Paula. Paula was an angel to us all, and still is! She was wiping my arse then, and she still pretty much wipes my arse now. She's basically become Bedfordshire's most sought after child minder, because she's absolutely excellent at it.

I missed Mum in all sorts of ways, but one of the things I was always praying for was the total thrill that she might be there to pick me up at the school gates. I would come out of my classroom imagining in my head that she'd be there to surprise me. She worked in London so couldn't really. That didn't happen very often, but I remember one morning she told me she was going to pick me up at the end of school, and I spent the day telling all my little mates that she was coming. (We were all little because we were children, just to clarify. I didn't have a group of friends who were especially small.)

I was SO excited. The bell rang and we walked out of our classroom. In my head it was always a bit like when you come out of the arrivals door at the airport, and everyone's lined up waiting and you feel dead famous as you walk past. And this time when I walked out, there she was. Tight leather trousers, tight leather jacket, massive-heeled boots, ciggy on the go, full face of make-up, and jet-black gorgeous hair. Still looking like an eighties rock star. And boy did she stand out like a sore thumb next to all the other mums, who would all tut at her and drag their husbands as far away as possible. My heart leapt with pride. 'DARLING!!!!!' she said, arms outstretched, and I ran into her arms as fast as I could. She always smelt of Elizabeth Arden flawless finish foundation, CK One and chewing gum. That smell of my mum will forever be my oxygen.

But for the most part, it all felt normal: it was our ordinary. We'd be running around the living room as kids, showing off in front of whoever might have come round for dinner or those who were there recording some tracks in my dad's studio. I remember once being pretty much butt-naked apart from my little pants, trying on Bonnie's high heels. She was so lovely to us, and we'd spend lots of holidays at her villa in Portugal.

One night – a school night – Paula put us to bed but then Mum and Dad arrived home, having been away. Mum gently woke me up and told me to get dressed and put my favourite 'lady shoes' on because we were going out for dinner. (My lady shoes were this red pair I was only allowed to wear for special occasions. They had a tiny heel and made cloppy sounds – I LOVED wearing them.) They took all of us to an Indian restaurant just up the road. It was probably only nine o'clock but it felt magically like the middle of the night to me. I remember swinging my legs back and forth because my feet didn't touch the ground, as Mum said I could have whatever I wanted. I'd tried Chinese spare ribs for the first time a few nights before but thought they were Indian, so kept trying to describe to the waiter what they were. He kindly kept bringing me out dishes and I kept sending them back. Now when I think about it, I can't believe Mum let me do that – but I think she was so desperate to give me what I wanted because occasions all together like that were so rare. I felt so lucky, and was probably the only kid at school to reek of garlic naan the next day, nodding off in maths.

We lived in a beautiful house. The Old School. It was called that because it genuinely used to be a Sunday school about a million years ago; it was also a church at some point. It was huge, dusty, bricky, covered in ivy and red and orange roses, with a big garden and an electric gate at the end of the pebbled driveway. Inside, it was a gorgeous mess. I hate myself for always moaning about the chaos, because when I think of it now, I'd give anything to go back there. Okay, sure, you couldn't find a pair of matching socks, and not a single sod knew how to work the TV. We had about a million remotes for each one, which we called 'the knobs'. (When I would ask, 'where's the knobs,' if I was at a friend's house for tea I'd be met with odd stares from my mate's mum.) And once you lost something, you knew you'd never see it again. The house was like a Bermuda Triangle, but dustier.

The thing that always makes me laugh looking back is that there were about eight bedrooms in that house, and yet me, Martha and George insisted on sharing one room together until I was about 13. We didn't want to separate. I had a queen-size bed, and Martha and George had bunk beds. Absolute chaos. Getting bollocked every 20 minutes because instead of sleeping, we were taking it in turns to jump off the top bunk onto my bed – we mastered the art of moving it to a perfect position to jump onto in order to get the best bounce. We would cry with laughter until really late and be little tired bastards in the morning when we had to get up for school. We missed the bus every single day and were always the last ones to turn up to registration. Everyone called us 'The Osbournes'. I kinda liked that!

The village we grew up in was a hamlet called Tebworth, in Bedfordshire. It was so tiny. It had one pub, a post office, and a really long lane that led to loads of crop fields and streams. We'd walk our dog, Rosie, down the lane with Dad at the weekends, and play 'cow splat': Dad would find the biggest cowpat and chuck a huge brick into it to see how far the shit would go. The idea being that us kids would all get covered in poo. It was hilarious. We'd get back home ruined and Mum would kick off. Great Saturday. Or Shaturday. Or SaTURDay. Sorry.

To everyone else, it must have seemed like we had a perfect life. And, in a sense, I guess that's true. I knew we were fortunate. Things were mad, but we were loved. I really want that message to be clear: we could not have been more loved. But as you get older, you become more knowledgeable, more aware of cracks, more aware of pain, and more aware that – actually – things weren't perfect like you thought they were.

From a very young age, I knew my dad was very much noticed by other women. Women at parties, at the shops, even friends of my mum's. I always noticed it and I hated it. I followed my dad around like an annoying little shit just double-checking nobody was trying to steal him from my mum. I guarded him and stared at women who I thought were trying to get my dad's attention. I think later on in life this little girl definitely practised the same behaviour with boyfriends. But we'll get to that later.

My parents loved each other. The one thing that was never lacking between them was laughter.

They would laugh and laugh and laugh, clutching their wine glasses in one hand, their stomachs in the other, while they wheezed and rocked. You know, that sort of laugh you get with your best mate in assembly when you think you might just pass out because you actually can't breathe. Sometimes I would sneak downstairs and sit just outside the main living room where they would be watching TV, laughing at *Parkinson*, or watching films, or I'd simply sit and listen to them chatting and laughing. Sometimes they'd catch me and let me sit with them for half an hour before I went up to bed. (That's how I first saw the film *Wayne's World* and it became one of my fave films of all time. Excellent!)

I would often sneak downstairs to try to persuade them to let me stay up with them for a bit. I wanted my own private 'eldest daughter' time with them while Martha and George were asleep in bed. I came downstairs once when Mum was away (knowing it was more likely that Dad would let me stay up), and he was making a quick dinner for himself as he'd got in late. He showed me step by step how to make it. It was a melon and Parma ham salad with a homemade dressing, loads of chopped things in it. I think this was when my love of food started! I loved all the colours of the vegetables and fruit, and bloody loved eating it. My dad is an incredible cook. He always made such a mess in the kitchen and it irritated the life out of Mum.

Our kitchen really was the heart of the home. It was huge and old and full of happiness when it was crammed full of people. It makes my heart physically hurt to think of it. From our fifth birthday parties, to the teenage booze-fuelled gatherings we had when our parents were away. The parties my parents had with family, neighbours, and every now and then a more work-based do where loads of celebs would come. I remember once our neighbour came storming into the house shouting, 'Whose bloody gold car is that on my drive?!' Then Des O'Connor poked his little head from around the corner of the kitchen and sheepishly put his hand up. Gutted, Des. (I swear that's completely true.)

All of this together probably gives you the impression that from the off I was quite precocious. I guess I could be both of those things in front of the people who knew me best, but I was actually really self-conscious growing up. Which was weird because ever since I can remember having thoughts, I knew that I was going to be in the entertainment world in some way. It was inevitable. I'd seen my mum be a famous actress and I guess, in some ways, I just really wanted to be like her. It was like repeat behaviour.

And, if I'm honest, I also wanted to be famous – for all the decent reasons, if there are any. I liked the idea of being admired and people knowing my name.

It was singing that got me first. I remember hearing Céline Dion when we were having tea at Paula's house one day. I was about six or seven and I thought to myself, 'Oh my God, how does that lady get her voice like that?' I gave it a go. The look on Paula's face was priceless, I still remember it now. She told me to do it again, so I did. I remember thinking, 'Oh, I can sound a little bit like that lady.' It was probably the first impersonation I ever did, but not my last! I love doing impressions; nailing a person's inflections and mannerisms is so much fun. I still do Céline on karaoke. But even then I didn't want to be anyone else. I didn't want to be Céline Dion or Whitney Houston or any of the other greats. I wanted to be Emily.

Saying that, I bloody loved me a persona. For a bit I was Tracey the pop star. I liked playing with my mum's lip gloss and, as soon as the wand brushed over my lips, it was like a spell had been cast. Over the speakers (in my head), a voiceover would play introducing me to the audience, and I'd whip my little blonde head round and look directly into the make-believe camera. My other go-to was Lola Red. Which, yes, I know, sounds a bit like a porn star name now.

But it was weird because I really was quite a shy child. All of this performing wasn't for anyone's benefit except mine and the bathroom mirror's. Mum would try to get me to sing for the neighbours when she and Dad threw their parties and I hated it. Singing felt too much like baring your soul, which is maybe why I settled more on acting in the end.

The first play I was in was *A Midsummer Night's Dream* when I was 12. I played Titania and it was a musical version: there was a big ballad and I won the drama award that year for it. That sticks out because I wasn't the best at school – for lots of reasons – and that was a dose of recognition that I was good at something. I wasn't *too* naughty or anything; I just wasn't fussed about sitting in a stuffy classroom, listening to things I didn't care about from teachers who I was pretty sure didn't care about them either. The subject I was always best at was boys – which is ironic, really, because they're still something I'm trying to figure out.

The People
Who Shaped Me:
The Cousins

As soon as I sat down to think about what was going to go in this book – a book about all the things that have got me to 29 years young – I realised that, if I was a ready meal, the packaging would read 'Emily Atack (60%)'. The remaining 40% is made up of weird and wonderful people and a glug of dry rosé wine. Those weird and wonderful people have looked after me, cared for me and gifted me some of their spirit. So, throughout the book I'm going to dot little spotlight pieces on some of these amazing people and how they've shaped me. And the first lot I want to shine a light on are my wonderful cousins.

Cousins are the best invention since the see-through Game Boy. They are basically 50 per cent sibling, 50 per cent mate. You look the same but different. You understand each other on a deep, deep level, and you have a smidgen more social etiquette towards them than your brother or sister. It makes me really sad for my friends who don't have that relationship with their cousins, because mine were the first best friends I ever had. They are still my best friends to this day.

The fact that your parents are also siblings is

often forgotten, but it's actually pretty cool when you stop and think about it. I think about me, Martha and George and when (one day, God willing) we have kids, I imagine our children being friends and my heart swells. Having so many aunties and uncles means I have a long line of first cousins who range from 13 to 36 and, to put it simply, there are no people on this earth I'd rather spend my time with. They are an eclectic mix of everything I love about people.

Most of them have northern accents like our parents, are model-tall, and they are all absolutely gorgeous. Growing up, we would spend spring days terrorising each other in a spare bedroom of my grandparents' house in Birkenhead, locking the smaller ones in bathrooms, nearly decapitating each other hanging out of windows and throwing sweets in the road. We slept in dens on the floor of each other's bedrooms, we stayed up late and ate midnight feasts until we were sick. We were bollocked on car journeys for swearing at bus drivers. We went to theme parks, sweet factories, Santa's grottos, and have gone on holiday together. My cousin Lydia is my make-up artist and is with me every single day. She lives three minutes' walk away from my house. Lydia and her brother Henry lost their dad

Simon a few years ago – my gorgeous uncle Simon. Simon was a choreographer, and danced for the greats like Diana Ross and Cliff Richard. Later in life, he was *the* Tinky Winky from Tellytubbies. Yep. You couldn't make it up. He was the guy inside the suit. Unreal! He was, is, such a huge compelling spirit in our family. Simon married my aunty Emma and gave us the gift of Lydia and Henry. He was gorgeous, inside and out. Watching the unimaginable grief they experienced was unbearable; all us cousins would stay up late messaging each other, asking who had checked in that day, asking who was seeing them that weekend.

They've taught me openness, love, friendship – things that I've looked to create with all my other friendship groups. They're my solid foundations that everything else is built upon and it doesn't matter what happens in the rest of my life – if all the walls are knocked down, I know those foundations will still be there. They make me think of those Ellie Goulding lyrics: 'When I'm standing with you, I'm standing with an army.'

The cousins have just started to have babies and there are weddings on the horizon. When Christmas comes around you'll find us girl cousins crammed onto a sofa, screaming, drinking fizz, talking about boys, laughing until we almost die. Even now, approaching 30, the thought of pulling into the driveway of an aunt's house for a birthday party, knowing the cousin crew are in; inside or in the garden – and thinking of that cheer of 'Wheeeey' as one more arrives – makes me laugh out loud.

They are the little added extra in my life, the bonus gold star in my sky. I couldn't live without them.

The Nineties
Best Bits

The TV was amazing – *The Queen's Nose, Goosebumps, Saved by the Bell, Sister, Sister, Sabrina the Teenage Witch.* I got a bit hot under the collar over *Neighbours* for a bit when I was very little. When we were a bit older, we'd stay up late on a Friday with next door's kids and Sky TV came along, WWE Wrestling (then WWF), The Box music channel and *Jackass* . . . then you'd flick over to Babestation for your first porn experience and scream at the girls twerking and chatting on their phones.

Tammy Girl – remember how amazingly slutty all the clothes were? Including the silky pyjamas. The photobooth in Tammy was well ahead of its time.

Sugar magazine – the Q and A pages were the best, and you could learn song lyrics from a back page of the magazine.

The internet – I mean pre-Insta, pre-iphone, house-phone internet. It took forever to load, cost hundreds of pounds to use, and there was that dial-up tone that sounded like you were going to the moon when you connected to it. No one could use it and make a phone call at the same time. It felt like an alien world.

Scented gel pens – caused no end of problems in middle school. Full gang wars over who had what scent.

Happiness was simply pens that smelt like grapes. Don't even get me started on the popcorn one . . .

Renting videos – we didn't have a Blockbuster near us, but the little convenience shop in the next village had a video rental bit at the back. Thrilling if we were allowed to rent one. It was a *bit * seedy, you'd go behind a curtain to find 3 walls of videos. Rude ones on the top shelf with ladies with their tits out on the cover. We almost always forgot to return them and had to pay a fine.

Beanie Babies – they were such a waste of money and yet we had millions of them. Again, another reason for many arguments and fall outs.

The Top 40 – it was on the radio on a Sunday and if you remembered to listen to it you could tape the songs you liked using a cassette.

Tamigotchis – except, okay, I never actually forgot about those very cute, utterly bizarre little digital pets. They were so great for the five minutes before you got bored with them.

The jelly aliens that live in goo – everyone would say that their one had given birth if you hold them together by their bums. It's a load of bollocks.

School Discos, youth clubs (always terrifying), Boys To Men ballads, Ben from A1's curtains, *Titanic*, playing Snake on the 3310... *sigh*

First Time
For Everything

First Kiss

I was ten, it was with a boy called James who lived next door to us. All the local kids would play down the crop fields – they were really fun days. We were all playing kiss chase one day and James kept going for me. I was chuffed cos I'd fancied him for about a week and liked playing with him, he was a good laugh. Sweet little ginger lad, looked a bit like Tintin. While we were playing kiss chase, he said to me, 'Have you ever got off with anyone before?' ('Got off' means 'snog', for anyone unfamiliar.) I said, 'Err, yeah, course, loads of times', and we agreed to count to three and give it a go. One … two … three. Then his little tongue hit my mouth and I was so morti-fied that I ran home, bright red, to have my tea. And I'll never forget my mum ACTUALLY said to me, 'You're all flushed, have you been kissing a boy?!' PAH, yeah right, Mum, chill out!! (Christ, she knew me so well even then.) So not really a first KISS as such. More of an embarrassing attempt that didn't go to plan, which I don't blame James for. I bottled it.

First Actual Snog

I was about 11 and in a park that was near to my house with some slightly older boys. I used to lie about my age a lot so I could hang around with the older kids. The boys were drinking cider and running around pretending to be drunk. There was one particular boy called Chris who I liked and he was paying me some attention, and he then kissed me out of nowhere. I've no idea how I blagged it, but we were snogging for about an hour until my little shite of a brother ran over and saw us and thought it was the funniest thing he'd ever seen. He said if Chris didn't buy him an ice cream from the ice-cream van, he was definitely going to tell Mum. I was on a bit of a roll and realised I was good at snogging, so then snogged Chris's mate Kyle about an hour later. So many ice creams bought for my brother that day. And he still told Mum anyway and I was banned from wearing make-up for a month. Little prick.

First Fag

It was also when I was 11 that I started hanging around with an older girl called Stacey. Stacey was my idol growing up, my real-life Beyoncé. She was naturally pretty, tall, slim, had pale freckly skin and was always changing her hair colour. Essentially a mega-gorgeous chameleon. She introduced me to most things in life, a Benson & Hedges super king being one of them. Her parents were smokers and were out one day while we were at her house, so we nicked one of her mum's fags and had it out the back door to the garden. I watched her and copied how she did it. I held the smoke in my mouth and blew it out. It tasted rank but I liked the thrill of it so did this a few times with her and the older boys, until one day I accidentally took it down and inhaled the smoke ... i.e. I accidentally smoked it properly – and promptly coughed my guts up.

First Drink

This is going to make me sound like I'm showing off. But the first time I ever got properly drunk was at a Paul McCartney concert. Because of the family connection we were in the VIP section, where there's always endless amounts of free champagne. I was about 12, but I looked 19, and I just kept secretly swigging the champagne. Because all my mum's side of the family are Scousers, the party vibes were in full flow and it was very easy to get away with being sneaky with the booze. I remember thinking, 'Oh wow, I think I'm actually drunk' … so then carried on and on. Next thing I knew, loads of aunties and Mum were gathered around me trying to pick me up, saying to each other, 'How much has she had to drink?!' Which I found hilarious because I was fine. I was having a great time! Of course, then I was sick ALL day the next day: my first hangover. It was also the first time I ever said, 'I'm never drinking ever again.' PAH! Kids, eh?!

The 'First Time'

Way too young. Painful, awkward, uncomfortable. Next.

First Thong

Stacey took me to a shitty little shopping centre when I was 11 or 12, where we'd hang around smoking with boys. She told me we were both going to go to New Look to buy a thong. I'd never worn one before. My mum had always said, 'Never wear thongs when you're older. You spend 15 quid on it and a tenner of it goes up the crack of your arse.' So I'd never seen the fascination with them. But Stacey stressed to me that it was the way to go, so I went into New Look with my £15 Mum had given me for the day (Mum thinking that I had gone to a car-boot sale with Stacey and her mum – still feel bad about that) and spent every penny on this tiny little black thong. I stood in the New Look queue absolutely certain that women were rolling their eyes and tutting at me. I felt like I was doing something illegal! And was also deep down completely gutted that I couldn't get a McDonald's on the way home because I was spending all my money on some stretchy black bum floss.

We both put them on when we got back to Stacey's and I had to pretend it wasn't hideously uncomfortable. Mum was SO right. Also, not worth the hassle of hiding it from your family. I managed to wash it myself so that nobody ever saw it and hid it in a special drawer, until one day my little brother got hold of it, was so horrified that he chucked it out my bedroom window and covered it in washing-up liquid and shampoo. I was secretly pleased, it probably needed another hand wash. He then told Mum who was livid. News of my infamous thong managed to reach the school and so the rumours began. Boys would sometimes ask about it. If they were lucky I used to give them a nudge and show them the strap - I should probably have bought more than one.

'Tom'

Then there's my first love. This deserves a whole chapter and … well, it's not the happiest of stories, for lots of reasons.

I was 13 and had just started Upper School. Things weren't exactly going great. My parents' marriage was on the rocks by this point, and I was being bullied at school by a group of really scary girls in the year above.

I'd been at the school for a couple of weeks before I started to notice a lad called Tom. Tom was two years above me. About five-foot-six, dark curly hair, blue eyes, skateboard glued to his left arm, and so many wristbands that covered every rock band you can think of. Tom stood out from everyone else. He was loud, hilarious, usually had something obscene written on the back of his school blazer, and was ALWAYS getting bollocked by a teacher in the corridor.

I was instantly drawn to Tom. I looked at him and genuinely thought, 'I want him to be my boyfriend.' I'd had crushes on boys since I was in nappies, but I'd never had this feeling before. Every time I saw him, or he walked past me or I heard his laugh,

I felt like I was on that ride at Alton Towers. The Oblivion, where you literally get dropped from a terrifying height into the ground and every single organ in your body feels like it's going to come out of your arse. (Horrific – yet thrilling – and you obviously go on it again.)

By about a month into being at the school, I'd pretty much worked out Tom's routine of where he hung around, what sort of times he'd be walking back from the tennis courts with the smokers, what time he would be in the lunch hall, and who his closest allies were, etc. (Not that I was his stalker or anything. I was just your average teenage, psychopathic girl.)

I was on my way to registration after lunch, doing my usual slightly longer route. This took me past his form group, who had to stand outside their classroom in a line before going in, so I always got a glimpse of him. When, suddenly, there he was blocking my path and held out his hand to shake mine. 'Hi, I'm Tom.' Oh God. Oh sweet Jesus. Holy mother of Moses. I was on the Oblivion again, that slow-motion bit of being carted horizontally up to the top of the ride, where you sort of feel like you're slowly being led to your death, but you are far too intrigued not to take the plunge.

I froze. I think I mustered a 'Hi', probably an embarrassing croaky one, and then I walked on. I went home and logged into MSN (Em_Is_Bad@ mail.com, if you're asking) and asked around if anyone had his MSN address. I found it, and added him. Now, for legal reasons, I obviously can't share his email address with you. Not because I'm scared of getting in trouble but because it was almost as shocking as Em_Is_Bad@mail.com But I typed it out just so I could look at it, and I mean this with every inch of my soul that when I see it written out, to this day, I STILL feel like my bowels are going to collapse.

I remember the first time he signed in. I thought I was going to be sick. It sounds so ridiculous but this is honestly how he made me feel, all the time. I didn't speak to him, didn't dare. So I was thinking of ways to ensure that another exchange would happen where I wouldn't be a quivering mess, and I would actually start a conversation so we could begin falling in love.

I found out about a night that was happening in Bedford, a 'battle of the bands'-type night. There were flyers going around school, and Tom came over to me and handed me one and asked me to come, his band were playing. I managed to muster some kind of over-the-top nonchalant response, and went home that night and begged my mum to let me go. I did the whole 'Mum, everyone is going apart from me, the school have put it on so it's not like we can drink or anything!' routine, which was kind of true (you just had to be 16 to go, and I'd just turned 14). But I'd promised Mum and Dad I'd stay with my friends, and would only drink a maximum two blue WKDs, and they could pick me up at a respectable 10pm.

It was a Friday night, and I'd spent hours and hours getting ready. I was so excited I couldn't even eat my tea. My mum knew there was a boy involved, and so she bought me a new top to wear and new shoes. The bullying at school had become quite bad, and so she was essentially treating me to this night out as I'd been having a tough time. She gave me £20 and dropped me and my (very reluctant) friends off in Bedford. We arrived at the place. Utter shithole, but I didn't care. Hardcore rock music blaring from the stage, blokes and women with huge red mohicans, tattoos and piercings. The smell of fags, beer and actual poo lingering on the graffiti-stained walls, while young lads moshed onstage, screaming into microphones about blood and hating their dads. I think some of the dads were even stood there watching, with their pints in massive plastic cups.

I stood out like a sore thumb with my brand-new blue silk halterneck top, flared jeans and pale-blue pointy-heeled boots, with my long blonde hair and face plastered in make-up. People I recognised from the years above me at school whispering to each other, 'What the hell is Emily Atack doing here?' This was undoubtedly the place where the 'greebos' and 'goths' came. And I wasn't in that category at school. So I had a lot of Marilyn Manson lookalikes glaring at me and shouting, 'All right, Barbie!' Time to neck a WKD.

WKD necked, and a few moans from my friends later, Tom came onstage and introduced his band. I stood at a pretty bloody good 'playing it cool' spot so that he could see me but not too obviously. My stomach was churning, and I started to think about my tea that I hadn't eaten earlier. I had another WKD, of course taking a sip every time I felt Tom's eyes on me. The band finished. I have no memory of them being good or not, I was just working out a tactic in my head the whole time for how I was going to see or speak to Tom afterwards without looking too desperate.

My friends were begging to leave but I begged them to stay just so that I could say hi to Tom.

are we there yet?

To my amazement, he came straight over to me; we chatted a bit and he asked if I would like to go somewhere with him outside so we had a bit more privacy. I nearly ruptured a kidney with excitement, told my friends I'd be five minutes, and we walked outside. We found a kind of romantic dark doorway round the back of the bar that smelt mostly like piss. He opened a beer with his teeth and offered me one. I sort of pretended to sip one while he lit a fag, and we chatted. I can't really remember what we chatted about, but I remember thinking I was the luckiest girl in the whole world. I was talking when, out of nowhere, he kissed me. My heels made me taller than him, so I remember leaning into the wall and slouching down a bit so that we were the same height. This wasn't my first kiss (high-five, Chris), so I knew what I was doing. I felt like our mouths matched perfectly. He tasted of beer and fags, and I fell in love with him there and then. We kissed for a long time, and his hands were sort of touching my bum and up my back. My heart was pounding. I couldn't believe it was happening. And I was already terrified about losing him.

I had loads of missed calls from my friends and it was nearly 10pm, so I had to go. He walked me back to the bar holding my hand. Everyone was

56

whispering and staring. I was chuffed to fucking bits. My friends were chuffed for me too, so I was forgiven for disappearing for an hour.

Tom said he'd text me when he got home, but then realised he didn't have any credit. I gave him a tenner from the £20 my mum gave me so that he could buy credit, and then he wouldn't have an excuse not to text me.

So the texting and MSN-ing began that weekend and, by Monday, every single person at school had got wind that we'd had a snog. It was front-page news of the imaginary school tabloids, everyone was talking about it. Even the teachers! (Made that bit up. They probably were, though.) The downside was it pissed off a lot of girls who fancied him, which didn't help the bullying situation.

He wasn't making a massive fuss of me at school just yet. He came over to say hi every now and then, but it was still quite tame. Then one night, he invited me to another one of his gigs and asked if he could stay over at mine afterwards as I lived closer to the venue. It took some persuading, but my parents eventually said he could stay – as long as he slept downstairs in the living room. Fair enough.

I went to the gig with a friend. It was basically just a massive piss-up in a hall full of hammered teenagers. Tom came straight over to me and snogged my face off in front of everyone. I was absolutely thrilled. (I should flag that by this point I had upped my greebo game slightly, so I didn't look too out of place. This basically involved me dressing more like Avril Lavigne rather than Britney Spears.)

I watched Tom's band play and, at the end of the gig, I noticed a dark-haired girl hovering around him. Flicking her hair, offering him fags. He was paying too much attention to her for my liking! So I asked him what time he wanted to go back to my house, seeing as he was staying. He turned to me and said he didn't need to stay over anymore, and he was going to go to another party with some friends. I felt like I'd been punched in the stomach. I knew he was staying because of this girl, and it made me want to die there and then. I got a taxi home and sobbed and sobbed. I knew at this point this wasn't going to be an easy ride. So I ended it and found a nice boy to go out with instead who was worth my time. Except obviously I did not do that.

After a few of these gig nights in a load of shit-holes, Tom and I became a proper boyfriend and girlfriend. On days where he wanted to pay attention to me, I was the happiest girl in the entire world. On the days where he ignored me, I went into myself and thought my world was ending.

He started to stay over at my house a lot. We weren't allowed to sleep in the same bed but I would sneak downstairs when my parents were asleep and be with him. I then started to stay at his and had to sleep in the spare room, but this time he'd do the sneaking and we'd stay in bed together for as long as possible. I felt completely addicted to this boy and needed him, and needed to be close to him.

One night, Tom's parents were out and we went up the road to his friend's house. The friend was older and had his own flat, where Tom and all his mates would hang around. Boozing, smoking weed, watching porn. Tom gave me some WKDs. Considerably more than I would usually drink. I was downing them and the lads were cheering, which obviously spurred me on to drink more.

I began to drink more and more. I would go to parties with Tom, we'd camp out in fields with all his friends, we'd sneak out of his house and go to all kinds of places where drinking and all sorts was involved. My parents tried to keep eyes on it all but I was just behaving how I wanted to by this point. I'd become so distant and withdrawn from my parents, who were by now having a really difficult time. I thought it best to just shut them out and stay with Tom as much as I could.

The bullying was making my school life extremely difficult. They'd spread awful rumours around about me, stick pictures of me up around all the villages with my mobile number on it – so I was getting abusive phone calls constantly. They were pushing me in the corridors, spitting at me, threatening me. I always told Tom about this but he pretty much ignored it and didn't do much to show sympathy or to help me. He'd left school by this point, so there was a degree of separation from the situation; maybe he didn't know how bad it was. Maybe he did and didn't think it was his problem.

I heard all kinds of rumours that he was cheating on me. That he'd shagged someone in a car park, shagged someone at a party, shagged his hairdresser regularly. Girl after girl after girl. People would tell me on MSN, or at school. Some girls even claimed to my face that they were the person he'd been with.

Every time I'd hear something new, a part of me completely died. I'd scream at him, be physically sick, and then stay with him. This happened over and over. He even broke up with me on a few occasions accusing me of being a psycho, but I would do drastic things in order to make him get back with me. I drank a bottle of vodka and cut my wrists at a party once – a cry for help, a cry for attention, a cry for Tom's attention. Looking back, I was spiralling. I was too young to cope with my breaking heart and cloudy drunk head. I woke up with massive bandages on my wrists and had to hide them from my family. I was hiding more and more from them now. My mum would beg me to open up and speak to her but I just couldn't. She started to see cuts on my arms and it broke her heart. I'll never forgive myself for harming my body in that way, and to this day I still have no idea why I did that. I didn't want to die. I just felt so out of control of everything and it was almost like a 'fuck you everyone, cos I can do this if I want!' sort of thing. A rebellion, I guess. I was also so terrified of losing Tom I saw it like I had no other choice. So I guess that was why. Even just writing all of this, these awful feelings of emptiness come rushing back to me. The excited rush of the ride was over, and I was just left with emptiness and fear. I felt like I'd been left at the bottom of the Oblivion ride completely alone and it had broken down. I couldn't see how I would ever get out of this darkness again.

I was about 15 by this point. I'd lost a lot of weight, and I was constantly in trouble at school. Bunking school to avoid it because of the bullying, and hanging around with older people doing older things. My mood had changed and I was always snappy with my parents. I just felt so sad, SO sad and heartbroken ALL the time. I was having house parties the second my parents were away, hundreds of people in the house, every single room occupied with people, smoke, girls with their boobs out, people puking, the lot. The house was getting trashed every weekend and the neighbours were slowly starting to despise us. People still talk about the parties in that house to this day. I hope to God those walls never, EVER start talking.

You might read this and think it all sounds dramatic, and that every teenager feels the same, and actually getting your heart broken by a lad and your parents divorcing when you are this age is very common. Which is true, it does happen a lot. If it happened to you and you still feel shit about it, like I do, then I'm sorry. If it happened to you and you got over it straightaway, then hats off to you. When you're in the thick of the storm of teenage heartbreak, weathering a hormone hurricane, you don't think it will ever end. I think of the girl I was,

Britney Spears dressed as Avril Lavigne. Sipping a WKD. Desperate for Tom to love me, for the scary girls to leave me alone. There are a number of things that happened in that period that will stay with me forever. Some things I'm not ready to recall publicly yet.

By 16, my dad had moved out, things were at their worst, and it felt like I was shut inside the washing machine on a never-ending cycle of emotionally distressing madness. I would say 16 was my toughest age to date. I felt like my life had fallen apart at times, and I was trapped in it. And then I met Daniel.

'Daniel'

By 17, I'd managed to ditch my toxic relationship once and for all, and Martha and I were hanging around with a really hilarious and fun group of boys. I'd been at school with them but they were a couple of years older than me, and it was only after I left at 16 that I'd had the chance to get to know them properly. They really looked out for me and gave me some of my strength and confidence back. They also looked after me, my sister and brother through my parents' divorce, taking us all under their dusty, smoky, but really warm and friendly wings.

We would often go to my friend Jim's parents' house because it was massive and they were always away. We'd play beer pong, smoke, listen to music and piss ourselves laughing in the garage until the early hours of the morning most weekends. I felt safe around them. They'd take me to the pub and we'd play pool, darts, and they showed me how to use the fruit machines.

My parents had pretty much left Martha and me to our own devices at this point because they knew we were safe and staying out of trouble. It was right in the middle of the divorce. Dad was living elsewhere, and Mum was trying to sell the house. I was having drunk sex with a lot of morons outside of my friendship group, thinking that this would lead me to another boyfriend. It didn't.

Then, one day, the boys introduced me to a lad called Daniel. I'd known of Daniel a bit at school. He was loud, obnoxious, cocky, very bright, but a massive bellend in my opinion. He was perfect. We got on instantly and sat in the corner of the pub saying how we couldn't believe we'd never actually spoken before, at school. I fancied the absolute arse off him. He would drive me around in his grey Nova with one white door; we'd listen to Dizzee Rascal's first album, *Boy in da Corner*, on replay (one of the best albums ever – get it on immediately) and we started snogging in his car every night and getting takeaway pizzas at our friends' houses. We completely fell in love.

Underneath the madness, Daniel was kind, sensitive, intelligent, ambitious, and he treated me like I was the only woman on the earth. He utterly adored me, and I adored him. He made me see what real love was, and saved me from what I thought it was. He was pretty much living at our house in Tebworth and actually took on quite a strong parental role in the family as my dad wasn't around at that time. He was great with my brother and sister, cooked us lovely dinners, and, because he was training to be a carpenter, he was very useful around the house. He also later trained our dog, Snowie, who we inherited after the passing of my grandad Mike. She was a bichon frise puppy who shat and pissed EVERYWHERE. I would watch Daniel chasing her up the road in Tebworth every time she escaped and he would quite literally jump in front of lorries for her. He was also wonderful with my mum. She loved him. They'd have slightly heated debates about silly things and my mum would just end up saying, 'Ah shut up, yer silly twat.' I felt like he was quite literally rebuilding my life again – slowly putting the parts back together, hammering in all the loose nails, sanding down the surfaces of our fatigued and weary hearts. (Jesus, I love an analogy.)

Just before I turned 18, I decided to move out of the Old School. My dad was giving up a flat that he'd been living in about ten minutes from where we lived and said I could have it for a couple of months for free until I found substantial income that would mean I could start paying rent. Martha had only just turned 16 but I looked at her and said, 'Let's get outta here!'

My mum then decided to pack up our wonderful giant bastard of a house and moved out herself. Moving out of there was probably one of the most painful experiences of all our lives, and Daniel was there for me through every single last pointless, dusty hoarding item that I packed up, and he helped Martha and me move into our flat. Mum moved to London to have some space and recuperate and find more work, and our brother George moved in with my aunty Amy and my uncle Bob, as the flat we'd moved to was only a two-bed. Also, he was only 14!

So here were Martha and I, 16 and 17, living on our own. Completely legal, but absolutely fucking mental. We had all our mates over every night and things got a bit out of hand, but we were having the time of our lives. We'd be up till 2am most nights, all the boys taking it in turns to do the 24-hour McDonald's run in their Vauxhall Corsas. But I had Daniel, so I always felt some kind of security. Martha was working on the reception of a tanning salon to fund her own cheap wine and happy meals, while I was convinced that I was going to all of a sudden become a famous actress in a Channel 4 sitcom: that was my focus. And I wasn't letting anything get in the way of that. After banging some doors down, I soon bagged my part as Charlotte Hinchcliffe in *The Inbetweeners* (more on this shortly), which financially allowed Martha and me to fund our lifestyle. Then we got the news we'd all been dreading. My grandma Betty's cancer was spreading, and she didn't have long to live.

After a painful few months of standing by her bedside and holding her hand, we lost her. I will never forget how Daniel helped me/us through that. My poor mum felt her entire world had crumbled around her. I'll never forget her saying that losing her husband and her mum around the same time made her feel like she was free falling. I tried to imagine that level of grief, and it sums it up perfectly. I suspect it does feel that way. It was Daniel's strength, kindness and understanding that got me through it.

My beautiful grandma dying was kind of the final blow for us all in this particular period of time. It changed everything. Everyone went a bit mental for a couple of years. I was now 19, 20, and my career was in full swing when *Dancing on Ice* then came along. Sadly, it was the last straw for mine and Daniel's relationship. It wasn't just the time I spent away, but the life I was now living was simply a million miles away from him and the life we used to have. I disappeared up my own arse for that period of time. I was very young, earning tons of money, dancing with an American man every day, then touring the country after the whirlwind of the live shows.

I will always feel guilty about how I left Daniel behind in that time. He had done everything for me and everything he could to be with me, but my head was just completely somewhere else. I was terrified that if I didn't put everything I had into my career at this moment, I'd lose it all again. I was terrified of missing the boat. I had to grasp every opportunity with both hands if I wanted to survive in this business. So I was being selfish. So bloody selfish. And I'm sorry.

After a few painful and tearful chats and hugs, Daniel walked out of my flat. We were both sobbing. I knew we were doing the right thing, but I'll never forget the look on his face, and I'll never forget the emptiness I felt in my heart.

Daniel and I are still great friends to this day. He has a wonderful girlfriend and he's happy, and that makes me so happy too. We were two kids who were there for each other when we needed it. I will be forever grateful for people like him in my life.

The People
Who Shaped Me:
The Girls

Despite the temptation to write an entire chapter dedicated to the one and only *Friends* (the best sitcom of all time aside from *The Office*) I think I should instead dedicate some time to writing about the wonderful people in my life who I call my friends. Like sitcoms, friends come in all kinds of forms – some are broad, loud, brash and brazen. Some are crowd-pleasers. Some are cool, understated and dry but full of heart. Some friends last for 47 seasons, and some stick around for just two series and a Christmas special.

But when it comes to my girlfriends, I'm really lucky that I've had the same core group since I was miniature. There is my oldest school friend, Lou – married with two beautiful children now. She knew and loved my freckled face long before the jungle revealed it like it was new. She'd laugh at something about me that nobody else would notice. We know and love each other's families. We have together endured every colour of the friendship rainbow – from love to pain to grief. We have had hard times and travelled different paths, we are in fact entirely different people – but we have common ground and that's love.

My best friend Skye was in my year at school – Skye, Lou and I were a trio. Skye for me is that friend who I would walk over hot coals for at four in the morning even if she's a flight around the world away – and vice versa. We all have one: that girl who's been in your life since you were nine. The one you sat next to in the school sandpit, and years later sat next to in the GUM clinic on a hot Saturday afternoon after a foolish night out in Nottingham, or accompanied you to a Spanish police station to obtain a crime reference number because you had your iPhone 'stolen' on the first night of the holiday. The girl who will walk behind you down the aisle with tears in her eyes and fluff your veil. The girl who, one day, will love your kids like her own – and come round to take them to the park, because you're on the lav with norovirus. Skye is that girl for me; she doesn't half drive me up the wall sometimes but she's part of my soul now. You know those cheap, crappy fridge magnets that say, 'You'll always be my friend – you know too much'? No one knows this but I invented that saying for Skye.

Skye and I joined forces with my sister Martha's friends in our teens (thank you mum for having Martha and me so close together in age), and we've not left their sides since. We call them 'the gaggle' because it really suits them – they are like bumble-bees on a hot summer's day around a melting ice cream. They're all under five-foot-four and have been friends forever – Martha was very lucky to have them throughout her entire time at school. They are badly behaved, they live for bank holidays, ASOS orders and Ibiza trips; they love rooftop drinking in the summertime and Saturday nights watching *The X Factor* in the wintertime. They are the most supportive and loving girls I've ever met. They are obsessed with each other. They are nice to each other, they respect each other, they absolutely lay into each other. They might not always have the words, but they have the time, the time for me, they have the want for my company, they love my cooking, they love me and I love them. If my cousins are the foundations of my castle, the gaggle are my battlements on the roof – they lift me up and make me feel on top of the world. I love nothing more than treating the gaggle to a table in a nightclub with bottles of champagne and sparklers and watching them swarm excitedly around it.

Visually it's also a treat: Skye and I are taller than the gaggle, who call us old wenches (despite the fact that we're only about 12 months older than them). On a night out we are like the two big geese waddling to the pond with the line of goslings following clumsily behind and clucking at our knees.

It's my girlfriends who keep me centred and grounded. They make me whole.

My Big Break:
Charlotte
Hinchcliffe

Living on our own so young was surreal. I guess it was a bit like what you experience if you go to university at 18 – that first taste of freedom and the opportunity to not get dressed before 4pm (or at all), never do any washing-up or even think about cleaning the loo. Jokes! Aside from the debris of the parties we were quite well house-trained. Unlike uni, there wasn't a maintenance loan in sight and so, as soon as Martha and I moved in, I thought, 'Okay, I've got to start making shit happen now so I can look after the both of us.'

I had a job as a waitress and then in a call centre, and I was shocking at both, probably because I knew that what I really wanted to do was to act. Luckily, my mum's agent said he would take a chance on me. I remember him, dressed in one of his impeccable suits, weighing me up with his eyes and saying he'd send me out on some castings – there was no way I'd get any roles first time round, but if the feedback was positive then he'd take me on permanently.

And so, aged 17, I tottled off to my first ever audition, for the guest lead in an ITV crime drama called *Blue Murder*. In a way, Mum's agent telling me I was never going to get it made me way more confident. I'd learnt the lines till they were coming out of every orifice of my body, strode with my head held high into the room, and was told about a week later that I'd got the job. I couldn't believe it, but also I could: I'd come through so much by this point that I was ballsy as fuck, and ever since I could talk I'd always wanted to be a performer. It felt kind of like my destiny.

The part was a really young WAG-type girl called Kelly Lang. My first ever character. She was so much fun to play. My first day on set I remember being nervous – but Caroline Quentin, the star of *Blue Murder*, was lovely to me and she really took me under her wing. She taught me some of the technical aspects of it: shots and eye lines and all that sort of stuff.

Shortly after that, an audition came through for something called *Baggy Trousers*, a new comedy on E4. I read the script and I thought, 'Oh my God, this is really, really funny.' I was so hungry for it: one, because it was amazing; and two, because there is nothing that makes you hungry like the actual thought that you might soon run out of money and be hungry. Martha was working too, but we were scraping by and I desperately wanted to provide properly for us. The audition was for the main guy's wannabe love interest, a certain Charlotte Hinchcliffe, and it was in Twickenham. My mum said she'd drive me but then her car broke down. I remember the feeling of my stomach dropping away in disappointment, but then reasoning with myself that this was the second ever job I was going for, and it sounded too good to be true anyway – the likelihood that I'd get it was tiny. I was about to tell Mum that we should just leave it, when a really kind neighbour offered her car up so we could get there.

So by some magic we got to Twickenham and I met Nadira Seecoomar, the casting director. It was a really hot day so I was wearing a little white dress and had made myself up in the only way I knew how: full face of foundation and thick black eyelashes – I looked cracking, if I do say so myself. I did the audition and Nadira told me how great she thought it was. The feeling of that praise when I was only 17 and desperate to make it was incredible, I was so chuffed. But then she said to me, 'You're wearing far too much make-up.' So I thought, 'Okay, brilliant, definitely didn't get that then.'

But then I *did* get through to the next round. The audition was with the producers and the two writers: Iain Morris and Damon Beesley. This time I went prepared – no make-up whatsoever. As I went in, Nadira gave me a wink and said, 'That's better.' The audition itself was quite a naughty scene between a boy and a girl talking about sex, except the boy part was being read by a middle-aged woman. I remember thinking, 'This is very weird that I'm re-enacting this with someone who could be my mum.' I'm so used to doing that now, but it was quite funny that first time.

The third round was similar but with more people in the room – the closer you get to the prize, the more people from the production team come to watch. I remember saying in that third audition something I would never in a million years say now. But I wanted this part so much, I thought, 'This part could really change my life. I've got to pay rent, I *need* this job.' In a way I was just fearless – plus I didn't know any different. So I announced to the writers and everyone in the room, 'Nobody can do this part better than me. This part was made for me. Charlotte Hinchcliffe is made for me.'

They sort of nodded politely and laughed a bit and said, 'That's great. We're really glad you enjoyed the script.' Christ I was excited. I got a call later that day offering me the part.

Walking into the first read-through was an out-of-body-type experience. I felt like I had a belly full of bees; buzzing with excitement and nerves at the same time, sort of like a first day at school. And it really did feel like that because we were basically in a classroom – read-throughs are always in stuffy, cold village hall type places, otherwise known as 'rehearsal rooms' but it's basically a youth club. I pretended to make notes on my script because I saw other actors doing it. I remember I brought a pad and a pen, and I always wanted more than just the fruit and biscuits on the table (still do).

I was intrigued to find out who was going to be playing Will, because I knew he was the character I was going to be rolling around with in the bedroom and snogging. Then Simon Bird walked in and he fit the character description perfectly: cute, black curly hair and glasses. 'Okay, we can work with this,' I thought to myself. Ha! There was a big age difference of about seven years between us and I think he was slightly mortified about it, but I was quite mature for my age so it didn't bother me in the slightest.

We went round the circle and introduced ourselves and the characters we were playing – simple things like remembering how to speak seemed to kick in when it got to my intro – and then …we made a start. I loved that first read-through. It was the first time I got to see the whole thing starting to come to life and even now I remember watching the chemistry between the boys and thinking they were great. It was at the read-through that I also met Emily Head, who played Carli – what a babe. We stuck together through the whole thing – she was so warm and friendly – and throughout the process all of us became good pals.

I loved going to work each day. I think sometimes, when you're watching TV, people don't stop to think of just how many people work behind the scenes on shows, but there are bloody loads of them, and the people who worked on *The Inbetweeners* were so nice. My make-up artist in particular made it such a nice experience. She was called Sarah Jane Hills and she was quite mumsy, and she made me feel at ease. I'd assumed they weren't going to let me wear make-up but had kept my fingers crossed that they might because of the character I was playing. And they did! I was the only actress who was allowed to.

One of the first scenes we had to do was the sex scene between me and Simon Bird. We were on location in a typically suburban house in Ruislip, west London, in a real teenage girl's bedroom. (What a claim to fame, eh? If it was *your* bedroom we shot in then I hope you put those sheets on eBay.)

My Big Break: Charlotte Hinchcliffe

Because it was the first time I'd ever done anything like it with a boy onscreen, I thought it was going to be really nerve-racking. But actually, in the end, I wasn't nervous at all and it was absolutely fine. *Obviously* – because who wouldn't want the opportunity to have a lovely gentleman like Simon Bird lie on top of them?! But seriously, I've found over the years that it's the guy who gets more nervous because there's obviously a certain thing that might happen which they can't control. Whereas I'm happy as Larry so long as I've got the flesh-coloured cups stuck to my boobs and sexy (it's not sexy) thong on. For most of the time when you're filming for something, you're standing around, freezing, in the arse end of nowhere, so getting to snuggle under a warm duvet chatting away to a nice boy has always been a part of the experience I've liked most!

I remember Simon climbing on top of me and he looked a bit nervy so I thought to myself, 'Right, I'm going to have to break the ice a bit here.' I went for: 'How does it feel being on top of a 17-year-old?'

He rolled his eyes at me. 'Oh, for fuck's sake. Thanks, Emily.' Lol.

We were a rabble. Most of the cast were pretty young and filming isn't an in-and-out job – the days are very long. If you ever remember going away on a school trip, it's that kind of vibe: you're around each other every second of the day, everyone's flirting and joking around. Joe Thomas, who played Simon, and Emily started going out which was really sweet. I struck up a particularly close friendship with James Buckley, who played Jay. We giggled all the time, he could really make me laugh. When you're young and you're working, it's nice to have someone you can cling onto a little bit – and James was that person for me. It never went any further than a couple of snogs at some wrap parties, but he was a good person to have around.

After the third series finished, we all went our separate ways. It's funny – when you're on a big job together, filming every day, you're in each other's pockets and you can't imagine not staying close friends with everyone. But when a series ends and everyone starts new projects, it's impossible to stay in touch like you did before. It was a bit of a shock then, but that's because it was my first big job. It's something I'm used to now. But maybe it was also a shock because that series was so important to me; it was such a massive part of my life for three years. It was my first major-part, and was where I learnt the ropes of the industry.

God, I'm grateful for kind neighbours and their cars.

Fame
(Not the Musical)

I'm quite grateful, to be honest, that my career kicked off before social media really got going. When I started out on *The Inbetweeners* people only cared about Facebook and Myspace – everything else was still pubescent, if you will. I'm not just grateful because I'm shit at it, but because I would have had no clue how to handle it. Going on TV doesn't come with a manual of how to approach that sort of stuff. Which is why when the first series aired and all these people began adding me as a friend on Facebook I went right ahead and accepted them. ALL of them. It was literally thousands – but I just thought to myself, 'Aw, this is nice, isn't it? Everyone wants to be my fwend.'

Then people started recognising me. Heads started turning a little bit; people would whisper when I was walking around shopping centres. They were more vocal about it on nights out or in pubs – then they'd come over and ask for photos. I quite liked it. I'd watched it happen to my mum all my life and so it was everything I'd wanted as a little girl. The only surprise was how quickly it could turn negative. For every ten people who came over, eight of them would be lovely but there'd be two who would be really nasty and say something awful. Weirdly, it was never girls – who I guess we always assume are quicker to be bitchy – it was men and boys.

But I could handle that. I can't really remember life before people being lovely and horrible to me at the same time. At school I had people either being nice to me or being absolutely vile. Whereas previously people had written things about me on the toilet walls, now they were in the newspapers. Fame seemed like an extended version of what I'd been through for years, except now I could afford loo roll.

That doesn't mean to say I was cool with everything that started going in the papers. It was eye-opening how much could be spun into a story. Not long after *Dancing on Ice*, I was stepping onto a road and a taxi pulled out and almost ran over my foot, so I knocked on the window to let the driver know I was there. A photographer snapped the whole thing and from the angle he was standing at, it looked like I was aggressively trying to smash the window in. The paper ran the headline 'ATACK ATTACKS A TAXI' – I was so shocked. If you don't do so already, take everything you read with a pinch of salt. But I did also think fair play to them because, come on, that's a pretty great headline.

The commentary on my body and my looks was worse. It was a really strange experience – because I suppose if a person slags you off, you actually never hear about it, do you? The point is, it's behind your back. Whereas when you're a celebrity, all the slagging off is in front of you. No one had ever called me fat before – a tart, a slut, I'd heard all of that sort of stuff, but I'd never thought there was anything wrong with my weight. Hearing the word 'fat' was painful, like someone was physically cutting me. I also wasn't very good at ignoring it – I'd properly go searching. I'd sit searching on Google for hours and trawl through the mentions of my name. I was so young, and when you're young you just want to be liked. You want to be popular and you get your validation from your peers. Now that peer group was on an insane scale and the feedback could be cruel. It was hard not to listen to it all.

It's only with age that I've stopped being as bothered. I suppose you get to a point where you realise you have your friends and their opinions are the only ones that count. I'm so lucky that I still have the same friends I've had since I was 13. Always having a finger in that pie kept me sane but it also kept me grounded (didn't mean for that to sound so wrong – definitely does). It's funny because people assume *The Inbetweeners* must have changed my life, and in some ways it did, but mostly I just carried on as I always had – living in the arse end of nowhere in Bedfordshire, hanging around with the same bunch of ragtag boys and beautiful girls.

If I've got to a point where I can brush off nasty stories in the press, unfortunately there are still things I find hard to dismiss. No one tells you that fame can actually be isolating. It's fine when you're with your long-term friends who knew you when the only thing you were famous for was your bra size, or at an industry thing when there are other 'celebs' around you. But the rest of the time you're in the real world, being a real person – and the way other real people can treat you ranges a lot. I've been at weddings where I've felt like people could actually see through me because no one will speak to me. I'll go home and see people I used to know from 'the time before' walking down the street, and I'll say hi to them and they'll ignore me; they won't even look me in the eye. You stop being invited to normal stuff because people think you're busy or won't want to come. People talk loudly about how indifferent they are to you *right next to you*. I was at an airport the other day when I heard a group of women talking about me. Some of them were being sweet, saying, 'Oh look, Emily Atack's over there – she's so nice, let's go and say hi.' And then their friends said, 'Oh God, really? Why on earth would you care about saying hi to her, she's so irrelevant. I refuse to watch her in anything.' And my heart crumbled a little bit. Did they know I could hear them? Did they care?

I'm so lucky, please don't think I don't know that. But when you're in any of the above situations, invitations to a new make-up launch or bar opening don't mean anything. Nothing is worse than being ignored, or hearing people choose to ignore you. I think some people think celebrities don't want to be bothered and that's why they stay away. I can't speak for everyone else on TV, but I'm telling you now: if you see me in the street and you would like to come over and have a chat or ask me to take 50 different selfies with you – that's fine! You are officially invited! (Caveat: don't be weird or anything and pull up a chair if I'm having dinner with my family, but normal friendly behaviour is very much welcome.)

Sometimes I feel like Julia Roberts in *Notting Hill*. NOT because I think I look like her (I wish) or am as famous as her – there is a point to the story, I promise! Do you remember the scene where Hugh Grant and his friends all offer up why their lives are the most tragic and therefore they deserve the last brownie? They go round the table and miss out Julia's character, Anna Scott, who is a famous Hollywood actress. She pipes up and says, 'Wait, what about me?' And then lists why being an actress isn't all fun and games – the diets, the paps, the personal maintenance etc. Everyone laughs and says not a chance. But that is sometimes how I genuinely feel, even with my friends who I love to death. There's this idea that everything is rosy in the garden of the public eye, and that even if something categorically shit happens to you that would still allow everyone else to have the last brownie, by being in the rosy garden you are automatically discounted from sympathy. I don't need sympathy all the time; I just need it when everyone else would need it. Everything is relative, whether you're on TV, or work in an office or a hospital or a school or a hairdresser's or a bank. Even if you can afford your own gold-plated chocolate desserts sprinkled with unicorn shit – you too will sometimes deserve that last crusty supermarket brownie.

I think, over the years, fame has sometimes made me more self-conscious, and sometimes made me more resilient, but that overall I'm still exactly the same person I ever was. Because, to quote my doppelganger Julia/Anna, 'The fame thing isn't really real.' In the end, we are all just girls, standing in front of boys, asking them to love us – or to get a round of cocktails in before happy hour finishes.

Moving to London

London was always the dream. When I was little, Mum would take me sometimes when she went to do voiceovers. Then when I was 16, I did some work experience at the same studio, and I remember thinking, 'This is the life.' I wanted to be in a fancy outfit, coffee in one hand, sunglasses down, strolling arm in arm with my friends through the crowds in Soho, watching posh people go by in their flash cars or carrying dogs in their handbags, rolling our eyes at tourists who stood lost in the middle of pavements, heading to trendy bars with the whole of the front window pulled back, the people inside spilling out onto the road with a drink in one hand and a cigarette in the other as the sun went down.

Finally, when I was 24, I made it. It was emotionally traumatising. Not because London's scary – it really isn't – but because it meant leaving Martha behind, and I'd never not lived with her before. She was staying in the flat in Bedfordshire and her boyfriend was moving in, so I knew she'd be looked after, but it still felt wrong. You know that feeling when you accidentally leave your phone at home and you keep going to check it but then you remember you don't have it? That's what it felt like. Like I'd lost a limb.

We packed all my stuff up into a van that my dad was helping me to drive to my new flat, and Martha and I couldn't even look at each other. We couldn't say goodbye; that would have felt too wrong. So we just said, 'Bye, then!' without so much as a hug, and I jumped in the front seat. I've never had to try so hard to fight back my tears – there must have been 92 lumps in my stomach that had been in my throat by the time we got to London.

I was moving in with my lovely friend Craig, who worked in PR and lived in Kentish Town. Dad carried my stuff into the flat with me and then said, 'Great, that's everything. See you later.' I was like, 'Oh no, oh no, oh no', because I was so terrified of being left in this new place by myself (Craig was at work). But *technically* I was an adult, so he didn't have any qualms about leaving me to it.

First things first: I looked in the fridge. Craig had already stocked it with a bottle of prosecco, which made me feel instantly better – empty fridges are BAD OMENS. I looked at the clock and knew that in approximately four hours he would be home and drinking it with me. I used the time to create my nest – it has become apparent to me over the years that when I'm in a new place, I have to immediately fill it with candles, throws, pictures and fairy lights so that I feel safe and contained. A fairy light-lit womb, if you can imagine. By the time Craig, and our other housemate, Abby, came home, I was feeling better. We ate our dinner off cheap camping stuff because we hadn't bought any proper kitchenware yet, drank the prosecco and then polished off a bottle of red wine. Which nicely set the tone for the years that would follow.

The time I spent in that flat is flooded with some of the happiest memories I own. Kentish Town, if you don't know it, is in north-west London, not far from Camden. It's a maze of shabby streets and some that would give Notting Hill a run for its money – ice-cream-coloured houses with smart white windows and flowers in neat pots on the sills. The pubs are epic – best pub crawls a girl could ask for – and there's an amazing music scene. Like most of London, it's both fancy and run-down; you can't swing a cat without hitting a celebrity, but there's also an upsetting number of sleeping bags in doorways that breaks your heart.

Our flat was on one of the last cobbled streets left in London, above a pub called the Assembly House. I love pointing it out to people now – there's a little turret on the top floor and that was where we lived. It wasn't anything to write home about: it was grubby around the edges, always dusty, we forever had mice, and it got wrecked from time to time when people came round and spilt beer on the sofa or in our shoes. But we loved it. You could climb out one of the windows to sit on a little bit of flat roof and look out over the jumble of streets – the view was beautiful, especially when there was a good sunset going.

My memories of it are all sunny. In summer we'd spend lazy days on Hampstead Heath, with picnics and drink all weekend. They were the days before hangovers, when Sunday drinking was the most beautiful thing in the world, especially when accompanied by a roast.

Craig was the perfect person to introduce me to the rest of London because of his job in PR. There were always bar openings to go to, new restaurants to try, and he introduced me to all his friends, some of whom I still see all the time now. I was going out with Jason the whole time I was there (more on this later) – between the odd jobs I was doing and his modelling career, things felt steady and unbreakable. There wasn't a lot of money, but there was enough.

If it sounds like I'm remembering it wearing

rose-tinted glasses, I probably am. I haven't thought about those years much recently because they are tinged with what happened with Jason; I'm so glad this book has reminded me of all the good bits in them! They were such fun years. There's something about London you can't quite put your finger on that makes you feel included, like you're part of the fabric of something bigger. I wasn't getting tons of work, but for the first time I felt like I'd made it, like I was living the life that had always been waiting for me.

The Kentish Town years ended after I moved to Camden with Jason, and although I moved back afterwards, time had shifted on – like it has a pesky habit of doing. Everyone's still game for a laugh, still likes the pub, still goes out, but we're probably a bit more worn-out these days and we can't fight the hangovers, or the grubbiness, like we used to. I live on my own now, which is too grown-up to admit to, but I'm still in north London. If I stop and think about my time here, I can feel the happiness rising up out of the pavements.

Funnily enough, I sometimes go to the place where I did my work experience for my own voice-overs now. Some of the same people work there still and remember me from when I was 16. We have a laugh about how nothing's really changed during that time. I love the familiar nature of Soho. From being a toddler on mum's arm eating Celebrations in a sound-studio's funky reception area to being a proper grown up running around to meetings and castings. Walking down Greek Street on a sunny afternoon, I still feel a flicker of pride in my achievements. I still feel like that 16 year old who was lost, getting coffee during a brief stint of work experience, but now with big sunglasses and a floaty dress on. And the coffee I'm holding is mine.

The People Who
Shaped Me:
London's Finest

Not all friends stick around for the whole show, but I've found the brief and beautiful ones can have some of the biggest influences on your happiness. Since I came to London I've made some incredible new friends, if only for one night. London churns out a tornado of characters – smoky, boozy, weird and wonderful, just like London itself. You're all friends with the same city and that's a good starting point. I have found myself clicking with someone by the loch in Camden one sunny Saturday after too much warm Pimm's.

People like my friend Joel (we call him 'great-time' Joel) who I met in 'London's smallest cocktail bar' in Kentish Town. A bar fashioned from disused underground toilets, it's tiny, it's fabulous. Martha and I were having a post-work cocktail and debrief about life. Joel, tall, handsome, a big fat Rolex on his wrist started chatting to us. We rolled our eyes, and looked away – weirdo. But he kept on. He asked us what we did, he was determined to get a convo going. I soon realised that he was a Northerner, Manchester – perhaps? He wasn't chatting us up, but just chatting. He worked in the bar trade, we talked about cocktails, we talked about work, he was interesting, he was nice. He joined our table. Martha and Joel got into some heated but hilarious debates about business. He was smiling over his Margarita, listening, laughing through giving his well-crafted opinion. I liked him so much that he's become one of my dearest London friends! We have lunch at the best places in the city, we have rosé at Soho House. He has ALWAYS got a stunningly attractive girlfriend who is too young for him. He comes to my work events and supports me, he was there at my stand-up gig at Clapham in the royal box. I had to laugh. I found a friend in a renovated toilet wearing a Rolex on a Wednesday night and that is why I love London.

London gives you friends like Joel, and friends that you have Sunday roasts with because you want to start drinking again to ease a hangover. It's the ones with black Merlot teeth, who demand a game of Scrabble in the pub, as they hurl the badly worn box down onto the table, only to abandon it ten minutes later. It's the skint ones, the rich ones and the ones who never go to bed. The ones who demand you stay out for one more on a Thursday and before you know it the sun is coming up. It's the PRs who message you, 'Fancy this?' followed by a ridiculous flyer to a party that looks too good to be true. You never actually go; you'd rather stay north and go to the wine bar you've been to 5,000 times. But it's always an exciting reminder that, in London, any time, any day of the week, something wildly tempting is happening around the corner, and it's up to you if you're up for a dip.

You might not know any of these people when you're 45 and living in the arse end of nowhere, but for now they bring you out of your shell and strangely but magically uncover parts of your personality that your best friends hadn't found before. For me, they were like the last elusive puzzle piece that I hadn't noticed was missing from my picture beforehand but suddenly made me feel all the more complete.

Showbiz: The Good, The Bad and The Ugly

The Good

I love acting. I love getting lost in scripts, I love disappearing under make-up and costumes and reappearing as someone else, I love working with great people. It doesn't matter what people chuck at me now when it comes to work, scripted projects are my biggest passion and will always be my preference when it comes to my next job. In 2014, I was in a low-budget film called *Almost Married* – it was about a guy and a girl who are about to tie the knot, but then the guy realises he picked up an STI while on his stag-do. (Critics choice here we come.) For the most part it was just me and two actors: Philip McGinley and Mark Stobbart. It wasn't extravagant or exciting, but we filmed in Newcastle for a month and it was just so fun. We went out every night and ate Japanese food and drank and just had a really good time. Sometimes when things feel a bit messy at home, the freedom of going somewhere different, of spending every waking moment with new people who can bring you out of yourself, is like medicine.

Dad's Army was also an incredible experience. We were filming in Bridlington, which is a picture-postcard town on the Yorkshire coast, and I was working with some of the most amazing people in the industry: Bill Nighy, Toby Jones, Danny Mays, Catherine Zeta-Jones, Michael Gambon, Tom Courtenay – people say never meet your heroes, but I met A LOT of heroes on that job and they were nothing but wonderful and incredible and amazing. The very first film I did, *Outside Bet*, was the same – it was with Bob Hoskins and he was such a gentleman. I remember after my first scene he came up to me and told me he'd been watching it on the monitor. He said to me, 'I hope you've got a fucking good agent.' What a babe.

American jobs are a different kettle of fish. The first American film I did was called *The Hoarder*, with Mischa Barton and Robert Knepper (if you can't place him, he played T-Bag in *Prison Break*). I had a few days off and I couldn't believe it but the team behind the movie agreed to fly Martha out to meet me. The shoot was in New York, so basically this meant Martha and I had six days to piss about

Manhattan together pretending we were from *Sex and the City*. When you're on a film shoot you get given something called per diems – it's an allowance per day to be spent on food and any necessities you need, normally it's about 100 quid. This time it was about 600 dollars as it was a much higher budget movie. Martha touched down at JFK, we nipped back to the Soho Grand (google it, it's epic) to spruce up, then went to a restaurant and lounge called STK and spent *all* my per diems on the first night. It was a FANTASTIC night. And a fantastic six days, truth be told – just imagine Martha and me strolling around Central Park with a bottle of wine each and you'll have a pretty good picture of what happened.

The Bad

The hilarious thing about acting is that everybody thinks it's the most glamorous thing ever, but for the majority of the time it really isn't at all – stories like the one I just gave you are very rare. Here's a day in the life of being an actor for you:

Eat crisps and stare at the ceiling.

Ha – just kidding. Although, when you're not working, genuinely you spend a lot of your time hating on the fact your friends all have nine-to-five jobs as no one's around.

But when you're on a job, it's all go: 5am you wake up in some kind of hotel. Sometimes they're nice, sometimes they're shit. A friendly driver comes to pick you up and you get whisked to the least Hollywood place ever: a trailer park full of, you guessed it, trailers and (my favourite) a catering truck. Most of the things I've shot for have been made in winter, so it's still dark outside and bloody cold. You go into your little trailer, which is effectively a freezer, and then a lovely runner comes to take your order for breakfast. I always go all-out and think, 'Well, I'm working so I'm actually allowed three hash browns, four sausages, five bits of bacon, nine bits of toast.' And then I sit there stuffing my face, dribble of ketchup running down my chin, while my poor make-up artist tries to do something to me.

Hair and make-up done, you get into your costume (which for me was not always season appropriate so you shiver some more) and wait for something to happen. Usually it's a good two hours. Normal people probably catch up on emails and get their laptop out, but I just sit and listen to music. If I'm still sleepy I'll put on some country and pretend I'm in a music video. Marvellous.

And then eventually you get called to set. You stand around with your hands stuffed inside your North Face coat for another hour while they're lighting up and rigging, having a chat with whoever's knocking about. You do about ten minutes of a scene. You go back to your trailer for another three hours. You come back. You do another tiny bit. And then you're done! You wrap at about seven o'clock, go back to your hotel, get a bit of room service, drink a bottle of red wine. Or you go into the bar and have a bottle of red wine with the crew and the cast members, have a few cheeky flirts with the actors. See which ones are single and out of those who you want to cop off with. (I'm kidding. Sort of.) And then you go to bed. Oh, the glamour!

I remember once on *Dad's Army*, we were all huddled in this freezing-cold trailer – Bill Nighy, Toby Jones, Michael Gambon, Tom Courtenay, Alison Steadman – eating out of these plastic lunch-boxes with plastic forks, the building literally falling apart around us. Toby Jones once had a screw plop right in his food from the ceiling above. We were all laughing hysterically because it was such a classic example of life as an actor. Cor, it's glorious, but it's definitely not glamorous.

The Ugly

I'd say 90 per cent of the projects I've worked on have been wonderful experiences. I've nearly always had directors and men treating me with nothing but respect and I'm so lucky for that. But there have been a couple of occasions that really were not okay, and it made me understand that women in this business have had to put up with bad, awful, behaviour for far too long.

There was one person I worked with – let's call him Frank – who said a string of really inappropriate things to me and then started sending me texts. The comments started with little things. I think he saw that I'm a very chatty person. I think if you're quite fun and full of energy people just want to be your pal at first, but he was older than me, lots older. 'You haven't given me a hug today. You've hugged all the other boys, why haven't you given me a hug?' All in a silly little, almost baby-like voice. I brushed it off but then he started saying slightly more crude things to me when people weren't in earshot.

And then we were doing a take where I was 'shock horror', having to play 'sexy'. I was required to bend down, I think they were after a sexy arse shot. Again, shock horror. We'd done the first take of it but then he came over and whispered something truly sexually inappropriate in my ear. I began to freeze up. I felt like my heart was slowing to a stop. 'Oh my God,' I thought, 'this has gone too far.'

Luckily one of the make-up girls actually heard and sort of whacked him on the arm and said, 'Frank, you can't say that!', and I could see the embarrassment in his face, because he'd been overheard, and he went bright red and just laughed it off.

'Oh, she knows I'm only kidding,' he said.

A day or so later, I was in the front of the car. We were all travelling back to the hotel and he started sending me texts from the back of the car: 'You haven't spoken to me much today.' Things like that, texts that out of context sound innocent but all together were unsettling and made me feel really uncomfortable. It was so weird because there was never any point where I gave him any kind of inkling that I was remotely sexually interested in him.

These little texts continued and I started to panic because he was going to be on my next job. There was a chance that this next job could shoot in the US and I of course was really looking forward to it. 'I'm gonna make sure our hotel rooms are really close together in America so we can go for dinner and stuff and have fun,' he would say.

I remember thinking to myself, 'Oh my God, he's going to be fucking knocking at my door every night.' I felt really uncomfortable about it and it made me dread this trip.

The volume of comments was getting more and more and so I just started to be really stand-offish with him. I thought, 'I can't be smiley.' Before, I'd blush – because I was genuinely embarrassed – and just try to laugh it off, but that hadn't worked, so I tried the cold shoulder route instead. He got more and more arsey with me because I wasn't responding to his advances

The shoot ended and, a fortnight later, all over the press were pictures of another actress in my role. I never received an explanation about why I'd been dropped; just one minute I'm doing it and I'm all excited to go, and the next thing I know there's another actress doing it. Sometimes stuff like that happens, it just wasn't meant to be.

Sometimes I think about how I might react to Frank now, would I stand firm? Tell him to fuck off? I'd like to think that now I would call someone out on such behaviour. Perhaps I would try a polite but firm, 'Don't say that to me, please.' Rightly or wrongly, I always thought about all the other people involved if you *did* speak up. It's hard if they're married with children, which they quite often are, because you think,

'I can't ruin this family. It's gonna destroy those kids' lives if they hear this about their dad.' Or the wife would be devastated. They may be a complete creep but I will hurt a whole load of innocent people if I say something. That's my personal thing. A lot of people won't agree with me on that and I completely understand. One less creep at work is another one we have beaten, no matter how minor their actions. But with that particular situation, I processed my thoughts and assessed the impact it had on me. I'm not scarred for life by it. I'm fine. Yes, it's shitty and horrible, but I'm okay. He knows what he was doing was inappropriate. He must do. He can live with that now.

As well as the impact on others, I think of myself. I never would have felt able to stand up to anyone in senior positions as a young actress, because they have all the power professionally. When I was younger, I needed all the work that I could get. This was a time when I was on a roll, getting more and more work and things were really looking up. The last thing I was going to do was put a huge spanner in the works. In effect, you don't really feel like you have the choice to do anything about it.

The one other occasion where I felt powerless to stop something was with a guy on the set of another project – let's call him Dave. There was a group of us on set, all around a similar age, talking about sex. I was being vocal in the discussion – I can talk about sex until the cows come home if I'm in an environment where everyone's comfortable with that. Dave was quite a lot older, and he must have heard this conversation. Because then he started talking to me about that kind of stuff, but not in a group situation – when it was just the two of us. I made it very clear that I wasn't going to talk to him about that kind of thing, now that the group chat was over. He tried it a couple more times, sort of quietly passing the odd naughty comment here and there. I ignored it. I stood firm.

But then one day I was filming a sex scene and Dave was there. Afterwards, I was walking to get some lunch on my own when he came up behind me and put a condom in my pocket and said to me, 'Let's go somewhere right now.' My heart just went into my throat. Out of a mix of shock and horror, I nervously laughed it off. 'Don't be silly,' I tried. 'What do you mean? I'm going for lunch.'

'Come on, let's go somewhere,' he said again, pulling on my hand. I had to really put my foot down and say, 'Absolutely not. That's ludicrous.' I got away from him as per the time before and just tried to block that out of my mind.

The night of the wrap party came round and we

were all drinking in the hotel. I was drunk. I wasn't single. I was with someone at the time, so I had no intention of doing anything with anybody. I was just having fun, letting my hair down, messing around with the cast I'd got to know really well. We were stumbling around the hotel corridors when we ran out of wine, so I asked if anyone had any left in their room, because we'd all been given a bottle or two. One of the group gave me a key and told me there was a mini fridge of booze in their room. I said, 'Great', took the key and went to the room. Opened the door, walked over to the fridge, opened it – no booze in there. And all of a sudden I turned round and Dave is standing there, in the room with his dick out.

I froze. I remember saying, drunkenly, 'No,' but I didn't have a clue what to do. I was drunk, for one, but not so drunk that I couldn't realise this was a really fucking tense situation. I asked him to let me out of the room and he said, 'I'll only go if you give me something.'

So then I kissed him. I just snogged him for a few seconds. Felt sick the entire time but I knew that was the only way I was going to get out of the room. He let me leave and the next day I cried my eyes out all day. It's always emotional after wrap parties, and of course there's also the hangover paranoia. But it was also because of what had happened with that man. *It's because I'm loud and silly and I get too drunk and I'm flirtatious with all the other boys. I dance provocatively. It was my fault.* As far as I was concerned, it was totally my fault.

I called Martha and told her all about it. She said, 'This shouldn't be happening to you.' She said, 'What do we do about this? We need to say something.'

I said we couldn't. We cannot say anything to anyone ever. I just wanted to forget that it had happened. Perhaps that makes me weak, I don't know. This is the first time I've recalled it to anyone other than Martha.

I'd love to say that with age, courage and experience, if it happened now, I'd kick him in the balls and leg it out of there as fast as I could. But I realise that for any woman (or man) who has found themselves in a situation like this, you just don't know how you'll react, or the impact it has after. But when you're drunk, standing in a room with a man who holds more power than you, instinct takes over, to get you the hell out of there. Whatever it takes.

I've read with horror about the stories from women around the world, from brief encounters with men at work to violent stories about something far more sinister. I've been amazed by the bravery of the women speaking out and sharing their stories – and I also stand with those who perhaps still aren't ready to as well.

The People Who Shaped Me: Team Atack

Everyone else I've included in these spotlights have been friends or family, who gradually over the years have taken me and moulded me like a lump of clay into the Emily you see now. But then there are the people who literally keep you in one piece from day to day and who never get enough credit for being the gods of your life. Let me tell you now, the people in showbiz do not get anywhere on their own – they all have brilliant teams standing behind them. Celebrities are a bit like dogs: they come in different shapes and sizes, they're mostly cuddly (you get the odd Rottweiler and annoying yappy one), and people like to watch them scampering around. Meanwhile, their team are like their humans, ferrying them from place to place, looking after them and, more often than not, walking behind carrying the poo bag.

My team is the best in the business and a big part of it is my primary agent, Alex, who knows the truth, the whole truth and nothing but the truth. Alex has seen me at my worst, my best and everything in between; he has championed me in this industry when nobody wanted to know. He knocked on doors, pushed and believed in me when I didn't believe in myself. He's made decisions for me that have guided me down the right path when I couldn't see the signs. He's helped me carve a steady 12-year career out of an industry where nothing is certain. He is constant and he is dedicated. The man is a machine. He's also like my brother – the poor lad was woken up by me banging on his door at 3am one night in LA, too drunk to find my room. We've chatted non-stop on long-haul flights and for hours on the phone. He has seen me trying to stuff myself into a BAFTA dress so tight that I thought it might kill me. Even when I've been exploding out of a corset with my granny pants on he tells me I look lovely. He's not a wheeler-dealer manager; he trained under one of the best agents in the world and it shows. I trust him completely.

I also have to give a big shout-out to my afore-mentioned cousin, Lydia, my make-up artist. She is the only person I trust to make up this big old head and she deserves to add 10 per cent client counselling tax to her invoice and to win a Pride of Britain award for the amount she has to deal with. Make-up artists are fascinating cogs in the system. They have to be present, yet invisible. Have authority, yet be malleable. In fact, I think out of all of the jobs on a TV set or photoshoot they have it roughest – imagine having to get up close and personal with someone's face you've never met or do a slightly scary celeb's hair. It must be arse-sweatingly stressful.

Everyone loves Lydia. She glides around a set with her kit bag on hip, a brush between each finger. I am so familiar with the sight of her face close to mine, with her glasses on the end of her nose as she dabs and probes and tweaks my face. She created my jungle-inspired crimped-hair look that has become my absolute go-to and always makes me feel fabulous.

Alex, Lydia and all the rest of the management crew (including Martha, but if I give her any more shout-outs her head's going to get too big for her body) have stuck by me through the good times and the bad. I don't know where I'd be without them.

The Elephant
in the Room

Food has always been a big part of my life. Whether it's in my aunty's kitchen or around tables pushed together in a restaurant, eating is how we get together as a family, it's what our holidays revolved around when we were younger and still do now. Indian is our go-to for any problem; there's nothing you can't face or beat if you've got a rogan josh and saag aloo in front of you. Food to me means togetherness and cosiness. It means an occasion. And I love that.

But loving food can be tricky when you're in an image-driven business, and even if you're not, it's stating the obvious to say there is an accepted form of beauty that we're all sort of conditioned to want to be from a very early age – as soon as we're old enough to watch adverts on the TV and see women on the sides of buses. I was definitely conscious of my weight from a very young age, I think maybe because I've always been quite physically aware of myself in general. It probably sounds vain but I'm sure it's true for lots of little girls: I wanted to be pretty and thin and look like Britney Spears in the 'Hit Me Baby One More Time' video. I was always quite slim growing up – I never seemed to go through a chubby stage like my brother and sister did (sorry guys). And I always had a really healthy relationship with food. I was always keen to try new things and I wasn't fussy. Which meant, unlike lots of kids, I wasn't bothered about chicken nuggets and chips. I mean, sure, I loved a McDonald's as a treat, or when my mum couldn't be arsed to cook, but I never had that fussiness of only wanting crappy fast and sugary food. In all things, I was desperate to be an adult and food was no exception: I liked seafood, and the sophisticated pasta dishes my dad would cook. While kids were snacking on bread and ice cream on holidays, I'd be asking my mum and dad to buy me some rollmop herrings like a little weirdo, and diving headfirst into the paella at lunchtime. So even though I ate a lot, I ate quite healthily for a kid.

By the time I was about ten or 11, I had started my periods and I grew boobs. I had big old boobies by 12 and was known as Boobzilla in my year at school. (Weirdly, I took Boobzilla as a compliment.) Because I'd hit puberty at a young age, my body became curvy and womanly pretty quickly. I was also quite tall. I'm a fairly average height of five-six now but the growth spurts that got me there happened not too long after I'd got my period, so at 13 I was a head above most of the other people in my year. So, because there was a marked difference in the way I looked compared to other girls my age, I was always very aware of my appearance. Once teenagedom hit, my parents' friends started to comment on how much I'd changed. 'My God, hasn't she grown up! She's like a model!' – that sort of thing. Their reactions made me start to kind of believe that I really did look quite different to most of my peers. I also wore a lot of make-up, which was rarer for young girls back then. I remember being the only girl I knew who was contouring and drawing on extra-thick lips at 12 years old.

Wearing lots of make-up, by the way, wasn't because I was insecure about my face and looks. After *I'm a Celeb* … I had a few people being very lovely to me and telling me that I should ditch all the make-up and 'unleash all my beautiful freckles'. Before the jungle I would never have gone down the street with a naked face, I do sometimes do it now and actually feel much more confident about it. But in truth, wearing make-up for me is actually a part of my identity. I'm not ashamed to love it. When I was little, I loved watching my grandma and my mum at their dressing tables and so, as soon as I was old enough to have my own powder set and mascara, it felt like the most natural thing in the world. I love make-up – the feel of it on my skin, the perfume of it, the versatility of it. Putting foundation on isn't about hiding my face, it's more like putting on my armour, to tackle the day. I feel powerful when I'm made up. I feel like me.

By 15, 16 I dropped quite a lot of weight because I was stressed and lovesick all the time, and instead of eating I was smoking and drinking in parks with my friends. But then at 17, once I was happier in myself again, I all of a sudden gained quite a lot. I had discovered wine, and getting takeaways with my nice new boyfriend Daniel. Seeing myself on TV for the first time I got a shock. I thought 'the camera adds ten pounds' was just a saying, but it really isn't. It's completely true. And once I had seen myself on TV, I knew from then on my weight was always going to be a complex subject in my life.

The more I worked in TV, the more I realised I was on the larger side compared to most actresses. When I played Charlotte Hinchcliffe in *The Inbetweeners*, it was the first time I had ever heard negative comments about my weight. I was one of the first girls on TV to be playing a sexy girl-next-door type, who wasn't a size 6. I was a size 10/12, but to people who were watching I was plus size, or chubby, or overweight. I guess because nobody was used to seeing this type of character played by a girl above a size 6 or 8. Social media back then wasn't as big as it is now, but I became obsessed with googling my name and searching forums where people were talking about *The Inbetweeners*, just so I could see if people were saying anything about me and my weight. Some people said horrendous things, some people said nice things like, 'Well I think she's a normal and healthy-looking girl which is a better role model to have for young girls!' But that hurt too because I wanted to be seen as thin. I wanted to be like every other actress and look the same as all the girls in the casting rooms when I went to auditions. I was always the biggest girl in there and I hated it. I felt like a big fat ogre towering above all these tiny, gorgeous, dinky little actresses, so I started trying to diet and working out with a personal trainer. By 18, 19 I was much fitter (and by fitter, I mean drinking vodka Diet Cokes instead of wine). And I made healthier eating choices (and by healthier, I mean ordering a salad with a side of chips). Looking back at photos around this time I can't believe how good I looked, and yet I still felt big, still felt like the odd one out at castings. Because

I was. It was the elephant in the room. Literally. Casting directors and people in the business would hint at me to lose weight, although it wasn't stopping me from getting sexy parts in films, and I was actually on a bit of a roll. But even when I was getting those parts, I still felt like my image wasn't good enough, and I wasn't thin enough.

Dancing on Ice came along when I was 19, which made the weight fall off me. Looking back, I was tiny – I was nine stone and had a full-on lollypop head. And yet I was still being referred to as the curvy girl. Around that time, I was in discussions with LA managers to make my first visit to the city. I remember Skyping one woman, who wanted me to fly over to meet her with a view to potentially signing me. I asked her when she thought it would be a good time to come and she said, 'Well, Emily, to be honest … we aren't even going to think about getting you over here until you are at least a size 2.' Her EXACT words. I hung up the call and made an internal, conscious decision to knock LA on the head as I knew I was never, ever going to be whatever it was they wanted me to be. I plucked up the courage and told my English agents that I just didn't think Hollywood was a path I could go down at that moment in time.

As I've gone through my twenties my weight has
been up and down. There are times where I've gone
a bit silly on the wine and the dinners out with my
friends, takeaways, dinner parties and so on. When
I've noticed I've gained a fair bit, I rejoin a gym,
cut down on the booze and go healthy for a while.
I am more than happy to accept that I am on the
telly and therefore it is part of my job to think about
maintaining a healthy image. And it's also important
for my own self-esteem that I'm happy with how I
look when I watch myself back, not to mention that
eating well and getting fit is good for your mental
health. But nowadays I never diet. I never starve
myself; I never deprive myself of the things that
bring me so much joy in my life. Because I don't
believe that is the answer. I love my job, and I love
that I've had the opportunities to play glamorous
and sexy roles, and posed for *FHM*, and have had
people tell me that I'm pretty. It's really lovely and
flattering, and I am proud of all those things. But
I came to the conclusion quite a long time ago that
I will never be that person who starves herself for
her job. I make sacrifices for my job in other ways,
but sacrificing paella on the beach with gallons of
white wine, pizza with my mates, roast dinners on
a Sunday, and my dad's giant bowls of pasta …

that is something I will never, ever deprive myself of. Because those things bring me happiness, way more happiness than a thigh gap ever could.

It's hard sometimes to find your place in the industry I am in, and it's even harder maintaining your place there once you've found it. My problem was I never really knew where I fitted. I was an *inbetweener*, I guess! Not skinny enough for the A-list beautiful leading-lady parts, yet not big enough to play the large funny girl. As the years passed, it made me think more and more about how I wanted to be defined and whether there was anything I could do to turn who I was – not thin enough, not fat enough – into an advantage. As a woman in the entertainment world, you do also have to be realistic about the fact that it can be a bit cruel as you get older. My boobs are getting saggier now, my arse isn't getting rounder sadly but flatter (ha!) and I can't play sexy schoolgirls anymore. But my personality – that's not going anywhere. So I thought: what if I could put myself out there and see what people think of my personality rather than just my weight, or my boobs, or my hilariously misinformed sex appeal? I am a good and kind person, and I like making people laugh. Maybe I should try to do that for a bit and see how it goes? Maybe people will be pleasantly surprised that I really am NOT what it says on the tin. That there's more to me than just the tits and teeth, and that I have a story to tell? Then the jungle came knocking. It was perfect timing.

There will always be times in my life when I feel crap about my weight, and then there will be times I'm feeling good. And I'm never going to be able to completely cut out making comparisons – we're all human, and we can't help but look at other people and sometimes want what they've got. There will always be someone on the beach who has a body I would kill to have, or someone who puts up a load of gym selfies on Instagram while I'm dying of a hangover in bed at ten in the morning, wishing I hadn't drunk all the wine in Soho and eaten two burgers at 4am in Balans on Old Compton Street. But actually, I'm getting to a point in my life where I can look at those beautiful bodies and think to myself, 'Good on them.' If that's what they want to put their energy into, that's great. Personally, I'd rather have the pizza.

I will still sometimes be the largest girl in the casting room when auditioning for a job. But the difference now is that I am fine with that. I am no longer apologising for who I am, because I've learnt that people like me for me. Being in the jungle allowed me to come out and show the country who I was as a person, and I am really lucky that most people didn't just think I was a twat.

I will continue to love my job, and work hard. At the moment, I'm working harder than I ever have before. But as me. And if anything ever requires me to be anything but myself … I would rather be the elephant in the room.

Five Foods
to Take on a
Desert Island

1. Assorted flavoured crisps with various dips. I find that no matter what, I am always in the mood for crisps and dip. I tend to go for Walkers Sensations Thai sweet chilli flavour with a caramelised onion humous. Crisps in a bowl and dip never fails to make me feel cosy and like I've created a fun little vibe for myself. And, let's face it, being on a desert island would be pretty boring after a while so you'd need to create a mini vibe. This combo is also perfect at any time of the day when you fancy a snack (though NOT before midday – crisps for breakfast is a bit depressing).

2. Eggs and avocados. You cannot go wrong with a show-off poached egg and avo for brekky. Providing that you've got the fire going like a legend on this island, eggs would go a long way. Fried, scrambled, poached or boiled – they're so efficient cos there's so much use you could get out of them. I would have eggs and avo every morning if I could be arsed – and on an island I would definitely be arsed cos there's bugger all else to do.

3. Rice. I learnt in the jungle that rice is a lifesaver. I'd take loads of rice, then go and catch loads of fish, crabs, lobsters, mussels, clams etc. from the sea and make an amazing seafood stir-fry with paella rice. I'd obviously have to learn how to catch stuff with a big spike, like Tom Hanks does in *Cast Away*. This would be great for lunch and fill me up for most of the day, and I'd feel like I was on holiday in Spain with my family. I'd probably end up feeling too guilty about killing the little fishies, though, so I'd wind up sacking that off and be left with plain rice.

4. Burgers with buns. I'd get those burgers on the go for dinner on my massive fire that I've started all by myself. And I'd have made some kind of fruity chutney sauce by now from all the fruit I've found and collected on the island (I'm imagining an island where it's very tropical and there's lots of colourful fruits knocking about), so that would go nicely on the burgers. (In the normal world I'd have sweet potato fries with the burg, but we're on an island and I can't think how I'd cook the sweet potatoes – let's be realistic.)

5. A cheese board. Obviously. Various different cheeses and biscuits. I'd have this at night-time before getting into my little desert island hammock. It would make me think of Christmas at my aunty Amy's, where every year I demolish at least an entire wheel of brie by myself. The fruity chutney I've made (see above) goes perfectly with it, and I can also use the cheese for the burgers. It's perfect. I could even crush up the biscuits to make some kind of crumble and use the fun, sexy island fruit to make a dessert! Too far …?

'Jason'

Of all the loves of my life so far, this is probably the hardest one I will have to write about.

It was 2010, not long after I'd come through my break-up with Daniel, and shortly after the *Dancing on Ice* madness had calmed down. I was approaching 21 and having fun being single, and had no intention of meeting someone serious for a long time. I was enjoying the single life of secret dinner dates, naughty late-night visits to hotels, and cracking on with a few people off the tele who would take you back to their £10 million mansions, show you a nice time and then in the morning their maid (yes this happened) would make you scrambled eggs before you hid under a coat and made a dash for a taxi that was taking you back to your very normal flat in Bedfordshire. 'WHAT IS MY LIFE?!' I would think, giggling to myself all the way back.

By the time I met Jason, I was having fun with one particularly famous boy: we were BBming each other and making long late-night phone calls (you know the ones – the type where you're a bit embarrassed afterwards about what you said). There were topless roll-arounds in various massive houses with various boys with massive personalities. I'd wake up in places like Fulham with my false eyelashes still stuck on my face, desperately searching for a glass for water.

I was in Milton Keynes shopping centre with my cousin Lydia and our friend Carl. Lydia grabbed my arm and said, 'Wow, look at this guy about to walk past Topshop.' I turned and honestly couldn't believe my eyes. A six-foot, brown-eyed, curly-haired boy was walking past. I had honestly never seen anyone so handsome. He looked like an actual Disney prince. Chiselled jaw, pouty lips, in Hollister shorts, t-shirt and flip-flops, tanned and completely perfect. I don't know if I believe in love at first sight but it's the closest I've ever come. I quite literally stood there and said to Lydia, 'Oh my good God. I need him to be my boyfriend.'

I started to sneakily follow him (yep, honestly). He went into a cool surfer type shop and then I realised that he worked there. I quickly formulated a plan. Try and get me to the post office to collect my undelivered parcels is an impossible task but watch me hatch a plan to track down a Disney Prince. I'd come back to the shopping centre the next day, go up to my friend Zach who also worked there, and get him to introduce me.

I strolled into the store the next day, sauntered casually up to Zach, making out I'd only come in to see him, then said, 'Right, the lad with the curly brown hair who works here. What's his name?' Zach laughed and knew straight away I was talking about Jason. Apparently, lots of people asked. Jason, it turned out, had only just turned 18. Christ. I was a cougar at 21. Zach introduced us and, that evening, we did the whole adding on Facebook thing and started flirting immediately. He said 'ha' after everything, which kept reminding me of his age, "Yeah I work there. Ha." "Yeah was so lovely to meet you too! Ha!".

But I looked past it. He was too fit.

After a couple of weeks of sitting by my phone waiting for him to text, belly-aching about how long to wait until texting back, wanting to fly into a pile of unicorns when he texted me first, I went out with my cousin Kate to Revs in Milton Keynes one Saturday night. Read: where I knew he'd be hanging out. We ended up snogging all night. It was glorious.

I started to meet him on his lunch breaks, which is where we were papped together for the first time. I was still a bit oblivious to the paps at that point, I certainly didn't expect them to come to Centre

MK! There was interest in who Jason was – he was very new to it all and it freaked him out a bit. So we started hanging out at my flat a lot instead. It was summer, and we spent most evenings walking around parks, sitting by rivers, then gazing at each other in bed till about 5am. I was arse over tit in love with him very quickly. He was so precious and gorgeous and I felt like I wanted to look after him and sort of show him the way a bit. I was his first serious girlfriend, so I was indulging in the maturity of that and how grown-up it made me feel. I liked the fact that I took the reins, I was the experienced one, the one in control for a change, and he hung on every word I said as though it was gospel. Even if I was slightly making it up every now and then. That was very new to me too. But it worked for us. He was my real-life Disney prince and that's genuinely what I called him to his face.

The thing with going out with a real-life Disney prince is that there are a lot of Tinker Bells flying around, extremely green with envy and cross that you are his Wendy. Hovering around with their blonde topknots, trying to sprinkle their fairy dust all over him, fluttering their wings and bending over with their extremely short dresses on and revealing their stunning tiny, toned and tanned bums (Tinker

Bell ALWAYS did that, didn't she?! Little madam).
And it was hard because, well … I was jealous. All
the time. Over every single girl that ever spoke to
him. He was 18 years old and extremely popular. He
knew everyone, especially all the young and utterly
breathtakingly beautiful girls he knew at Hollister
and beyond. I had it in my head that every single
one of them fancied him and I hated it. I was always
friendly to them when I met them – I am certainly
not that horrible girl who scowls at other girls for
no reason. Never have been. I even became quite
pally with a couple of them. But it did make me
feel insecure. It made me feel old and fat and not
as cool as they all were. I also knew that Jason was
so young and new to relationships that I was always
scared his head would turn, or he would test the
boundaries. I had doubt. And I hadn't had that
with Daniel, so it made me panic. I felt like a little
girl again, terrified about my dad running off with
another woman and leaving my mum.

Jason had an amazing family that he was living
with who I became close to very quickly. They lived
about half an hour from my flat and I was spending
most weekends at their house in the countryside. His
lovely mum, his stepdad, gorgeous younger sister
(about 15 when I met her) and a hilarious younger

brother (around seven when I met him) – together we became like a little gang, like I'd had with my family when we were younger, I guess. They lived in a beautiful big house, big garden, huge fridge always full of fun stuff (mainly wine for his mum, stepdad and me to drink). His grandparents also visited a lot and I became really close to his grandma. We'd sit and drink prosecco in the garden and gossip about EVERYTHING.

I spent summers in their garden, drinking with their neighbours, having takeaways, taking their dog Marley for a walk (although I moaned about that bit – wish I hadn't now). Watching Jason and his little brother play football in the garden while I sat and painted (it sounds so fucking middle class when I write it down). I spent winters there putting up Christmas trees, playing chess with his little brother, playing cards with Jason on the sofa, laughing in the kitchen with his sister about ridiculous things. I adored his family as though they were my own. That house made me feel safe and stable. They treated me like a member of the family, and I will always have so much love in my heart for them.

Jason and I had a loving, fun and close relationship. But there were occasional bumps along the way when it came to girls, sometimes with my silly jealousy, but also sometimes because he did give me reasons to feel that way. He was so young, and I truly believed he tried his best to be the man I was trying to mould him into. I struggled with our age gap every now and then because it would show when it came to things like friends and family. I spent a lot of time with his, whereas he didn't take much interest in mine. I would also try to take him with me to friends' parties, or weddings, and he always had an excuse as to why he couldn't come. He would rather play on the PlayStation or go and play football with his friends when I needed picking up from an airport – this was always the sort of stuff we'd clash over. It wasn't his fault; he just wasn't in the same place as I was a lot of the time and that was simply because of our age difference. I know he adored me, but he just didn't quite understand the priorities and the security that I needed. I'd battle with this a lot, but because, overall, we shared so much and we loved each other so much, I just accepted it most of the time. I didn't want to lose him simply because he chose the PlayStation over my best friend's birthday.

When I moved to Kentish Town, Jason began spending more and more time with me there so he eventually moved in. Craig's boyfriend Macgowan then moved in and we were a fun little four. We'd have our ups and downs but we were enjoying living together. Jason had become a model by then and was getting quite regular work, as was I with a few bits to keep me going. We were good. Life was good. We'd spend the week in London, then lots of weekends at his family's house. We'd sing Justin Bieber songs the whole way there and back in Jason's car, bicker about something, fall silent for a moment, then one of us would burst out laughing and the argument would be over. I loved him. I really, really loved him, and he loved me. I could never be angry at him for long. All he had to do was give me a certain smile and I would absolutely forgive anything. It was sometimes like a mother and son irritation! That sounds fucking gross, but what I mean is that I never felt he was doing any wrong as such. He was just a cheeky little shit sometimes and knew he'd get away with it if he cuddled me a certain way or gave me his white, toothy Prince Eric smile. (That's Prince Eric from *The Little Mermaid*, if you didn't catch the reference. I won't be able to listen to the song 'Part of Your World' ever again without thinking of him.) Until one day, unfortunately, something happened that I was unable to quite forgive, and so we 'went on a break'.

In this break, I went away on a work trip with my mum. She was directing a play out of town that was running for a few nights and persuaded me to go with her thinking it would cheer me up. I was heartbroken. Utterly miserable. After the show, I was sat in the bar with some of mum's friends, and actually started to have a good time. A boy came in and joined the group. There was an immediate spark, an immediate attraction, and we started laughing and having fun straight away. I spent the weekend meeting up with him and we established a really great connection. He was older, hilarious, and we were just so similar. I went back to London. We carried on speaking for a little while and then that dried up. I didn't think much else of it other than that I'd had fun over a weekend with someone who made me feel better about my break-up.

Jason then got wind I'd met someone while I had been away and was devastated, to the point where I got a car at three in the morning to go and comfort him and we ended up getting back together. I still loved him. We wanted to fight for our relationship.

After long conversations and making new promises to each other, we moved into a flat together on our own in Camden. It sounds mad when we'd only just got back together, but you know what it's like when you're trying to fix things. We thought creating our own little home together with pictures of us both on the walls, and having dinner parties with our friends, would sort everything. And it does for a while. I'm sure lots of girls can relate to this period of time during relationships that have been through the mill. You nearly lose each other, you come back together, the sex becomes exciting and adventurous again, the flowers and surprise dinners happen again, the late nights of chatting come back, the sacrifices you make become more apparent, and you speak in a nicer and more amicable tone to each other. 'No, of course – you do that tonight, that's totally fine, babe! Enjoy yourself!' And your voices have gone up three keys higher because you're being super-lovely to one another.

While this was all happening, though ... there was still a doubt niggling away, far in the back of my mind. I completely pushed it out and shoved it in a scary-thought drawer because I had to make this work. I was terrified of losing my fairy-tale prince again. But I just couldn't help but think I had already lost something that I couldn't get back. Trust, maybe. Something had gone.

I got a late-night message one night from the man I met on the trip with mum. We started chatting quite a lot. Absolutely nothing bad. The conversations honestly went from sending songs to each other by the band we both liked, to our favourite sandwiches. It was friendly, fun chat, but obviously because of the weekend we had spent together, I knew what I was doing was a little bit naughty. But he made me laugh, we made each other laugh, and we understood each other.

The weeks ticked by, I was on a downward spiral. Jason and I were growing further and further apart. I would lie in bed sobbing silently while he slept next to me, because I knew it was over but I just didn't know how to articulate anything. And the thought of not having Jason in my life was still too painful to fathom. I was heartbroken that since getting back together, I just couldn't get back what we had before. I still loved him so much. I still loved the smell of his neck, his clothes; still looked at him and thought he was the most gorgeous boy in the world. But it was too little too late. I don't know what you call this kind of end to a relationship, really. I have been dumped before but there was something hugely traumatic involved in this kind of ending, it was just closing down, it was the end of the road, for no real reason. I didn't understand. So, one day, I plucked up the courage to tell Jason I wasn't happy.

I was lying in bed waiting for him to come to bed too. I was crying when he came in, and I just said the words, 'I'm unhappy.' Simple as that. They just spilled out of me. I can't really remember what was said, apart from teary words of regret and sadness and reminiscing. We were both heartbroken. We knew deep down it was the right thing, but it's just so fucking hard. When you're breaking up with someone, it's like you're about to die and your love flashes before your eyes. Your love with that person, all your memories, from the second you met to now, all in chronological order, completely flash through your mind as though death is about to take you. And I guess a part of you does die. That's how it feels anyway. My love flashed before my eyes, and it was gone.

We agreed to move out of the flat but still had a month left on the lease, so we were still living together for those few weeks. We were still being nice and kind to each other, cuddling at night-time, crying; I still stroked his hair. And we helped each other with living arrangements. I was going back to the Kentish Town flat and he was moving to a flat-share. I'd been seeing a therapist for the last few months and I was by now on very strong antidepressants. My drinking was bad, my sadness unravelling. And I was slowly going down a very sad and dark path of self-destruction. If I wanted to end my relationship with Jason, I had to do it with a clearer head. So any late night texting, any potential meet ups with rebound men or men that lingered on the outer rings of my life that I knew would pop up at any given moment were off limits. So that was over, my relationship was over, and I felt empty.

Jason and I said our goodbyes and I moved the last of my boxes back into the Kentish Town flat. I knew this really was it, no going back. I kept thinking, 'How can this be the right thing if it hurts this much?'

One day I went out and drank so much that I came home, fell and hit my head on the side of the bath and knocked myself out. My flatmate, Alex, who had also just moved in, found me on the floor and called my parents. Enough was enough and they came to see me.

I was a mess. So, so, so, so, sad. Heartbroken. Questioning everything. Was it all my fault? Probably. I always seem to blame myself for these kinds of things. Maybe if I wasn't so this and so that, blah blah.

With a bit more distance I can see that the fact of the matter was the relationship had run its course. But where does that leave you? Why does that happen? When you have nothing more to pin it on but a simple 'dead end' sign. It's like the end of the film *The Truman Show*, when the boat crashes into the set at the edge of the horizon. Nowhere further to go. But I don't regret trying again. Sometimes you have to go back to really realise. That final go at things gave me consolation that what we had was gone.

Jason has moved on and I'm happy for him. We don't have contact anymore. I think sometimes that's just the way it has to be. It doesn't mean I don't think about him and our time together. He will remain very special to me, and I am sorry for always nagging him to turn the football over. I didn't mind it so much really.

All kinds of people will come into your life. Some will hurt you and make you feel like you're constantly on a terrifying Alton Towers ride. Some will fix the broken pieces of your soul back together and be your pillar of strength. And some will look so much like a Disney prince that you will want to keep them in a little box forever. (But you can't – I should really stress that.)

In the end, I realised that in relationships – be they long and intense or short and exciting – will shape you. With each one I evolved into a different version of myself, and for each one I learned a little bit more about who I am. I think the one that will last is when you've learned enough about yourself to not settle. I will always have a lot of love in my heart and will fall quickly, I just do and I will always let something go that isn't meant for me, eventually. Even if that is really fucking hard.

How to Get Over Someone

Days 1–4:

Stock your house with your favourite foods and plenty of wine. It's definitely acceptable to buy all this either in your pyjamas or in clothes he/she left behind at yours. If you can't move, voice-note a shopping list to your best friend. If your best friend isn't around, download Deliveroo.

Your sofa can become your new best friend for a few days. Take a load off. Netflix was invented for days like these (it wasn't but I like to think it might have been). Whatever you do, DO NOT watch *The Notebook*. DO NOT WATCH THE NOTEBOOK. Watch *Making A Murderer*.

'Anyone around?' If you are at home, alone, newly heartbroken and wanting some company – send that message. If you are at home, with your boyfriend/girlfriend on the sofa and you receive that message, that is the message from a newly single friend who needs to go out. You better wash your bum and get the Rimmel instant on because you're going out in support of the heartbroken. Sorry love.

For the heartbroken ones – go easy on your friends. Even if as soon as you rock up to the pub someone says 'So how's Adam?' – when they've forgotten Adam is a fuckwit who has been sending dick pics to a girl he met in Ibiza. Yes, I know your heart is now crushed like a Rice Krispie cake you've dropped on the floor and then ground into the carpet, but your friends will need some time to adjust and not everybody has the words.

Days 5–9:

Wash your hair, tidy your room, if you're feeling up to it change your bed sheets. Message your friends, 'I'm making pasta,' and have them all round to chat. I do suggest cooking, it's therapeutic and distracting and I think you'll enjoy it. Something simple though, this isn't the time to try and master a soufflé. 'The thing is I kind of always knew it wasn't right,' someone will say. 'Honestly, be glad this has happened now and not in six months,' will say another.

Limit yourself to only an hour of stalking his social media a day. Don't go cold turkey, but don't overdose either. In fact, no delete him. (I'm not great at this am I!)

When your friends have gone, have a bath, listen to a podcast, light a scented candle. Shave your legs, paint your nails – giving yourself that bit of care and attention will make you feel loved. Self care, sister.

Days 10–14:

Go on, head out into the night, but delete his/her number first. Let's be honest, before you delete it you're going to write down the number on a bit of paper and put it in your knicker drawer. You will still be able to find your knicker drawer at three in the morning after a BNO. And nowadays deleting someone's number is not deleting someone's number – you will find it, in an archive somewhere. But at least try to!

Eat your tea before you go out. White wine-no tea is a disaster. Try not to sleep with someone because your heart will still be sore. But if you do sleep with someone, remember, protection is your friend. Getting pregnant or an STI at this point will not be helpful to your recovery and will guarantee a huge bout of 'hangxiety' the next day.

Days 15–30:

Go to the gym. Cut your hair. Buy yourself new knickers. Work on being healthy and happy and finding out 'what it is you really want'.

Days 31–60:

Have a ponder over dating apps and possibly download some, but also probably delete them as quickly as you swipe right to the fit boy two miles away. A year from now, repeat all the above.

Running the
Rat Race

Christmas is one of my favourite times of the year. As you've probably got the picture by now, my family bloody love a party, and Christmas is an excuse to have a glorious one, and then another one, and then another one, all the way up to New Year. Plenty of booze, plenty of food, plenty of singalongs, a gigantic tree, endless excuses to get tarted up – and plenty of time to recover each day on the sofa in front of *Home Alone* with a medicinal cheese board.

Christmas is also a time when, despite the total joy at the prospect of having Baileys on my Coco-Pops for two weeks, I have often felt reflective and down if I don't have a Christmas-jumper wearing boyfriend by my side to shower with presents and to sleep on a blow-up bed with.

It's so annoying. I've got my health, my family, my friends, my cheeseboard ... What more could I possibly need!?

Then, the old Christmas engagements start popping up. I'm here in a Santa hat and Mum telling me off for coming in late and eating all the ham whilst girls two, three years younger than me are putting up ring selfies in the park with 'A perfect

Christmas' as the caption. Oh hell. (Sidenote: I've always wanted a Christmas wedding, I want the snow, the sparkling decorations, the trees, *Home Alone* music playing as I walk down the aisle ...)

Christmas can be hard when you are without a significant other. I just wish we could all be happy at the *exact same time*. When we were growing up, everything happened to everyone at a similar point. Sure, some people got periods when they were nine and some people got them when they were 15, but no one's really racing for the time when wearing white knickers becomes a case of Russian roulette. When we're younger, we all grow a little taller each year, we all finish school and move on to new things at the same time, we're all on the same trajectory together. But unfortunately, that doesn't happen when it comes to relationships. Gutted.

Parking the tragedy of the situation for now, logistically it's a pain in the arse, isn't it? Why were we not taught at school that from our mid-twenties onwards we should have taken out an ISA and started saving just for all the weddings we'll need to cover? Alternatively, the lesson could have been: limit your friends to five – five is a number you can just about cover. If you have more than five friends, I'm afraid you can kiss goodbye to being able to afford a deposit on a house before you're 35. Especially. Takes deep breath. If you're invited to the hen do . . . This is what will happen:

You are walking down the street one day, minding your own business. Suddenly your phone is burning a hole in your pocket – it's vibrating like there's no tomorrow to the point where you're actually quite enjoying it. But you can't leave it in your pocket, there's clearly some sort of emergency. You pull your phone out and see that, no, the flat you live in is not on fire. Instead you've been invited to a new WhatsApp group by a number you don't recognise. The group is invariably called 'Berlin Bitches'. 'Madrid Mamas'. Or my personal favourite: 'Amsterdaaaaaaam, girl'.

You open up WhatsApp. You were invited to the group at 2.15pm. It is now 2.17pm and you already have SEVEN HUNDRED messages. The group admin – the maid of honour – is nearly always a girl called Bex, and she is the dictionary definition of passive aggressive. On the surface, she's the loveliest person you've ever met, but underneath every word she's bubbling with rage. She's like a Rottweiler with a St Tropez spray tan that's getting darker by the hour. What Bex wants more than anything is for you to part with exactly £1,378 asap – and, no, don't you dare suggest waiting for payday, anyone who does categorically hates the bride. You may indeed ask what the £1,378 is going to get you: you'll be flying to a capital city or beach resort somewhere in Europe and staying in an Airbnb with no windows and one too few bunk beds. Yes, it does include something else: the bride's portion of the bill – she deserves it because she's found the love of her life and is incredibly happy, whereas everyone else is a failure and must pay their own way. Except everyone who has already got married – you're just being generous.

The itinerary, which you can have an opinion about so long as you keep it to yourself, will be something along the lines of a boozy boat trip with the first watered-down gin and tonic free, a pole-dancing class where Bex and anyone else who goes to the gym can show off their skills, a jaunt to a male strip show with a very beige buffet and plenty of games such as penis piñata, which, yes, you will also be expected to contribute money to. The cost of all this plus food and alcohol will likely be another £932. AND, YES, YOU WILL BE PAYING FOR THE BRIDE.

Over £2,000 and three days of your life spent with people you'd never choose to hang around with and you'll never get back later, you can start looking forward to the actual wedding day. After you've sorted the gift, outfit, travel and hotel, you don't know when you'll be able to go on a holiday you'd actually like to go on, with people you'd choose to go with, ever again. But, of course, the actual wedding is beautiful. The bride looks stunning, there's an open bar (warning: not all weddings come with these) and the speeches have all been amazing. You felt a little tremble in your gut looking around at the other smug couples gazing wistfully at each other while the bride and her new husband said their vows, but you're really riding the wave of love.

Now you're looking around your table of fellow singletons. Your mum likely said something to you along the lines of, 'Ooo, you're going to a wedding? Might meet a nice man!' Ha, as if life is that kind! There are only two specimens on your table to choose from: the rogue cousin from America they don't like but couldn't *not* invite, and a guy you slept with five years ago who struggled to keep it up with a condom on. If push comes to shove, all right, you'll take that one for the team, but now you've paid the expense of a double room it might be better just to make the most of having it all to yourself. Or not.

The entirety of this experience is then repeated as many as four times in a summer. If you do eventually get a boyfriend, you will have to add another four to your calendar for his friends, meaning all your weekends in June and July will no longer belong to you.

An unmarried friend of mine recently reminded me that 50 per cent of marriages end in divorce these days. She seemed to find solace in this, whereas all it made me think was, 'Oh my God, by the time I'm 35, half my friends will get divorced and then remarry and I'll have to do this routine ALL OVER AGAIN.'

Deep down I *know* getting married doesn't equal any sort of success, but then why does life seem like a race towards it? I *know* that when a friend of mine gets married it doesn't take away the likelihood of me doing the same, but it does feel like a big flashing sign reminding me I haven't done it yet. Who sets these rules? Who makes us feel this way? Why does someone being happy, even when we love them to absolute bits, make us feel a little bit sad?

I don't have the answers. What I hope is that soon the adult train we're on will magically take me through a station where I'll learn not to compare the milestones I've completed with other people's.

But.

If I'm really, *really* honest.

I think I'd rather just marry a beautiful man and be too busy being blinded by my fuck-off engagement ring to look out of the window when we get there.

Under
Pressure

Being in the entertainment industry is like running continuously on an uphill treadmill, the gradient gets higher and higher and your feet move faster and faster. You get one job that you're really happy about, but no one really wants to talk about it – they just want to know what you're doing next. There's no sitting still, ever. It's like constantly battling for a promotion but, instead of it being every year, it's every month. Each job has to be more splashy, more sparkly, more noisy than the last, and if you don't keep the fireworks popping then you run the danger of being forgotten about and becoming irrelevant. Like a Catherine wheel. Like a Catherine wheel that's whirling and fizzing around but not really going anywhere. No big bang. No big ooo-aaaa moment. A bit like a sparkler, you have a small window to wave it around while the light burns bright, but do it quick, because in a few moments time, you'll be withered and burnt out and chucked in a bucket to cool off.

OK, maybe I'm being a bit dramatic, but that's kind of my job.

All this pressure does have an effect on you, it can't not. It does for everyone. It also means you're constantly left feeling a bit unsatisfied. I was quite lucky, to be honest, with how my career kicked off because most actors have to graft for a long time before they get a big break, but my big break came when I first started out. And, after *The Inbetweeners* and *Dancing on Ice*, opportunities did start rolling in, but I think everyone was waiting for me to get this huge movie. I kept getting parts and being told, 'This'll be the big one. This'll be the big one.' I am so proud of all the films I've been in and I loved doing them, but none of them were blockbusters. And it got so exhausting waiting for the biggun to come. In the end it's what led me to making different choices – going on *I'm a Celeb* ... and deciding to give my own one-woman show a go.

I could have tried harder, that's something I will always have to accept – and I have. I could have trained; I could have read Shakespeare; I could have gone to more plays and studied them; I could have eaten less. But I was never going to be *that* person. I'm sure I've only ever got to where I am through being 100 per cent entirely Emily Atack. I worked with my assets. I was blonde, I had boobs, I was slim: there will always be roles for those girls. There will always be *FHM* covers for those girls. It worked for me and I've never regretted doing it. I look back now as a woman and roll my eyes and think, 'It shouldn't be that way', but it was – and I'm not complaining at all. I've got the *FHM* plaques up in my house and I'm proud of them. I truly believe that everything I've done – taking my top off, being a bit of a pin-up for a while – has led me to where I am now. And where I am now is sitting on my squidgy arse on a sofa, looking back at those photos going, 'Phwoar, I looked good – let's all have a good laugh that I used to pose in my pants like that.' It's all material now for my stand-up!

I got enough jobs to keep me ticking over, and through doing that and not bullying myself into starving my body for the perfect role, I think I actually maintained the elusive work-life balance. I was never going to choose not to go to my friend's birthday and drink vat-loads of wine with her before an audition – I knew there would be girls going for the same part as me who were as good as me or better and that there was a chance I'd get it, and a chance I wouldn't. I wasn't going to put all my eggs in the work basket and not see the smile on my friend's face when I bought the 17th round of tequilas. Life was too short then and it's too short now. If I didn't get it, I didn't get it – there were other gigs. And to be honest, without wanting to sound big-headed, I don't think I ever lost out on an audition because I was hanging out of my arse. I've never had bad feedback from an audition. If I didn't get a part, I think it was because I didn't fit sometimes: my weight, my background. There's a lot of rejection in acting, and it can hurt if you really want the part and you've demonstrated your commitment by not going to the pub with your mates the night before. But it makes you stronger; you pick yourself up and get on with it, you count your lucky stars that there have been roles before, you trust there will be roles again. It gives you more and more armour until you're brave enough to make leaps you might not have taken otherwise.

In 2014, there were a few scary months where I was getting rejected for everything. Good, but not good enough. I was reaching the end of my tether with it all. The audition for *Dad's Army* was approaching, and then something awful happened: a really wonderful, dear friend of mine died in a car crash. I was devastated. He was only 30. I spent the weekend afterwards with all my friends, hugging one another, sobbing, utterly heartbroken. The audition was on a Monday and there was no way I could go. I looked at myself in the mirror, puffy-eyed and grey, feeling so lost and empty, and thought, 'There is no way I can do this.'

It's such a cliché for people to say that a person who's died would have wanted them to carry on, not to put off doing something, but no jokes I felt like I could hear him saying, in his Essex accent, 'Don't be such a silly fucker. Go to the audition.'

For the first time, I knew I really didn't care if I didn't get the part. Rejection just didn't matter compared to this tragedy that had cleaved my heart in two. So I decided to go. I marched into that room, I had no nerves whatsoever, and I probably gave the best audition I've ever given. I got the part.

People like to quote sayings such as 'If at first you don't succeed, try, try and try again' and 'Nothing worth having comes easy'. It's taken me years to realise it, but I don't believe in any of that. Do your best – do *your* best. If it works out, it was meant to be; if it doesn't, try again, but if you can't be bothered to try again, don't worry about it. Maybe decide on a different path. There are plenty to choose from. There's so much pressure nowadays to kill ourselves at work, or to achieve a goal we're actually not as bothered about as we think we are. If this resonates with you, don't let it get to you. Some industries, like acting, are uphill treadmills. If you don't want to run on them, don't be afraid to get off.

The People
Who Shaped Me:
Grandma Doris

Doris is my dad's mum and she's my last living grandparent. She lives in Yorkshire and has done her whole life, and for many years ran a clothes shop in her local town centre. A stunning woman with bags of style – her wardrobe is to die for. At 87, Grandma Doris still puts on her make-up and diamond earrings and goes on cruises and long holidays to exotic locations. She still spends hours on the phone, chatting to friends each night. She's the sort of lady who you'll find nattering away to a shopkeeper and, when you ask her how they know each other as you leave, she'll reply, 'Oh I don't know him, love.'

She is the stereotypical proud grandparent in every sense of the word – our school photos line the walls and surfaces of her immaculate bungalow and she still sends birthday cheques to us in the post even though by our age all her kids were parents themselves. In a big silver frame on the table in her hallway, next to the house phone, is a blown-up photo of me, my dad ... and John Barrowman at the *I'm a Celeb* ... wrap party! (Impressed by the quick printing technique there, Doris.)

For my cousin Faith's hen do, Grandma Doris and her friend joined her and 15 girls in Las Vegas. She marched up and down that strip and stayed up late on the slots – she doesn't even drink so that is some epic stamina. One night, at the strip show the girls had organised, one of the giant muscly men yanked her onto the stage and performed the Magic Mike 'Pony' dance on her lap. I think she kissed him on the lips!

She lives on her own now, but cared for my grandad Roy for years at their house before he went into a care home. Grandma Doris and Grandad Roy married young and raised my dad Keith, his identical twin Tim and their brother Simon well, surrounded by music – all three are exceptionally talented musicians and can play just about every instrument there is. I only ever knew my grandad Roy as an older man; he suffered two very big strokes when I was young and so I was only ever really aware of him being slightly held back by ailments. But he was a funny and talented man who I loved very much.

I've taken a lot from my grandma Doris – or I try very hard to. She's a bright, strong, ballsy and beautiful woman who doesn't let life knock her. I am so lucky to have her – she, out of everyone in the family, is my biggest fan. She follows it all, she watches every show I do and I'm pretty sure that, through her systematic canvassing at her local market, she was personally responsible for 50 per cent of the votes I received in the final of *I'm a Celeb* ....

'I'm Depressed'

These are two words I hear a lot, and I'm sure you do too. I use them all the time and my friends do too. Correct me if I'm wrong, but 'I'm depressed' OFTEN means in young people's terms 'I'm hungover' or 'I wish I hadn't done that' or 'I've got so much work to do and I haven't done it cos I've been getting pissed all weekend'. But sometimes it may just mean something more than that.

From a very young age I've felt susceptible to sadness, feeling scared, anxious, like I want to cry all the time, and I didn't know why. I've always been a happy person in general. Anyone who knows me will usually describe my personality as 'bubbly' and 'outgoing' and 'fun', and, sorry to sound like David Brent here, but, yes, I am all of those things, sure. However, there's always been something inside me somewhere that feels like a lost kid in a supermarket. You know, that sinking feeling you get the first time you lose your mum in a supermarket and you think your world is about to end and you can't get past the never-ending sense of doom and emptiness. I sometimes feel like that – I feel lost, I feel homesick for a home that doesn't exist, I feel like I want to go

home but I don't know where that is, even though I
have a million homes surrounding me full of people
I love and that I could go back to whenever I please.
I still feel like something is missing and that there's
an empty hole somewhere in me, and I've pretty
much always felt that way.

I remember listening to music and it really
affecting me, as did films and the stories my mum
would read to me or make up on the spot. I was
sensitive and very open to feelings, which has been
a great thing in my life and makes me empathetic,
but it has also at times been to my detriment. I find
myself, and always have, getting very emotionally
invested in things. When it comes to happiness,
I fully commit to that emotion when I'm feeling
upbeat, but the same thing happens when I'm feeling
sad, and I fully commit to that too.

I've found that the majority of people in the
creative industry are this way; my parents and most
members of my family have been like this. As I've
grown up and become more knowledgeable about
the word 'depressed', and learnt about chemical
imbalances in the brain, or traumatic pasts and
various other causes of depression, I've always tried
to ask myself what the reasons are for my feelings.
I've felt like this at times since I can remember even

having thoughts. I remember once we were putting up our Christmas stockings for Santa when I was about six or seven, and I recall feeling so happy that I actually felt sad. I was heartbreakingly happy. I was crushed with love for my mum as I watched her put the carrots and brandy out on the side for Santa; my heart broke for my dad as I watched him (terribly) putting up the last of the lights in a bush outside our house. And the amount of presents we got!! I've always been funny with presents. I don't have a materialistic bone in my body so I never really fully appreciate a present. Does that make any sense? I feel like someone else should have my present, someone who needs it. I don't need a present. Christmas morning, devastated. So fucking happy and yet devastated at the same time – WHY?! I'm crying as I even write this. It's bizarre. I guess with me, when something makes me happy, I am so terrified of it being taken from me. Nothing in terms of material possessions (I honestly couldn't give a shit if my house got burgled tomorrow – I would hope that someone who was desperate enough to nick my stuff now has a couch to sit on; I can get another one) – it's my family, my mum and dad, my siblings, my past, my future even. The fear of having any of those things taken from me fills me with dread every day. Subconsciously, mainly – I'm not saying I sit there sobbing all day, every day, about all these things.

I think this is what confuses people about 'depression', its insidious nature. Some of the greatest comedians in the world have been the most depressed, it doesn't discriminate – funny people, or the richest or most famous, or someone who seems on the surface to have everything they could wish for, anyone can suffer from it. 'What have you got to be depressed about?' is a question I hear a lot – and it really pisses me off. It's absolutely nothing to do with what you do or don't have in your life. It's like someone saying, 'What have you got a migraine for? There's no reason to have one.' You can't explain it, you just have a migraine.

I think, for me, I never want to tell anyone I sometimes suffer from feeling like this because I'm known as being so happy, and I don't want to disappoint anyone, or I don't want them to think my whole outward persona is false. It really isn't. When I'm at a party or a barbie, or at work, or in a jungle, I really am presenting to you my true self, which is a friendly and happy person. I identify myself as a happy individual who loves life and loves People, Places and Things (that play's a bit depressing, though!).

I just sometimes feel sad and I can't really explain why. I've had therapy, I've been on antidepressants, stopped boozing for periods of time, been to the gym every single January, read self-help books … and I've come to realise that actually just accepting that sometimes I feel this way is way less stressful than always trying to figure it out. 'It's okay not to be okay' and all that.

I think we're all now made to think we should be running around with unicorns up our arses when, actually, sometimes maybe we just have to accept that we might feel shit sometimes, and at specific periods more than others. Some days it's just a little bit more difficult to get out of bed, and I'm just learning to be at peace with that. You can do things to help yourself along the way, like put olives in a bowl, light a candle and put a facemask on, or listen to your favourite Spice Girls song.

Being fearful of my past and my future will probably always creep in every now and then, but I'm learning to embrace the *now*, whether I am in a good or bad place mentally. Because I'm here, I am alive. Because now is MY present, and the now is the greatest gift of all.

Sister, Sister

So you've heard a lot about Martha. The sister, the agent, the fun police. So here she is in her own words. Marf (as we call her) might be scary boss lady now but just to really embarrass her, I'm pleased to say that her nickname as a baby was psycho sausage because she looked like an uncooked sausage. She was a large baby, had no teeth for ages, and was always cackling like a mad old man. If you are lucky enough to have a sister you are close to you will know that it's impossible to describe the relationship and do it justice in words. Impossible. No other person can make you flip your lid like it but you'd drop everything to be there for them, Over to you, Marf.

I was meant to start writing this chapter last night but I had to postpone it until this morning as I was up until just gone midnight scrolling through over 18,000 images on an old iCloud account of Emily's.

A few weeks ago, one spring Saturday morning while I was drying my hair with Saturday Kitchen on in the background (it was a non-hangover, smug kind of Saturday), Emily called me. If Emily calls me before

11am on a Saturday (or most days, in fact) I know that a) something is probably very wrong or b) she hasn't been to bed yet. I answered and she said with panic and a break in her voice, 'There's naked pictures of me on Twitter.' My stomach lurched, I am silent. I looked, yep, there they were. A few RTs, a few faves, many, many absolutely vile comments.

We soon establish these are from iCloud, an old one, hacked and leaked online. Fuck.

I would expect most people would have their sister as their first port of call should their breasts somehow have made their way onto the internet against their will, so nothing unusual there. But the difference here is that it's not only my personal duty to help her with this issue, but my professional one too.

I am one of Emily's agents/managers. Her little sister first and foremost – but, along with a guy named Alex Segal, I manage and represent Emily in her working life. We would call ourselves 'her people' if we were dicks.

Much like a real leak from your bathroom, the next few hours were spent going down the usual pathways to try to assess the root of the problem and contain the damage caused by the leak. We summon a conference call with her publicists to discuss the matter. One by one people get added on the line: 'Hi James', 'Hi

Marth' – everyone sounds like they've been out last night, much less bright-eyed and bushy-tailed than if this was a Monday call. We talk numbers – how many pics? Two? Three? Eighty-seven? 'Emily, do you think there's anything worse on there?' We call a lawyer; he joins in the conference call: 'Hi Jonathan.' We pay through the nose for said lawyer. We get a call from the Sun. We call Apple. We call Mum (awkward).

So, for now, Smug-Saturday is on hold. I had planned to get coffee and browse around H&M with my fiancé Mark, but that will have to wait until tomorrow. He gets it. Between myself, Alex, Emily's publicists, her lawyer, we make a plan and assign roles – you check this, I'll look at that, I'll call her back. I am never anything but astounded by the speed and the efficiency of the people I work with. There is not a single weak link in the chain in Team Emily.

Where were we? Oh yes, the violation of Emily's sexual privacy. The reason I am recalling this story is because in this business of show it is so easy to forget the crux of what you are dealing with. The job is to put out the fire – you often forget the fuel at the pit of the blaze. Emily, her private photos, her body, put out to the public against her will. It's just awful. Emily has to recount stories to men she barely knows about what parts of her body might appear on Twitter next. She has to (in detail) let us know of anything she feels may come to light. It's embarrassing and it's humiliating.

As her manager, her agent, during these operational moments to put out the fire I forget that she's my sister, and I think it's important I have that separation – otherwise our working relationship wouldn't work. But once the team have gone back to their Saturday trip to the zoo and back to their newspapers and tea (until tomorrow's papers land), I am always left with a feeling of such horror for my sister – not my client – but my big sister. I want to wrap her up in cotton wool. I ask if she's okay. She always says yes.

So, last night, at midnight after we got access to the hacked files, I sat and I went through each photo one by one. Selfie, selfie, selfie, pics of our baby sister, more pics of baby sister, Mum, Dad, selfie, selfie, selfie, night out, night out, night out, hangover photo, hangover photo. This is not just her life, but our life, our life as a family, and for someone to have access to those private moments, 95 per cent of which have not been shared on Instagram – so were never intended to be in the public domain – made me feel sad. Pics of our brother in hospital strapped to a machine, pics of our late uncle Simon, pics of our grandad, pics of our uncle Steve on his last day of radiotherapy, pics of moments we have shared not with her followers or fans for likes or for RTs but private moments snapped and shared on WhatsApp or kept sacred in a folder marked 'Family <3'. Someone has all of these, someone somewhere has them all. When someone in the public eye gets their privacy violated it has a ripple effect throughout that person's whole world.

Working with family has taught me to be a good manager, I care for everyone I look after with a great deal of intimacy and empathy as if they were family. I care for every person as if they were Emily as best as I can. She sets the benchmark.

Working together has always been part of the plan. Even as toddlers I'd push her around in a pram even though I was 18 months younger. I would stage-manage Emily as a kid in the garden and ensure her performance in the paddling pool was perfected before she went on and entertained a good turnout of kids from the village. I never wanted to be famous or in the public eye but Emily did. She couldn't really do anything else but perform.

I am particularly proud of her achievements that perhaps didn't gain her the huge profile she has now. Away from the jungle, away from the hype, the fake tan and celebrity men, she has quality jewels in her comedy crown that I'll always be envious of. She has worked closely with comedy legends, including Victoria Wood, Julia Davis, Tracey Ullman, Ben Elton, Bill Nighy, Toby Jones and Jennifer Saunders. Many of these people hired her personally after rounds of auditions. She has captured casting directors' eyes and won roles by her quick and effortless comedy timing and the sparkle in her eye. When she was cast as Daphne in the remake of Dad's Army among the lead cast (alongside Catherine Zeta-bloody-Jones), I nearly exploded. She looked sensational in that blonde wig and army gear, like she was plucked from that era. We saw pap shots of her online, marching along this huge set-up final shot alongside Michael Gambon, Sarah Lancashire and Felicity Montagu (as a huge Alan Partridge fan the fact she was working with Lynn was almost too much for me). In the end titles, on her freeze-frame 'You have been watching … Emily Atack' I burst into tears at the screening.

These are the moments where I am her sister, not her agent. I often have to keep a poker face when she achieves great things – nobody wants a manager who actually secretly wants to be the talent, even worse if you're their sister, cringe. So, I keep calm and collected, but of course I scream and jump around and tell my fiancé about all her achievements when I get home each night.

When she came runner-up to the great Harry Redknapp in I'm a Celeb ..., I was in a tent in Australia with my dad, gripping his arm, while Mum was up on the bridge waiting to greet her. We were down at the base of the camp, watching on a screen with all of the families. When they announced John Barrowman had come third I was stunned. Runner-up – oh my God, Emily, you've done it. Watching her wild knotted hair and freckly, tear-stained, skinny face – that new face everyone was talking about was one I knew so, so well – come second was one of the proudest moments of my life. I am her sister in those instants, not her agent.

Being so close in age meant we shared almost everything growing up, friends, a bedroom, clothes. Everything except our taste in boys. Even at the age of 11 I couldn't fathom Emily wanting to hang around in the back of someone's Vauxhall Nova in a sea of McDonald's wrappers and smoke. The only time Emily hasn't wanted me around was from the age of about ten to 13. She was very naughty in these days and hung around with boys with crispy curtains and gold teeth and push bikes, and they all smoked. I didn't dislike these boys, in fact some were quite entertaining, and I think some of them thought I was quite funny, but I always felt like it was time to go home after an hour of chatting at a gate at the park. I wanted to go back to Mum and dance on the kitchen table (which we often did when nobody was at home).

I was fascinated by Emily's looks as a kid. She looked far too old for her age. But it was enchanting; in middle school she looked like a pop star. I used to steal her clothes a lot, much to Emily's dislike, and, in all honesty, they didn't really fit. I had a bit of a belly and buck teeth and Emily had a washboard stomach and a padded bra and white eyeliner.

I remember once wearing a light-pink halterneck top of hers to the park à la Mariah Carey in the 'Heartbreaker' video. Upon my arrival on my micro scooter, my can of cream soda in hand, an older naughty boy with a Slipknot hoodie shouted 'Belly's gunna get ya!' at me. I didn't really understand what he meant, but soon clocked that he was talking about my pink puppy roll that was proudly sticking out from beneath the top. Emily was greeted with wolf whistles and playful nudges.

I once saw her kissing a boy by the village hall – it stopped me in my tracks. I had never seen her kiss anyone before, I was traumatised. I remember thinking I wasn't sure Father Christmas would like that.

I remember climbing into a tent around the back of a load of garages where Emily was hanging out one summer day; she told me to go away. I declined to listen and stuffed myself into the hot green cocoon. Boys without tops on – I remember thinking their nipples were very dark in comparison to our brother George's who (at the time) was like a little pink micro pig. Within five minutes of me taking up too much room a boy who looked a bit like a lizard, was making wisecracks and laughing at me under his breath; he then kindly pointed out that I had very hairy legs. I looked down at my milk bottle bruised legs stretched out in front of me, covered in a moss of white wisps – he was right and I was embarrassed; it was time to leave. I went home immediately and hacked my legs to bits with Dad's Bic razor and got very told off by Mum when she found hairs and blood in the bath. In a bid to completely turn the bollocking around I explained to Mum that Emily was hanging around with scary lizard boys and kissing them in the tents down by the garages. Needless to say, Kate dragged her home and Emily banned me from hanging out with them for the rest of the summer holidays.

Their loss. While I used grassing up Emily as a good bid to take the heat off me for my impromptu summer shave, I remember telling mum because really I wanted Emily to come home. I didn't like that tent, or those boys. It wasn't right. It would be best if she came home and played with me and George for the rest of the evening in the garden and had some Cheerios.

Moments like that as a younger sister shape you. As a younger sister you watch on, you see how your sister, the person you are most like in the whole world, moves so differently, is received differently. In a weird way I began to realise that if I was uncomfortable, it couldn't be good for Emily. For example, in the tent, I was sure they weren't nice lads, I knew it wasn't fun, but Emily was so relaxed and consumed by the situation that she couldn't see the boys from the lizards! I had a genuine fear I may never see her again. Lost forever in the tents.

It was like I was beginning to lay little concrete blocks within me. If I didn't like it, it can't be good for her. So on I went, for the next 20 years, and I still do to this very day. Laying the blocks and building up the fortress that I use time and time again to shield her from the shit when bad things come to a head.

Tom, Jason, Daniel, bullies, school, admin, homework, morning-after pills, and now work, you name it – I am there with operation 'Help Emily' whenever she needs it. As teens I learnt to drive, I printed her scripts, I cut up pillow cases to make headscarves for her auditions when we realised at the last minute the casting notes said '1950s'. The one time I had nothing to give her and the fortress closed for the season was during our parents' divorce. Emily put a roof over our head, she made the phone calls, she brought the Domino's pizza, she paid the council tax (sometimes) and she held it together while I fell apart. She saved me.

And so, here we are today, and really nothing has changed – I'm still trying to get her out of tents with guys. I am still in awe of her when she walks onto a red carpet. I feel I have a lifetime of experience to make the right call for her, but sometimes I get it wrong, sometimes I need to let it go. It pains me to tell you but I was on the fence about the jungle; she was certain that it was the year to do it and she was right.

I'm getting married next year and Emily will of course be my maid of honour and by my side on the day. I sometimes think she is worried she's losing me, but, married or not, the fortress will always be open.

It's a Jungle
Out There

Taking part in *I'm A Celebrity* ... is one of the most insane things I've ever done. You do often forget that it is a TV show – the biggest one on UK television, in fact. So while you see the bugs and the hammocks and cold showers you are also part of a major operation. It's thrilling, it's HUGE. Here's a few bits you may not know about The Jungle experience.

– I slept the best I have ever slept in my life in that camp. While this might not be the juicy gossip you were after, I thought that was extremely telling about how we live our lives normally. The second my head hit the pillow I was out. For eight, nine sometimes ten hours. The fresh air, the exercise, the warmth no doubt helps, but I felt such peace of mind. No phone making your eyes ache, no Twitter making you feel anxious, no emails, no digital invasion, no alcohol, no sugar. My mind would drift into peaceful, light dreams (usually of food). You have an alarm clock in there (yes even in the Jungle someone is getting you out of bed). 'WAKEY WAKEY CAMPERS RISE AND

SHINE,' the voice of Gods would boom out across these huge tannoys every morning. Well I guess it's fair enough, they did have a show to make every day.

– 'EMILY, GET UP!' the voice would boom after 40 minutes of me not stirring. Everyone else would be slowly getting up, bleary eyed, walking to the shower. Not me, I'd roll back over, back into this soft, pure slumber that I cherished. I haven't slept that well since and I probably never will, but I learned what true peaceful sleep is in there, and it means pretty much getting rid of everything in our life that we consume too much of.

– The hunger is real. You only eat what you win, and other than that, it's beans and rice. We all got on brilliantly but food can cause even the smiliest of campmates to kick off and get narky. After making it to the final with Harry and John you get to order your dream meal – it is cooked from scratch by a chef and you can order whatever you fancy. My meal – starter: Baked Camembert with sweet onion chutney and bread (and half of John Barrowman's pizza). Main: an American style stacked burger with bacon, cheese, onions, relish and sweet potato fries. Dessert: I was craving peanut butter and chocolate and cream so I had them whip up a a chocolate and peanut butter cheesecake! I then had some of Harry's sticky toffee pudding too. For my drink I had a glass of cold Provence rosé (my fave wine). It went straight to my head, I was giddy, I was in heaven. I think it was one of the best moments of my life. No, in fact, Harry gave me his Bailey's – and then THAT was the best moment of my life.

– The money is great, but for me I was probably one of the lowest paid of the series. When you have legends like Noel Edmonds, Harry Redknapp, Nick Knowles in there you can kind of gather that you're probably in the bargain basement! But I hope they think they got good bang for their buck! Haha.

– The security guards are fit. Whenever you do a task you have security with you and some of them were HUNKS. Like action man hunks. After three weeks of no action, your eyes start wandering! I got told off for trying to chat to one of the guys when I was being taken down to a task – trust me to seriously attempt to go on the pull in the jungle, smelling like pond water with dreadlocks. They aren't allowed to speak back to you, nobody is, not the crew, not the camera guys – definitely not the fit security guards. I saw one of them at the wrap party, one I had seen a few times while in there. After a lot of champagne I made a beeline to go and chat to him but within 30 seconds my dad appeared and dragged me away! Killjoy.

– Lock down was wonderful, contrary to popular belief. You have a few days before you go in – you hand over your phone, your luggage and then you just wait. I was in a hotel for a few days alone with nothing to do but read and wait. Wait for someone to come and collect me and tell me 'it's time'. I was excited. But let me tell you I absolutely hated jumping out of that plane. It hurt, I was absolutely terrified, the harness crushed my vagina and I'm still picking the wedgy out of my arse.

Love

Being *in* love – what does it mean?

Since I was about four years old, I've been aware of love in my heart. When I was about six I started to dance with my curtains in my bedroom, and wrap them around me pretending they were my boyfriend/Aladdin. I would have dreams of being loved by a Disney prince, and wake up completely devastated that it was just a dream. I would weep for hours at a time over the boy band Hanson (the long-haired kids that looked like actual pretty females) and then, a bit later on, any Westlife song would send me over the edge. I cried constantly over boys at school, I'd develop crushes on waiters on family holidays; I constantly felt like I was lovesick.

As a grown woman, I'm not that different. I might not dance with my curtains anymore (only on Fridays …), but I constantly find myself in a state of despair about being 'in love'. I'm now approaching 30, trying to figure out what that really means. Here's what I have so far.

When you are *in* love, you are *in* something. Then I thought, 'What else can you say you are *in* other than love?' When I googled 'I am in ...', searching for alternatives, this is what I found:

- **I am in ... search of**
- **I am in ... need of**
- **I am in ... debt**
- **I am in ... trouble**

It almost seems like when you are *in* something, you are lost and out of control of the situation – meaning when you are in, you can't get out. So maybe when we casually declare, 'I am in love', we should really think about what we are saying.

I've definitely been in love before, and every time I have, I've been lost in it, no control. I'm searching for it, I need it, I am lost without it. I am in debt to it. Then I thought, 'I have so much! I *have* so much! What if I *had* love instead? Maybe *having* love is something that can bring happiness?'

If you say you have something, it implies that it is already yours, you are in possession of it. If you met someone and said, 'Yeah, he's great, we have love', surely that would be better than being *in* love because it's something you both confidently share?

Falling in love – that phrase has already set itself up for a negative. Falling – when you fall, you hurt yourself, or at least you nearly hurt yourself. Falling can NEVER be a good outcome, and yet I constantly just stick plasters on the wounds and chuck myself onto the spiky rocks, hoping that one day someone will catch me, or I will at least land safely.

I don't think we can have aims in love because there are all different types. I think in the past I have definitely confused love with lust. I have lusted after relationships that I cannot fully have, and I became addicted to that hit of euphoria every time I had them for even a small amount of time. And so, because of that intensity, I thought it was love. I thought pain was love, and chaos, and longing, and if I didn't feel those things about someone, I thought, 'Well, I can't be in love then.' It was like I needed the pain and uncertainty to be fulfilled or to keep me interested.

In the Ancient Greek language, there are different words for different types of love, and there are at least four ways to describe the concept of love in its various forms:

Agape – The love religious people have between them and God – considered the highest form of love. It's a selfless love.
Eros – intimate, passionate, romantic love.

> *Philia* – the love you feel for your friends.
> *Storge* – familial love, between parents and kids, or between siblings.

As I was reading up about those meanings, it did make me realise that if you are a very loving person, a very 'deep' person who explores all kinds of chambers and tombs of feelings, you will go through life and feel every single type of love. Some people don't. Maybe some only experience a more 'basic' version of it. Some people's hearts and heads just don't open those scary doors because it might possibly be just too terrifying for them to fathom.

Unfortunately for me (or fortunately, some might say), I have always been a daredevil when it comes to my heart. I play with fire, get burnt, make the same mistakes, move on and make new ones, and I am open to emotion, making me completely susceptible to pain. The phrase 'I wear my heart on my sleeve' doesn't even begin to cover it. I hand my heart over on a royal red fluffy cushion while I'm down on my knees, hoping and praying that it will be enough for someone, and enough for them to know that, although broken, it doesn't give in, it's everlasting.

What I'm slowly learning is that I am, and will ALWAYS be, this way. It's something I cannot change. I have so much love in my heart I literally sometimes don't know where to put it all, so it spills out of me like lava. And, just like lava, people run from it, terrified. But I'm learning to just accept and be okay with that. You can change a lot of things – you can even educate your brain to become more knowledgeable by having therapy and reading self-help books etc. – but your heart isn't one of them. This is the one I have been given – damaged, battered and bruised, but everlasting.

So I will keep loving, tripping, falling, spilling and forever hoping and praying that one day I will find a soft landing.

The People Who Shaped Me: TV-Land Friends

TV friends come and go. You do a job, you fall in love with each other for those few weeks and then you move on. Passing them occasionally on a red carpet or at a party, you give them a quick squeeze and that's about it. Some stick. Leigh Francis, aka Keith Lemon, is one of my dearest pals. Leigh gave me jobs when I really needed them, and saw something in me before anyone else did. He let me be funny, he has never cast me as sexy in any of his shows. He's one of the few blokes who saw through the sexy schoolgirl thing and let me be me. He is an extremely loyal man. As part of his many sketch shows I've been Michelle Keegan to his Mark Wright and Louis Tomlinson to his Harry Styles. We have never pissed ourselves laughing as much as we did when he made me play Slimer in the *Ghostbusters* episode for *The Keith & Paddy Picture Show*. He yelled 'BOGEY GHOST' at me for six hours while I was painted bright green and wearing a bald cap. Leigh is one of the few remaining traditional all-around talents who can do it all; he is hugely successful, clever, artistic and a comedy genius. He's taught me so much over the years and I am so grateful to him.

Other 'TV friends' who I've come to love over the years include Ollie Locke, Holli Dempsey, Jason Maza, Laura Whitmore, Liz Holmwood, Steve Dunne, Joel Dommett, Kieran Richardson, Russel Kane and Daniel Mays – these kinds of familiar faces are the ones you come to rely on. Seeing them pop up at a lonely party makes you instantly know you're on for a good night, and they've thrown me a lot of bones that I won't ever forget.

Alex Johnson, a major film casting director, gave me the role of Daphne in *Dad's Army* and then, two years later, a leading role in a film called *Patrick*, alongside Beattie Edmondson and her mum, Jennifer Saunders. I played a PE teacher in that film who was always eating cream cakes. The director of *Patrick* was called Mandie Fletcher. Mandie stripped me of my make-up – 'Send her back, she looks like a model,' she would say to the make-up team, who would walk me back to the make-up truck to wipe off the tiniest trace of foundation. She would tell me off for 'flirting' in my acting, and spoke to me about how conditioned I was to 'play sexy' – when really she just wanted me to be funny and simply let it all go. 'CUT. GO AGAIN!' she shouted, over and over, take after take. She didn't stop until she had what she wanted. 'Perfect,' she'd then say and wink as I finally found myself. I loved my performance in that movie. No make-up, no love interest, no tits out. I learnt A LOT about myself on that film. It was the last movie I did before *I'm a Celeb* ....

You remember more than anything the moments along the way that make you feel accepted. But then you remember the people and the situations when you felt like a big fake-tanned fish out of water. I feel that girls like me, who wear fake tan, who speak openly about sex, who go out, who watch *Love Island*, who love Ibiza and bottomless brunches, are so often boxed into a corner of stupidity – it's wrong, but you get used to it.

When you're that kind of girl, you're not allowed to be funny, you're not quick, you're not a writer, you're not qualified to speak on social or political issues, you are certainly not a stand-up comedian. I have been booked as the bimbo before and it sucks. After the jungle, I was booked on a late-night chat show and I soon began to feel that I was there to be the butt of the joke – the host seemed frosty, the audience didn't laugh at my jokes, the whole thing felt chaotic. I performed like a circus clown for over two hours, did everything they wanted from me and I just wanted to cry. My agents had told the producers I wouldn't answer any questions about

James Buckley (there had been a story in the press the day before about James and me falling out). Within five minutes of the recording, one of the hosts asked, 'I want to know about James Buckley, what happened there.' The others on the sofa cooed, 'Ooooo.' My face said it all and they moved on quickly and apologised afterwards. They cut it out of the edit but it hurt; it felt like they didn't care about me, or my wishes, or my privacy, it felt like, 'Get the blonde jungle girl on and make her say stupid things.' It made me feel like shit. That is not who I am or who I want to be. I told Martha and Alex. Noted for future.

There is a running theme here about the people who stick around, the good guys and the people you remember along the way, especially in work. You learn to laugh along with the people who can only see the surface-level you – the boobs and the tan – but that's okay. I hope to continue to keep surprising people and showing them there's more to me. I wrote a whole stand-up tour about turning 30, and people actually liked it. The *Guardian* gave me three stars and so did the *Evening Standard* – I would have taken one star for my first show, I'm just happy people came! I write comedy sketches, I do impressions, I sing, act and I love poetry. Look beneath the Estée Lauder Double Wear (best foundation ever) and you might find a smart lady chilling in there – a lady with thoughts, opinions and, dare I say it, the power to do something different.

It seems the people who make an impact on you are the people who really love you for who you are, it's the people who encourage you to be yourself. It's the people who don't just encourage you, but who literally beat your authentic self out of you – like an old dusty rug. At 29, I think finally all of my colours are starting to show through.

What 30 Looked Like ...

At 15

It looked so far away that I didn't give it one speck of thought, except every now and then when a teacher admitted they were 30 and then I thought they were ancient.

At 20

Thirty would be the age when everything was sorted. I'd be living in a mansion with my very rich and beautiful husband and have already pushed out at least one baby and probably be pregnant with another. Martha would be living down the road, also married and with a baby cooking in her tummy, and my double deluxe fridge would be covered in postcards from George. I'd have been in several major movies and my husband would be one of the leads from those films – probably an American who had moved to England because he loved me so much, but luckily we'd held onto his small-massive bolthole on Hollywood Boulevard so we could pop back there routinely.

At 25

Jason and I would be newly married after he proposed to me in Florence. We'd be living in our own flat somewhere in London, thinking about moving out to the country in the near future to live close to his parents. We'd be planning to get pregnant in a year's time if I thought work could take it (I'd be the lead in an ongoing series for ITV by this point, following the success of various British films). Martha would be engaged and living down the road, and my fridge would be too small for the postcards from George so instead they'd be all over the radiator.

At 29

Twenty-nine has been the best year of my life so far. Thirty, I'm sure, will have its own ups and downs, but I feel more in control of everything than I've ever felt before. I don't pretend to know what 30 looks like now. Instead, it is the most breathtakingly beautiful blank page.

10 Reasons
I Know
I'm an Adult

1. I live on my own. I got my own place for the first time recently. It did wonders for my mental health. I did not feel alone, I did not get scared in the night. I cherished my own space and that feeling of total privacy. If you've ever wanted to, and are in the position to, go for it.

2. I save money. Saving is a luxury from a past generation. If you do make sacrifices and save a bit of cash each month, I salute you.

3. I have a new expressed interest in House Plants. It's good for you in that you have to keep them alive . . . and very Instagrammable.

4. I realise that New Year's Eve is 99 per cent of the time the worst night out of the year.

5. I sometimes iron my clothes before I wear them.

6. If I say I'm going home after one or two drinks, I do.

7. I exercise. Much to my dislike I'm learning that this is not optional. Moving your arse means you might live a bit longer. You might feel 10 per cent less sad on a Sunday. I give in to it.

8. I drink more water. Loads of it. Even when I'm not hungover!

9. I accept the things that aren't meant for me – jobs, boys, the last mega loaded nacho at dinner.

10. I'm getting better at remembering birthdays.

10 Reasons
I Know I'm
Not an Adult

1. I'm lying to you about going home after one or two drinks.

2. When something goes wrong, the first thing I want to do is call my mum.

3. I sometimes have to check my Uber receipts after a night out to remember where I came back from.

4. I don't use fabric softener.

5. Phrases like 'switching your Energy tariff', '0% APR' and 'cashback ISA' are a foreign language to me.

6. I still get put on the children's table at Christmas lunch.

7. I can't drive.

8. I still get surprisingly light hangovers.

9. I never pick up my missed parcels from the post office.

10. I have lost 10 passports.

Are We
There Yet?

Okay, kids, how many of you got what I was trying to do with the book title? (Hmmm, suddenly worried I've spent too much of the book talking like you're sitting opposite me. Sorry if that's been annoying – far too late in the day for me to go back and change it now – it's just really strange writing a book all on your tod when you're used to chatting AT people for a living. Anyway, I digress.)

Hopefully you'll remember, like I do, asking the question again and again on long journeys when you were sat in the back of the car, squeezed shoulder to shoulder with your siblings, empty Capri-Suns and Wotsit packets littering the footwells. After the umpteenth time of you repeating it, your mum turned around and said something like, 'If you don't stop arguing I'm going to crash the car!!!'

But as an adult, I think quite a few of us carry on asking the question, except the difference is we're now in the driving seat and it's no longer about reaching whichever family member's house we were heading to, it's about life. Have we made it yet? Are we doing what we want to do yet? Are we successful yet? Are we the happiest we'll ever be yet? Have we reached the know-the-answers-to-everything stage of adulthood yet?

I went into *I'm a Celeb* … feeling sore and bruised. I was heartbroken over Jason and I wasn't where I wanted to be. I could see 30 looming on the horizon and it felt like I was in Tomb Raider, that PlayStation game where my friends would make Lara Croft swim but then drown her. I felt like I was in *Jurassic Park*, and the T-Rex (life) was coming for me with his small nasty hands and big teeth. It was exhausting.

After three weeks away from the real world, spending time with Nick Knowles (chilling in his hammock and knowing everything about every-thing), Anne Hegerty (who gave zero fucks) and John Barrowman (who made me silent scream-laugh in that Dolls House covered in spiders), and pushing myself to do things that would have scared the shit out of me a year before, I felt restored. I came out feeling like I'd had an epiphany: that everything was going to be okay in the end, that I still had everything left to play for and that I was enough, just as I was.

Now, having written this book, I don't think the jungle taught me that – I think I knew it all along; it was just that the jungle gave me the time and space to realise it. I've had some tough times in my life, but I've come out the stronger for it. I've been so lucky to have incredible people around me who have nurtured me, supported me, picked up the pieces when things have fallen apart and given me amazing opportunities. I've been utterly, utterly heartbroken, but I'm so happy I've been given this huge capacity to love. I've made a million mistakes along the way but I've also done things I'm so, so proud of. I can look at myself in the mirror, with or without my make-up on, and tell myself that I'm kind and generous and have things to share with the world. The jungle didn't make me strong; I was already strong because of everything that had happened before.

I'm not asking myself the question 'Am I there yet?' anymore. I'm no longer that kid sitting in the back of the car needing my mum to tell me that. I don't always feel like a fully functioning adult either, but then I'm not really sure anyone ever thinks that about themselves. What I am is a complicated, flawed human being with blonde hair, boobs and a brain, who wants to entertain people for as long as they're interested in letting me try.

The biggest lesson has been understanding that this mystical 'there' we're all aiming for isn't real. Maybe it comes from all the fairy tales we

grow up on, where there was always a convenient happy ending that closed the story, usually
involving a prince and a big wedding. I'd still like
the big wedding, at Christmas, if that's okay, and
lots of babies would be great too. I just don't
want the 'ending' anymore. I'm more interested
in beginnings

When I started writing this book back in January
2019, I was sitting on a train heading to Manchester.
Considering it's now June, you'll be pleased to note
I did in fact reach Manchester and get off said train.
But, figuratively speaking, the 'journey' is still going.
People drop the word 'journey' a lot on tele, and
even though it sounds a bit wanky, I definitely think
I had one on *I'm a Celeb* ... and it was marvellous.
But it didn't stop at the end of the show. I'm still
on it now. In the last six months, I've made some
of the biggest and boldest choices about my career
and done things that have really petrified me, like
my stand-up tour, and I want to carry on doing
that. I want to keep pushing and finding out about
myself while being content with all that's happening
in the present, rather than aiming for some target
way off in the distance that I think is there but I
can't quite see.

I really hope that if you're feeling lost, whether

you're 19, 29 or 99, you're as lucky as I've been to have people around you who love you and will support you and provide you with the space you need to realise that you too are good enough, just as you are, and that tough times always pass in the end. Don't let other people's achievements sidetrack you and don't worry about the future. None of us are 'there yet'.

We are all exactly where we need to be.

Acknowledgements

Thank you to my editors Emily Barrett & Pippa Wright and the whole team at Seven Dials/Orion Publishing Group for this incredible opportunity. You have been the most amazing partners and I've loved working with you all.

My beautiful and talented parents Kate and Keith. You taught me to love and to always be kind. Be free, passionate and expressive. Your support knows no bounds and I couldn't have written this book without any of those things you have instilled in me.

My aunty Amy and uncle Bob. Your kitchen is the centre of my universe. Where all the ideas happen! Thank you for your endless love & support.

My cousin Lydia. Your strength, beauty and positivity blow my mind. You help me every single day, and encourage me to be the best version of myself I can be. An actual real life angel.

are we there yet?

My agent Alex Segal. You gave me a shot when no one else would, you saw beneath what everyone else saw and gave me back my confidence in the business. A wonderful agent with my best interests at heart, and a true friend above all else.

My brother George. All round legend. Thanks for letting me steal most of your jokes.

My sister Martha. Without you I am nothing.

 KT-416-138

Please return or renew this item HAI
by the last date shown. You may
return items to any East Sussex
Library. You may renew books
by telephone or the internet.

East Sussex
County Council

0345 60 80 195 for renewals
0345 60 80 196 for enquiries

Library and Information Services
eastsussex.gov.uk/libraries

04584066

RADIANT

↔

Recipes to heal your skin from within

HANNA SILLITOE

Photography by Joanna Henderson

Hanna Sillitoe is the food blogger behind the website www.mygoodnessrecipes.com. She gained a wide online audience when she started sharing her journey to health over social media, and now has followers from all over the world who use her plan and credit her with curing their skin complaints.

KYLE BOOKS

To you the reader. I hope this book gives you back control over your health, skin and life, so that you feel empowered to heal naturally and completely, forever.

I trust you in turn will tell your story, and by doing so help inspire others to do the same.

An Hachette UK Company
www.hachette.co.uk

First published in Great Britain in 2017 by
Kyle Books, an imprint of Kyle Cathie Ltd
Carmelite House
50 Victoria Embankment
London EC4Y 0DZ
www.kylebooks.co.uk

10 9 8 7 6 5 4

ISBN 978 0 85783 392 1

Project Editor: Tara O'Sullivan
Editorial Assistant: Amberley Lowis
Copy Editor: Stephanie Evans
Designer: Tania Gomes
Photographer: Joanna Henderson
Food and Prop Stylist: Emily Ezekiel
Production: Nic Jones and Gemma John

A Cataloguing in Publication record for this title is available
from the British Library.

Printed and bound in China

For a full list of references, please see www.mygoodnessrecipes.com/radiant-references

The information and advice contained in this book are intended as a general guide. This book is not intended to replace treatment by a qualified practitioner. Neither the author nor the publishers can be held responsible for claims arising from the inappropriate use of any remedy or dietary regime. Do not attempt self-diagnosis or self-treatment for serious or long-term conditions before consulting a medical professional or qualified practitioner. Do not begin any dietary regime or undertake any self-treatment while taking other prescribed drugs or receiving therapy without first seeking professional guidance. Always seek medical advice if any symptoms persist.

CONTENTS

INTRODUCTION 5

THE SKIN PLAN 39

THE RECIPES 52

HELLO, HOW ARE YOU?

This is the bit where you reply, 'I'm fine, thank you,' regardless of how you're actually feeling. We all do it. It's our inbuilt autoresponder. I know, because I spent years saying it, when the truth is I wasn't fine at all: I was miserable, and in constant discomfort and pain.

Over the following pages I'm going to share with you my story. For twenty years psoriasis, eczema and acne dominated my life. I became increasingly unhappy and unwell, until I finally resolved to do something about it. Not by popping a pill to mask the symptoms, but by cleaning the tank and changing the fuel. By altering the way I thought about food forever.

These days, when people ask me how I am, I can genuinely say 'I'm very well, thank you!' I'm full of energy, fit and healthy with clear, glowing skin.

INTRODUCTION

As far as skin, health and weight are concerned, I'm far from genetically blessed. I don't come from a particularly privileged background either – kale and quinoa were certainly never staples in our household! I'm an ordinary, northern girl and I've had to work hard to conquer an autoimmune illness which plagued me for most of my adult life. Now I want to help you do the same – to feel better, inside and out.

My mission is to make this journey easy for you, to explain things simply and talk you through my skin-friendly recipes step by step. I'm not planning to bamboozle you with fancy ingredients and I don't want you to feel intimidated or discouraged by unfamiliar foods. If you're not used to preparing meals using wholesome, fresh ingredients, trust me – it's so much easier than you think.

This isn't another fad diet or temporary detox promise. Completely transforming my diet totally changed my life, the lives of my friends and family and so many of my online followers. My complexion is glowing, my psoriasis, eczema and acne have disappeared: that's something I never achieved with prescription medication. The energy I have now is remarkable – a far cry from the temporary, caffeine-stimulated pick-me-ups that previously enabled me to dawdle through my day.

The saying 'beauty comes from within' and the old adage 'you are what you eat' ring so true in every sense. My poor diet, and the stress I put my body through, were very much reflected on the outside. I battled psoriasis throughout my twenties. Red, scaly patches on the surface of my skin, caused by a poorly functioning immune system. My bad diet would exacerbate the problem, which in turn would stress me out, which would cause another flare and so the cycle went on. But, let me tell you, there is hope. Because now, my skin is clear, I can think straight, I no longer get sick, I sleep peacefully and wake full of energy when the sun rises. I'm not exaggerating when I say this way of being is absolutely life changing.

PROBLEM SKIN

A few facts and figures for you:

» At least 100 million individuals are affected by psoriasis worldwide.

» A survey by the National Psoriasis Foundation found that almost 75% of patients believed their psoriasis had a significant negative impact on their quality of life. Another survey reported that at least 20% of psoriasis patients had contemplated suicide.

» Research shows that the psychological effects of skin conditions such as psoriasis can equal those experienced with heart failure or cancer.

Those are frightening statistics. And this is just one skin condition, out of the many severe skin problems that have a devastating impact on so many people of all races and ages around the world.

People are more aware of skin problems such as acne and eczema, but psoriasis is less well-known. It is an autoimmune disorder activated by an over-responsive immune system. When the immune system functions properly, a highly complex collection of processes work together as our first line of defence to prevent disease. However, this defence can go wrong, causing autoimmune disorders. The body thinks there is a problem, and the immune system goes into overdrive and sets out to defeat the perceived problem. Except there is no problem. So the immune system attacks perfectly healthy tissue, replacing it far too quickly and erratically. For psoriasis sufferers the result of this unnecessary response is red, flaky patches spreading all over the body.

If you've never suffered from a skin condition, it's hard to describe the effect it can have on everyday life. For me, coping with psoriasis, eczema and acne meant that ordinary things such as buying clothes stopped being a pleasure, and became more like a mission to find something that would make the angry red patches covering my body look a little less obvious and feel less painful.

I completely changed my life through reeducating myself on the benefits and detrimental effects food can have on health and well-being. My psoriasis, eczema and acne cleared up, and I lost five stone in weight without trying. My recurring kidney infections disappeared, my bleeding gums healed and my energy levels bounced through the roof. I truly believe – with a little commitment and time – you can achieve the same.

ME AND MY SKIN

I've struggled with a lifetime of bad skin. For me, whenever there was a problem on the inside, it was instantly reflected on the outside.

As a teenager I got spots. Lots of spots. No matter how many topical skin-clearing products I tried, they just wouldn't disappear. I exfoliated and cleansed and toned, I tried daily moisturisers and overnight creams, but nothing worked. I caked my face with makeup, blocking my pores and making the problem ten times worse. Acne plagued me throughout my teenage years but that was nothing compared with what was to come.

I was fifteen when I first noticed a little clump of itchy, red dots on my tummy. Over the course of a week they seemed to spread and multiply. My GP diagnosed scabies – a contagious skin condition caused by tiny mites that burrow into the skin. I was given a cream and an antibiotic to stop the infection spreading. However, I'd been misdiagnosed; not only did the cream have zero effect, but the antibiotics were stripping my gut of any good bacteria and, as it turned out, were making my skin problem much worse.

Subsequent visits to my doctor and a dermatologist correctly diagnosed psoriasis. I still remember sitting there helpless in the GP's surgery, being told 'there is no cure'. The best I could hope for were periods of remission through using steroid creams. Steroids decrease inflammation, relieve itching and slow the development of new psoriasis patches. Although they can be effective in the short term, long-term steroid use can cause skin to thin, eventually leading to stretch marks. Not great, huh?

I used those creams. I used emollients, bath oils and shower lotions. The moisturisers were super greasy. Some burned my skin, some smelled of tar. I remember my boyfriend at the time telling me he'd driven past a set of road works and the smell reminded him of me! He wasn't being cruel, but I felt horrified at the thought of smelling like hot tarmac. I used medicated shampoos to treat my scalp, which looked as if it had a severe case of dandruff.

> PSORIASIS *and* ECZEMA TOOK OVER MY LIFE, PHYSICALLY, MENTALLY *and* EMOTIONALLY.

Psoriasis and eczema took over my life physically, mentally and emotionally. Despite this, I considered myself a confident person; I tried not to let my skin's appearance destroy my self-esteem, but it was a constant battle. I couldn't dress like everyone else. Vest tops and dresses got stuffed to the back of my wardrobe, replaced with jumpers, trousers and long-sleeved cardigans. I felt self-conscious and unattractive. The discomfort prevented me from sleeping, and stopped me studying. I'd use makeup to try and disguise the red, scaly plaques and tried blister plasters to cool the patches and ease the itching, but nothing seemed to work.

By the time I went to college, my skin was horrendous. Teenage dramas coupled with the pressure of exams didn't help, and the junk food I ate was stoking the fire. By then, I had acne, eczema and psoriasis. I ditched sports and rarely walked anywhere: my skin conditions made even basic activity uncomfortable. I was sapped of energy, and so it became a vicious cycle. On top of an already terrible diet, I discovered cigarettes and alcohol.

I spent the early part of my career working as a DJ in bars, when smoking indoors was still legal. By my mid-twenties I was easily going through twenty to forty cigarettes a day. Full-bodied red wine was my preferred poison; I could happily drink my way through a bottle each evening. I had a brilliant social life and, because of the industry I worked in, most of my friends were male. Keeping up with the lads on pints was standard. My skin absolutely hated alcohol.

Amidst the poor diet, the smoking, drinking, pain and endless medications, there were periods of remission. In truth, my skin never really healed completely. Even during those short times when I managed to achieve some sort of clearance, there were always temporary and occasional patches. There were days when I braved wearing shorts or sleeveless tops, but the fear of someone staring at my skin was always present. You would assume people would be too polite to comment, but they're not.

I'll never forget the time I was coming home from a week away with my boyfriend in Egypt (my skin seemed to like the year-round sunshine and salty waters of the Red Sea). We were queuing at the check-in desk for our return flight to Manchester. As we approached the desk, the girl waiting to scan our passports started pointing at my skin. My heart sank. I'd travelled to the airport in a strappy top, confident enough to go sleeveless for the first time in months. I honestly thought a week in the sun had done a lot to minimise the scaly patches on my arms, but this girl clocked them immediately. Pulling me to one side, the girl gestured for her colleague to come over and they began asking all sorts of questions. I soon realised what they were getting at – was I contagious? Perhaps she was just doing her job. The cruelty was unintentional and, after all, she had no idea how hard it was for me – but by now the entire queue of people were watching this interrogation. In that moment, any confidence I'd gained during our week away completely vanished. I felt horrendously self-conscious, miserable to the point of despair and highly embarrassed for my boyfriend.

The Turning Point

By the age of thirty-five I was sick. Really sick. A combination of predisposed genetics, countless antibiotics, steroid medication and the rubbish I'd been fuelling my body with over the years had finally caused my immune system to begin failing big time. My body had started attacking itself. As well as my skin problems, I suffered recurring urinary tract infections, my blood pressure was dangerously high, I was overweight and permanently exhausted.

At its worst, eczema covered my eyelids and plaque and guttate psoriasis spread across my arms, legs, boobs, tummy and scalp. Plaque psoriasis is the most common form of the disease with red raised patches covered in silvery scales affecting my knees, elbows and forearms. Guttate psoriasis appeared as tiny red droplets all over my body. At first I would notice a handful of these little dots which would begin to multiply and eventually join to form big red patches. The itching would keep me awake at night and the feeling of my clothing brushing against red raw skin would leave me crying in pain.

It was during one such flare-up that my friend Rachel and I had to go down to London to meet a client we were working for. Knowing how important the meeting was, I dragged myself out of bed, covered my body in coconut oil and wrapped my skin in clingfilm. It was the only way to relieve the intense, burning pain and it stopped my clothes brushing against the red raw patches on my stomach. During lunch, I was trying hard not to rustle as I moved! It's funny looking back, but it was a desperate measure at the time.

By this stage, so much of my skin was affected that my doctor wanted me to consider a medicine called Methotrexate, a chemotherapy drug. The idea was to suppress my immune system, to stop the overreaction. In theory it made sense, but some of the potential side effects included acne, low energy, itching, hair loss, stomach ulcers, seizures, hepatitis, infection, kidney disease and lung or liver failure. Was it really worth risking serious organ failure? It was possible it would have no effect on clearing my psoriasis at all. It certainly wasn't a long-term cure.

This was my turning point. After 20 years, I'd finally had enough. I refused the medication and began some research of my own.

UNDERLYING ISSUES

Our skin's function, and the part it plays in keeping us healthy, seems to have been superseded by the importance of aesthetic appearance. The models with apparently flawless skin who grace the front covers of glossy magazines, celebrities airbrushed to within an inch of their lives – we know the images are Photoshopped, yet we still strive to attain that same, impossibly smooth complexion.

Psoriasis, acne and eczema were the three specific skin complaints I struggled with most over the years. Although they vary somewhat in appearance, I fully believe most skin problems appear as the result of an underlying issue. While it's true that some are caused by allergens, even these are often exacerbated by inflammation and toxins in our system.

There are five main organs of detoxification: the skin, lungs, kidneys, colon and liver. Our skin is physically our biggest organ of elimination, because of its large surface area (two square metres). The best way to detox is through our other organs of elimination. However, if these are overloaded or not operating optimally, our skin takes on the role of freeing the body of excess toxic compounds. Whatever you're seeing on the surface of your skin is most likely down to an underlying problem. Think of it as a symptom of disease rather than the disease itself. Creams or emollients are at best a temporary fix and treat only the symptoms. The trick, I realised, is to target the underlying cause.

WHAT OUR SKIN DOES

Our skin shields us, protects us from the elements, helps us to regulate body temperature and reacts to hot and cold. It's full of nerve endings and receptors that constantly gather sensory information from our surroundings. Our skin looks after us by performing countless protective tasks, yet we so often neglect to look after it correctly.

Before we consider how best to achieve and look after a healthy, beautifully radiant complexion, it's important to understand the basic function of our skin.

There are three main layers of the skin:

The epidermis – the outermost layer. It provides a waterproof barrier, makes new skin cells and gives our skin its colour. When the epidermis is healthy, it acts as the body's first line of defence, protecting us from bacteria, viruses and infection.

The dermis – the layer beneath the epidermis. It's much thicker and contains tough connective tissue, hair follicles and sweat glands, as well as the vital nerve endings that enable us to feel things. It carries blood to our skin and makes oil to keep our skin soft and smooth.

The hypodermis – the deeper subcutaneous tissue made of fat and connective tissue. It is the layer that helps keep the body from getting too warm or too cold. It stores fat and attaches the dermis to our muscles and bones.

We spend a small fortune on chemical-laden skincare products. Sadly these products will neither treat underlying problems, nor in most cases improve the health of our skin. Attaining a beautiful, radiant complexion is a process that begins from the inside out. Our skin reflects what is going on within the body. What we see on the outside is simply a manifestation of the body's internal needs and unless our skin is getting the vital nutrients it requires, it simply can't perform its task. I know from experience that by feeding ourselves the correct combination of vitamins and minerals through good nutrition, our skin can not only function correctly, but it will also look and feel hydrated and radiant.

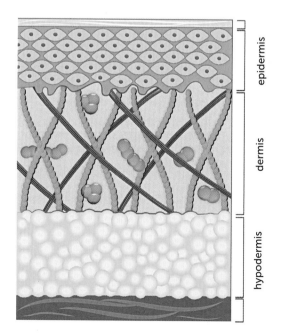

FOOD AS MEDICINE

Over all the years I was treated for my various skin conditions, not once was diet suggested as a potential factor. In fact, one doctor told me point blank it would have no effect whatsoever. It's a story I hear time and time again. It's so frustrating to see prescription creams and medicines (which come with a long list of potential side effects) being dished out when the only offshoot of a nutrient-, plant-rich regime is glowing health! Diet and natural topical salts and oils are often referred to as 'alternative therapy', but without that list of harmful side effects, shouldn't this really be our first course of treatment?

People with long-term conditions use a significant proportion of health-care services (50 per cent of all GP appointments; 70 per cent of days in hospital beds), and their care absorbs 70 per cent of hospital and primary care budgets in England. These persistent illnesses, such as heart disease, stroke, cancer, diabetes, obesity and arthritis, add up to the leading cause of death globally. They also leave in their wake lifelong disability, compromised quality of life and burgeoning health-care costs.

The most frustrating part is that this worsening of chronic conditions is preventable. According to the Center for Disease Control and Prevention, much of the chronic disease burden is attributable to a short list of key risk factors:

» Tobacco use/exposure to secondhand smoke

» Obesity

» Physical inactivity

» Excessive alcohol use

» A diet low in fruits and vegetables

The problem is getting worse, but the good news is that each of us has the power to begin taking ownership of our well-being.

Conventional medicine is quick to treat the symptoms of skin conditions. That not only leaves the causes untouched, but prescribed medications also come with their own side effects, which often contribute to the root of the problem or create new ones. The end result is a vicious cycle of ill health.

That's a loop I was caught up in for a long time.

I would slather on steroid creams to suppress the rash on my skin, but as soon as I stopped it was like unleashing a monster. The underlying cause would get more angry and the flare-ups grew worse. I was on perpetual courses of antibiotics to treat recurring kidney infections. At one stage I was in horrendous pain and urinating blood. While I panicked, the doctor simply prescribed a stronger medication which, although successful in treating the infection, stripped the good bacteria from my gut, exacerbating the skin problem. My health was like that 'whack-a-mole' game – just as I was bashing one problem over the head with a hammer another three popped up. The pattern became seemingly endless.

Throughout my sickness, none of my doctors or dermatologists ever asked me about my lifestyle. About what I ate, how much water I drank or whether I bothered to exercise. I think most of us see these factors as contributing in some way to our overall welfare, but get them right and they don't just add to our health, they will form the very essence of our entire well-being.

With a handful of exceptions, chronic skin problems do not occur overnight. They tend to develop slowly, usually over many years. Redness, itching, rashes and an extremely dry or oily complexion are subtle signs that mark a gradual loss of health. We tend to ignore them or treat these symptoms with medication to make them go away. They're not the only early warning markers. Have you ever taken drugs to resolve high blood pressure, insomnia, sinus problems, headaches, migraines, diarrhoea, constipation, indigestion, sore throat, IBS, ulcers, hay fever, colitis, immobility or a lack of energy? Sure, you may have successfully alleviated the symptoms, but you neglected to address the underlying cause. By understanding the process that leads to inflammation, which causes disease and dysfunction, we can make long-term sustainable dietary and lifestyle choices that promote true health and longevity. Our skin is trying to tell us something. Masking the message is not the answer.

FANNING THE FLAMES

The gut is the gateway to health. The ancient Greek physician Hippocrates is known as the father of modern medicine. Much of his wisdom, which is over 2,000 years old, has stood the test of time. He said: 'All disease begins in the gut.' Granted, not all disease originates in the gut (genetics too have their part to play), but with processed meals and high-sugar foods, stress and lack of exercise, the Western lifestyle is hardly conducive to good gut heath.

Leaky Gut

Gut bacteria can greatly affect our health, both physically and mentally. There is growing evidence that many chronic metabolic diseases do, in fact, begin in the gut. This is intrinsically linked to the different gut bacteria residing in our digestive tracts, as well as the integrity of the gut lining.

Through a combination of poor diet, lack of exercise and an overuse of medicines, the lining of the gut wall can become permeable. Inflammatory foods such as gluten and dairy, or toxic ones such as excessive sugar and alcohol, can all contribute to poor gut health. Toxins come in the form of medications such as steroids or antibiotics, and environmental toxins like mercury and pesticides.

There are trillions of bacteria in the gut known as gut flora. Some of the existing bacteria in the gut are friendly, some are not. It's vital to keep the balance healthy, through eating well, reducing stress, exercising and avoiding trigger foods and toxins. The quantity and composition of gut bacteria can greatly affect our overall well-being. If they are out of kilter, components called lipopolysaccharides (LPS), or endotoxins can leak into the body. When this happens, our immune system recognises these foreign molecules and mounts an attack against them, resulting in a chronic inflammatory response.

INTERNAL INFLAMMATION

It's thought that many of the symptoms of disease we see today are linked to internal inflammation. The causes of inflammation are incredibly complex, and the way in which it is linked to diet is only just beginning to be explored.

Inflammation is part of the body's immune response. Initially, it's beneficial – for example, if you bang your arm, the tissues need care and protection. Without inflammation, infections and wounds would never heal. However, sometimes it can become self-perpetuating. More inflammation is created in response to the existing inflammation. Sleep deprivation, stress, a poor diet, genetic predisposition and certain environmental factors can all exacerbate our body's response.

Chronic inflammation falls below the threshold of perceived pain. You don't feel sick to begin with, but a fire is quietly smouldering inside you, upsetting the delicate balance among all of the major systems: endocrine, central nervous, digestive, and cardiovascular/respiratory. In a healthy body, these systems communicate brilliantly with each other. With chronic inflammation, the seamless communication becomes distorted.

Psoriasis runs in the family, but that's not to say I was guaranteed to get sick. Even if the genetic predisposition is there, you still need to add a range of factors to trigger the disease. Stress, a poor diet, antibiotics... they all gradually add up, until a tipping point is reached. That's usually when we're finally pushed to do something about our well-being. It's also the time at which that becomes most difficult because the sickness has well and truly taken hold.

We've become so used to popping a sticking plaster over the problem and using medicine to control our symptoms that we're completely missing the point – to cure the underlying disease. As a result when the plaster comes off, or the course of medication ends, we wonder why the sickness returns. Often with a vengeance.

Using plants to treat chronic illness is so often dismissed as a kind of quirky alternative medicine. In fact, it's likely humans have used plants as medicine for as long as we have existed. Archaeological excavations have found remains of medicinal plants being used as early as 60,000 years ago.

Don't get me wrong: I'm not vehemently against all forms of medication. Antibiotics have their place, of course, but they're handed out so readily these days. Yes, they kill off infection, but they also strip our bodies of the good stuff and there are alarming reports of bacteria evolving to become ever more resistant to antibiotics. They weaken our systems and

leave us vulnerable to yet more disease.

I was miserable and lazy, so when my doctor told me that diet would have no bearing on my skin, I just kept trying new medication without any incentive to make the healthy lifestyle changes my body was screaming out for. These days, many doctors are far more open to discussing dietary change. The important thing is to do your research and listen to your body. And, let's face it, a healthy diet full of fresh fruit and vegetables can be no bad thing.

It was my doctor's suggestion of trying a chemotherapy drug that scared me into trawling the internet to search for an alternative to more medication. In my head, the concept of what's on the skin's surface reflecting a problem within, already made sense. I was determined to find and fix that problem. Reading Jason Vale's story and watching the Joe Cross movie *Fat, Sick and Nearly Dead*, gave me hope. These advocates of juice detox both healed their autoimmune skin problems through diet alone. My main hurdle was my love of food! Sure, I had the willpower to get through short-term juice fasts, but ultimately I had to come up with a long-term sustainable plan – and that had to involve food.

WHAT TO AVOID

Before this begins to look like a long and daunting list of things you can never enjoy again, remember it's all about balance. Eating well the majority of the time will give your body the energy it needs to deal with those days when your lifestyle isn't as clean and on-track as it could be. We're individual and complex, so while the general aim for all of us is to reduce internal inflammation, your skin may react particularly strongly to certain foods and moods. Through a process of elimination and reintroduction you'll eventually find what works for you. I've found the following to be particularly problematic when it comes to skin and I still avoid them:

» Caffeine

» Alcohol

» Sugar

» Processed and junk food

» Nightshades (see page 14)

» Dairy

» Wheat

» Strawberries, peanuts and oranges

» Smoking

» Stress

CAFFEINE

Caffeine is the most commonly used drug in the world. So many of us use it daily to alleviate fatigue, improve concentration and increase alertness. While I was never a huge fan of coffee, I would start most mornings with Diet Coke straight from the fridge. It was my thirst-quencher, my hangover cure, my wake-up call and my caffeine hit all rolled into one.

What was I thinking? How was my body ever going to function properly? I often receive emails from people who can relate to this because they're doing exactly the same thing. It's akin to filling a high-performance racing car with contaminated diesel. Not just once but over and over again. Repeatedly pouring in a poor-quality fuel, allowing the vehicle to operate (just), but continually damaging the engine. The body fast builds a tolerance and soon it decides it needs that morning injection of caffeine to function at base level.

There's no doubt about it, excess caffeine is bad for our skin. It stimulates the nervous system, causing our adrenals to secrete cortisol. Cortisol is a hormone which helps the body respond to stress. Those same stress hormones that prepare us for a 'fight or flight' response also have the potential to trigger skin conditions such as acne. Cortisol depresses the immune system, making it much more difficult for our skin to fight off bacteria, which multiply inside clogged pores. It impairs the body's ability to absorb nutrients from food. That's a really big potential issue for those of us with skin problems, because so many of them can be worsened by deficiencies in minerals such as zinc and selenium.

Aside from its direct effect, cortisol also encourages the body to secrete insulin. Not only can insulin trigger over-production of new skin cells, it

also increases the body's inflammation levels, which can exacerbate an existing skin condition, causing skin to appear redder and more swollen.

In addition, coffee and cola are highly acidic. This acidity can cause severe disruptions in our gut flora, potentially leading to an overgrowth of bad bacteria in the intestine. The condition, known as dysbiosis, also triggers gut inflammation, which can in turn lead to intestinal permeability – more commonly referred to as 'leaky gut' – and persistent low-level inflammation, often manifesting itself as skin dryness and angry, red patches on the skin's surface.

ALCOHOL

Alcohol is a natural diuretic: the more you drink, the more dehydrated you become. It literally saps the moisture from every part of your body, skin included. One of my biggest fears when I made a commitment to changing my diet was giving up alcohol. Much of my social life revolved around pubs, bars and restaurants. But my skin was so bad during my post-Christmas flare-up, certainly not helped by excessive alcohol consumption, I knew I needed to make some tough choices. One of those was quitting the booze.

My alcohol intake varied but there's no denying I was drinking way too much. Okay, so I wasn't starting each day with a large glass of red, but I was certainly ending it with one. Often an entire bottle. It sounds crazy when I say it now, but that bottle of red each evening, usually justified by the stress of work, or needing to relax, or one of the million other excuses I used, actually seemed normal. It's only by taking a step back that you realise just how hard your liver and kidneys have to function to eliminate what is essentially a poison and you begin to question why you're pouring it down your neck in the first place.

Alcohol is a toxin to the cells that detoxify your body. Your body has to work very hard to filter it. It hinders the production of vasopressin, an anti-diuretic hormone. Your kidneys have to work overtime, sending water to the bladder instead of your organs.

Alcohol's effect on our skin is extensive: it robs the good (hydration) and leaves the bad (dryness, bloating and redness). Drinking too much deprives the skin of vital vitamins and nutrients. Vitamin A, for example, is essential for cell renewal and a lack of it can cause the skin to look dull and grey. Over time, drinking heavily can have other, more permanent, detrimental effects on the skin. Rosacea, a skin disorder that starts with a tendency to blush and flush, is often linked to alcohol: the 'drinker's red nose'.

Being so depleted of vital electrolytes and fluids through excessive drinking causes the skin to exhibit signs of bloating. When we're lacking the water we need to function, our body will store whatever it can absorb, wherever it can. Consequently any water you do take in will cause your tissues to swell.

Aside from the damage we can do from consuming alcohol, applying it externally can also cause problems. Many skin-care manufacturers use alcohol in their apparently complexion-enhancing lotions and potions. Check the label, because alcohol as a major ingredient in any skin-care product is most definitely a problem. Moisturising formulas loaded with ethanol, isopropyl, methanol or denatured alcohol tend to have this lovely, weightless feeling to them when applied. The other reason manufacturers use alcohol is to penetrate the skin's protective barriers (i.e. the epidermis and dermis). It allows better absorption of active ingredients such as vitamins and retinal, but in the long term using creams containing alcohol destroys our natural defences: the skin's protective barriers are there for a reason, designed to safeguard our inbuilt protective membrane and keep our complexion effortlessly healthy.

SUGAR

Sugar is fast gaining a bad reputation as diet enemy number one. To describe it as a sweet and silent killer might sound a little extreme, but the havoc that refined sugar wreaks on every organ in the human body should not be underestimated. Refined sugar is made from raw sugar that has undergone a refining process to remove the molasses. This process involves up to 32 separate processes of crystallisation, mingling, melting, carbonation, filtration, de-colourisation and re-crystallisation. Once it's been through this process, this kind of sugar no longer holds any nutritional value. You may have read stories blaming sugar for causing weight gain, diabetes and countless other health complaints,

but what does it do to the skin?

Excessive sugar consumption can lead to dryness, puffiness and those terrible dark circles under the eyes. It's highly acidic. Acidic foods are something we want to actively avoid to reduce internal inflammation and in turn skin problems (see chart on page 20). It's really important for the health of our skin to eliminate all foods that are pro-inflammatory. Foods such as sugar, sweets, ice cream, white pasta, ketchup, pre-packaged snacks and fizzy drinks are some of the worst culprits and I have found they can lead to an inflammation flare-up throughout my body, potentially causing stress, redness and visible swelling on the skin's surface. Inflammation encourages an immune-system response; therefore, if the inflammation is chronic, our immune-system cells are constantly patrolling the body, causing more harm than good. Autoimmune illnesses such as psoriasis are activated by an over-responsive immune system.

Another important factor to consider is that digested sugar permanently attaches to the proteins in our skin through a process known as glycation. Over time, the end products accumulate and destroy our collagen and elastin, the proteins responsible for keeping skin firm and supple. Glycated collagen cannot regenerate as effectively, causing the skin to sag and wrinkle. Aside from increasing the appearance of ageing, glycation can also exacerbate skin conditions such as acne and rosacea.

PROCESSED AND JUNK FOOD

You really don't need me to tell you how bad junk food is for you. The clue is in the title. Processed foods are extremely low in essential nutrients. They contain added chemicals, plus cheap fats and refined vegetable oils that are often hydrogenated. Hydrogenated oils are vegetable oils whose chemical structure has been altered to prevent rancidity in foods. This process increases shelf life and reduces costs for food manufacturers. Also known as trans fats, these oils increase bad cholesterol and can block the production in the body of chemicals that combat inflammation.

A good rule of thumb to improve the health of your skin, is to eat foods that keep your blood sugar levels steady. Almost all processed and junk foods are full of ingredients that will cause blood sugar to soar. This rapid spike triggers the metabolism to boost insulin in response, which in turn creates a flare of inflammation. Over time high insulin levels can make skin drier, thicker and flaky, often blocking the pores and resulting in acne.

The more you consider what's been added and taken away from real food to create processed junk, the less appetising it becomes. We're drawn in by bright, artificial colours, intense flavours and smells, and often a sugar or salt overdose. Fast food such as pizzas and burgers, crammed full of salt, sugar and white starchy carbohydrates, are high GI (glycaemic index) causing blood sugar to leap. It's important to focus on foods with a low GI. If you take the time to prepare your meal from scratch using raw ingredients, you'll know exactly what's gone into it.

NIGHTSHADES

The potential problems associated with fruits and vegetables in the nightshade family can be a little confusing; after all we were brought up to believe that fruit and veg were good for us! There's a bit of science to explain here, but I'll try to keep it simple.

Edible plants of the Solanaceae family, known as the nightshades, are not advisable for anyone struggling with autoimmune skin conditions such as psoriasis. (They're also worth temporarily eliminating if you suffer from rheumatoid arthritis, to establish whether or not they're exacerbating the condition.) Before you rush to bin your tomatoes, it's important to emphasise that they are not a problem for everyone, nor relevant to every skin complaint, but psoriasis sufferers would do well to avoid them.

You've probably heard of the most poisonous of the nightshade family, the plant known as belladonna or deadly nightshade. There are actually over 2,000 species in the Solanaceae family, a few of which

are classed as edible, of which the most common are tomatoes, potatoes (but not sweet potatoes), aubergines and peppers (but not black pepper). These plants contain natural chemicals called alkaloids which essentially act as natural pesticides – think of them as a sort of in-built fly spray. While the plant is growing, these chemical compounds protect it from insects; in other words, they are meant to be toxic.

A healthy gut can cope just fine with alkaloids, but those of us with autoimmune skin issues or a compromised digestive system can be a little more sensitive to them. Alkaloids, after all, can prove incredibly powerful. The glycoalkaloid alpha-tomatine in tomatoes, for example, is so potent that it can be used in vaccines to ensure that the recipient develops immunity against the virus they are being inoculated against. Certain alkaloids can rev up our immune response, which is the last thing anyone with an overactive immune condition wants from their food.

The alkaloids in nightshade vegetables are believed to provoke gut irritation. It's thought they can attack the healthy cells that line the intestinal tract, making it more permeable – the condition known as leaky gut (see page 10).

YOU REALLY DON'T NEED ME TO TELL YOU HOW *bad* JUNK FOOD IS FOR YOU. THE CLUE IS IN THE TITLE.

If you search online you won't find a great deal of peer-reviewed studies to support the nightshade-inflammation connection, largely because there's so little funding for that area of research. There is, however, plenty of anecdotal evidence and blog posts from people who have found that nightshades aggravate their autoimmune illness.

Everyone is different, so, as always, it's important to establish whether these foods are posing a real problem for you. I can give you all this information and point you to studies and articles about nightshades and their effects, but the only way you can tell if they are a problem for you is by observing the way your body reacts to them. As with any food sensitivity, the only way to find out is to exclude all nightshades from your diet and see what effect this has. If you suffer from psoriasis, rheumatoid arthritis or any other autoimmune condition, I would suggest it's worth avoiding all nightshades for a month or two. Then, reintroduce them as a test. Eat them at least four times over a two-day period, then stop again, and monitor your symptoms for 72 hours.

If you don't feel you can cut nightshades out entirely, peeling potatoes will help as the alkaloids are mostly found in the skin. Avoid green tomatoes since unripe nightshades are higher in alkaloids and cook nightshade vegetables whenever you eat them as this will reduce alkaloid content even further. They can be a difficult food group to reintroduce, so if you do find you're sensitive to nightshades, it's worth considering permanently eliminating them. The vitamins and nutrients in these plants can be sourced elsewhere, so they're non-essential to your diet and there are some great alternatives, such as sweet potatoes instead of regular potatoes and my recipe for Tomato-less Sauce (see page 94).

If you are not sensitive to them, however, there's absolutely no reason to eliminate this group of foods from your diet as a precaution.

Common edible nightshades are:

» Tomatoes

» Aubergines

» Potatoes (excluding sweet potatoes)

» Peppers – includes hot and sweet varieties plus spices like paprika, chilli powder, cayenne, pimento and Tabasco, jalapeños, habaneros, chilli-based spices (excluding black pepper)

» Goji berries (wolfberries)

» Cape gooseberries

» Black nightshade or garden huckleberries (not to be confused with huckleberries, which, like bilberries, are part of the heather family)

» Tobacco (see pages 17–18 for more on tobacco and smoking)

DAIRY

Dairy was one of the very last things I eliminated from my diet for good. I dramatically reduced my intake for a time and initially switched to more alkaline variants such as goat's cheese and yogurt. But after I had spent a fortnight in Thailand where dairy foods barely feature, the improvement in my acne was so dramatic I decided to cut out dairy altogether.

As humans, we're the only species on earth that continues to drink milk beyond infancy. And not our own mother's milk, but the milk of grazing animals! It is really rather strange when you think about it. About 75 per cent of the world's population is lactose intolerant, meaning they cannot digest milk properly. Lactose intolerance is rare in Europe, North America and Australasia, where dairy farming has been practised for centuries, but it presents a real problem in Asia, Africa and South America, where milk and cheese are not such a significant part of the diet. Studies document how we have evolved to accommodate the dairy products we eat. Our bodies have had to adapt in an attempt to tolerate a food group we were never designed to consume, and for some people this hasn't worked.

Dairy is very, very hard to digest, even in those of us who don't have a diagnosed allergy. It's one of the most acidic, inflammatory foods we can eat. To take care of our skin, we want to eat as many anti-inflammatory foods as possible. All animal protein is inflammatory to some degree but it is specifically dairy proteins that have been linked to skin problems. Even organic varieties contain natural hormones and growth factors that, once absorbed into the bloodstream, often lead to, or exacerbate, acne. If you suffer from any type of skin problem, try eliminating dairy for a couple of weeks. You should notice an improvement in your condition, your energy and your complexion. If you really miss it, try reintroducing it gradually to see whether you suffer an adverse reaction. If your symptoms return, it's certainly worth trying to quit for good.

I'm often asked, especially by parents who are eliminating dairy to heal their children's eczema, whether a lack of dietary calcium is of concern. The connection between calcium consumption and bone health is actually very weak, and the

connection between dairy consumption and bone health is almost non-existent. Countries with the lowest rates of dairy and calcium consumption, like those in Africa and Asia, also have the lowest rates of osteoporosis. We can get all the calcium, potassium, protein and fats we need from whole plant foods – vegetables, fruit, beans, nuts, seeds and seaweed. Almond milk and coconut milk offer much less problematic, alkaline alternatives to dairy, and coconut oil makes a terrific butter substitute in baking.

WHEAT

Do you ever get that sleepy, fatigued, bloated feeling after eating a bowl of pasta? If so, it could be a sign that you're gluten intolerant. Gluten intolerance can manifest itself as digestive issues such as gas or bloating, inflammation, swelling and pain in the joints or as psoriasis on the skin. For many people, identifying a wheat or gluten allergy can be the missing link to clearing skin and resolving a whole host of underlying health problems.

The reason wheat is thought to be such an issue for those of us with skin problems is primarily that it's high on the glycaemic index. High GI foods prompt raised blood sugar, in turn triggering insulin release. Not only are elevated insulin levels linked to increased sebum production that can clog pores and lead to acne breakouts, but more worryingly they also promote chronic inflammation throughout the body. Acute inflammation that ebbs and flows as needed signifies a well-balanced immune system. However, chronic symptoms of inflammation, those that never recede, are warning the body that the 'on' switch to our immune system is stuck. It's poised on constant high alert. This triggers it to remedy non-existent problems, potentially resulting in an overactive immune response (autoimmunity).

Refined carbs, such as sugar and grains, can wreak havoc on the makeup of your intestinal bacteria, feeding problems such as candida (a form of yeast) overgrowth. Gluten might be making your gut more permeable and when your gut is leaky, toxins, microbes and undigested food particles – among other things – escape from your intestines and travel throughout your body via your bloodstream. The immune system needs a warning signal before reacting to these large food particles. Candida overgrowth, bacterial overgrowth and inflammation along the intestinal wall all tell the body to release this warning signal and send the immune system into overdrive.

It isn't always easy to diagnose gluten intolerance. 'Chicken skin' on the back of the arms can be a result of a fatty acid and vitamin A deficiency, secondary to malabsorption caused by gluten damaging the gut. If you suspect gluten might be causing your health and skin problems, try removing it from your diet for at least two to three weeks before you consider reintroducing it. It can take months or even years to clear gluten completely from your system, so the longer you're able to eliminate it, the better. If you feel significantly worse when you reintroduce it, gluten is likely to be causing health problems for you.

STRAWBERRIES

Certain foods carry a higher risk of being potential skin irritants. Strawberries are one example. Those hundreds of tiny little pips on the surface of a strawberry can really irritate the gut lining. Remember, what we're trying to do by resolving skin problems internally is heal the gut wall and calm inflammation. Teeny strawberry seeds are not conducive to either. Strawberries can also contain over fifty different chemical pesticides applied to protect them when growing; they're one of the most highly sprayed fruit we eat. It may be that you're absolutely fine with them, especially if you grow your own or buy organic, but if you're struggling to heal a skin problem it's worth eliminating strawberries for a little while, just to see if they pose a problem.

PEANUTS

It took me some time to realise peanuts are a real problem for my skin. For a while, peanut butter on rice cakes became my go-to snack. While my psoriasis and eczema stayed away, I noticed lots of tiny raised spots around my nose and mouth. After much trial and error, eliminating various foods, I eventually identified peanut butter as the culprit. Having since researched the effects of peanuts, I have learned that they commonly cause an overreaction of the immune system. Peanut

intolerance is recognised as one of the most severe food allergies because of its prevalence, persistence and the potential severity of an allergic reaction. (I've since replaced my peanut butter with almond butter which is much more alkaline and, aside from the temptation to finish the jar in one go, it doesn't cause me any problems!)

ORANGES

Like nightshade fruit and vegetables, oranges provide a lot of health benefits and tons of vitamin C. If you don't struggle with eczema, dermatitis or psoriasis, there's no reason at all to avoid them. They do, however, seem to be a common problem for eczema sufferers, especially children, and it is down to their salicylate content. Salicylates are naturally occurring chemicals found in many plants. They act as a type of natural pesticide to protect plants against insects and diseases. Salicylate sensitivity can manifest itself as itchy skin rashes such as hives (urticaria) and eczema.

SMOKING

You don't need me to tell you smoking is not good for you. Research reviewing the damaging effects of smoking on our health is pretty conclusive. But when it comes to skin, the problems go even deeper.

Tobacco is a nightshade (see pages 14–15). It is also known to cause heart, lung and circulatory problems, as well as cancer and other health issues. Studies have shown there is a direct correlation between smoking and instances and severity of psoriasis. Inhaling nicotine is thought to increase the risk of developing psoriasis because it directly affects the immune system. A specific form of localised psoriasis known as palmoplantar pustulosis, which affects the palms of the hands and the soles of the feet, is much more common in smokers than in non-smokers.

Even if you don't suffer from these very specific skin conditions, smoking is generally incredibly detrimental to the appearance of your skin. Smoking tobacco decreases blood flow, potentially damaging the connective tissues that help maintain a healthy complexion. Skin fibroblasts (the cells in connective tissue that form collagen and elastin) are polluted by tobacco smoke. Not only does smoking hamper the blood supply that keeps skin tissue looking supple and healthy, it reduces the levels of vitamin A and hydration in our cells.

Numerous studies have found that premature wrinkling is associated with smoking. In addition to wrinkles, smoking increases the risk of gauntness and facial skin discolouration. There's evidence to indicate inhaling nicotine decreases the ability of our skin to regenerate and repair wounds and nicotine withdrawal during the night can cause a restless sleep pattern, leading to dark circles under the eyes.

Whichever way you look at it, smoking is undoubtedly bad for your health and damaging to your skin. I speak as an ex-smoker, so, believe me, I know how tough it is to quit. But if you're striving for clear skin, those cigarettes absolutely have to go.

STRESS

There is only so much food can do to reverse serious illness. We're often unaware that our emotions can have a powerful effect on our well-being.

Stress can directly impact the health and appearance of our skin. When we're subjected to stress over a period of time, our digestion can go a bit haywire. Blood is directed away from the digestive system to deal with the problem of stress and in turn everything becomes more acidic. Unbalanced digestion and gut inflammation can lead to skin dryness, oiliness, blemishes, acne, or sometimes a combination of these complaints. Stress makes our skin more sensitive and reactive, and problems such as eczema, psoriasis, rosacea and dermatitis are common symptoms of underlying anxiety. Stress has been shown to weaken the immune system, cause high blood pressure, increase fatigue and depression and even lead to heart disease. High levels of stress can also make it harder for existing skin problems to heal and prolonged exposure to stress can lead to premature skin ageing.

In life, a certain level of stress is unavoidable. It isn't the stress that kills us, it's our reaction to it, but this is something we can actually change. Our greatest weapon to combat stress is the ability to choose one thought over another. If you find yourself continually highly stressed, be it in your job, your social life or your relationship, you may need to make some bigger changes to begin feeling truly well again.

The introduction of a clean diet and exercise will certainly reverse some of the physical effects of stress. As we begin to eat, look and feel better, we're swapping the vicious circle of ill health for one of perpetual wellness. Just as the compounded effects poor diet, lack of sleep and unresolved stress have on each other (and ultimately on our well-being), the gradual build-up of the positive changes we implement will instead work to construct a chain of wellness. The more of those changes we make, the stronger that chain of wellness becomes.

I found making constructive, physical changes to my diet simpler than trying to eliminate emotional stress. For me, the focus on nutrition strengthened the chain, so the lifestyle and emotional adjustments fell into place more easily as a consequence. Your switch to a high-alkaline diet also begins to counter the strain of internal acidity which is undeniably exacerbated by modern-day stress. Your mood lifts, you sleep better, you have more energy, you wake earlier. All these factors give you more time, taking pressure off, reducing stress. You may find it easier making small adjustments in all aspects of your life to begin creating that circle of health.

CAN STRESS CAUSE WEIGHT GAIN?

Stress is an important, unconsidered factor fuelling the obesity epidemic. Have you ever found yourself in a situation where, no matter how hard you tried to diet or how much you exercised, the weight just wouldn't shift? A huge amount of research over the past two decades indicates stress makes it hard to lose weight.

Cortisol is normally released in a specific rhythm throughout the day. It should be high in the mornings when you wake up (this

> IT ISN'T THE STRESS THAT KILLS US, IT'S OUR REACTION TO IT, *and* THIS IS SOMETHING WE CAN ACTUALLY CHANGE.

is what helps you get out of bed and start your day), and gradually taper off throughout the day (so you feel tired at bedtime and can fall asleep). Stress disrupts the natural cortisol rhythm. And it's this broken cortisol rhythm that wreaks so much havoc.

To complicate matters further, the 'fuel' our muscles need when we struggle with stress is sugar. It's perhaps one reason we crave carbohydrates. Our system responds to stress with a hormonal signal to replenish nutritional stores – which may make us feel hungry. Eating in response to stress can also be a learned habit – for some of us it relieves the stress. It's easy to do and it's comforting. Continually overeating, of course, puts additional strain on our digestive system which in turn can affect our skin.

LEARN THOSE LABELS

One of the toughest lessons for me, and the one that catches most people out when they're first transitioning to a skin-friendly diet, is deceptive food labelling, especially when it comes to foods claiming to be healthier options. The manufacturers of this stuff are more sneaky than those flogging us cake! At least with cake we know it's cake – we understand it's not a particularly healthy choice. But if you're looking at a packet of cereal bars with the words 'healthy' and 'natural' emblazoned across the box, you'd be forgiven for assuming they're reasonably sin-free. Lots of these apparently healthy cereal bars contain just as much sugar as some chocolate bars.

The most important part to read is not the nutritional information but the ingredients list, which always shows what a product contains in descending order. So if it contains sugar (in any guise – for example, glucose, sucrose, corn syrup, fructose), ditch it. If it contains artificial colourings or flavourings, ditch it. If it's full of chemical ingredients you can barely pronounce, ditch it. You can make great snacks yourself at home from scratch. All it takes is a little time and practice. The benefit, aside from the fact they taste amazing, is that you will know exactly what's gone into them.

Forget how many calories a particular food contains or how much fat is in it. Fat will not automatically make you fat and not all calories are created equal. The myth of calorie counting as an efficient measure of what we should and should not be consuming is a dangerous one. Yes, it's true that all calories hold the same amount of energy, but our body is more complicated than that. Different foods go through different biochemical pathways and the macronutrients within them have diverse effects on our brain centre, which controls hunger and eating patterns. For example, your skin is not going to get the same benefits from you eating a plate of junk food as it will if you make yourself a healthy, nutrient-rich avocado and walnut salad which may, in very simple terms, match a burger and chips in terms of calorie content.

When it comes to eliminating foods to keep your skin clear, it's vital to focus instead on reading labels. If you're preparing healthy, clean meals from scratch, checking ingredients lists may become almost irrelevant, but there will be times when you're stuck somewhere – an airport, for example – and you simply have no choice but to buy something prepackaged. The obvious ingredients to check for are sugar, additives, preservatives and flavourings. But if you're particularly sensitive to something which triggers a reaction in your skin – nightshades, for example – read the ingredients on the packet and check for things like potato starch.

ACID/ALKALINE

Avoiding potentially inflammatory foods is the first step to healing skin. Introducing a clean, high-alkaline diet, lots of fresh still water (sparkling water can be slightly acidic), a combination of vitamins, salts and oils, plus skin-friendly foods and juices, all tailored to reducing inflammation, will not only replenish your system, but can also defeat sickness and skin disease long term.

All the systems in our body are delicately balanced. Take body temperature. It should be between 36.1°C and 37.2°C. It only ever fluctuates by 0.5°C unless we get sick. That's an incredibly fine tipping point. One of the first things we do is take our temperature as an indicator of illness and yet we rarely pay much heed to another finely balanced figure – our body's pH. This is a measure of acidity or alkalinity and people are starting to realise it has a real impact on health.

You may already have heard of foods referred to as acid or alkaline. Forget what you think you know about the acidity of a particular food. Lemons, for example, you might consider to be acidic (in that they contain citric acid), but while they're acidic in nature, they actually have an alkalising effect on the body once they are digested.

When we metabolise food and extract the energy (calories) from it, our body is burning the food. This happens in a slow and controlled fashion. As part of this process, food leaves behind an ash residue – just like when you burn wood on a fire. Scientists can tell how foods will react inside the body by incinerating them and analysing the mineral content of the ash.

If the mineral content is highly alkaline, the food will likely have an alkalising effect on the body. Fresh vegetables, most fruit, nuts, seeds, pulses and filtered water are considered alkaline. At the opposite end of the spectrum, sugar, junk food, processed or refined foods including white bread and pasta, sweets, fizzy drinks, alcohol and drugs are considered acidic.

A diet rich in alkaline foods played a hugely significant role in reversing the symptoms of my acne, psoriasis and eczema. Redressing my acid/alkaline balance provided the catalyst to clearing my skin completely. Of all the things I learned about food, the importance of an alkaline diet is perhaps the simplest and most powerful principle. This

FOOD CATEGORY	MOST ACID	ACID	LOWEST ACID	LOWEST ALKALINE	ALKALINE	MOST ALKALINE
Fruit		Tinned fruit, processed fruit juices	Blueberries, cranberries, bananas, plums, rhubarb, prunes, pomegranates, raspberries, strawberries	Cherries, tomatoes, oranges, pineapples, peaches, avocados, raisins, limes	Dates, figs, blackcurrants, grapes, papayas, kiwi fruits, apples, pears, melons, mangoes, grapefruit	Lemon, watermelon
Beans Vegetables Legumes Pulses Roots		Pickled vegetables, potatoes	Cooked spinach, green string beans, butter beans, chickpeas	Asparagus, mushrooms, cabbage, peas, cauliflower. turnips, olives, sweet corn, watercress	Okra, celery, beetroot, squash, carrots, green beans, lettuce, courgettes, sweet potatoes, parsnips, rocket, onions	Freshly pressed green juice, raw spinach, broccoli, parsley, cucumber
Nuts and Seeds	Peanuts, walnuts	Pecans, pistachio nuts	Pumpkin seeds, sesame seeds, sunflower seeds, cashew nuts, macadamia nuts	Brazil nuts, coconut, hazelnuts	Almonds, chestnuts	
Oils		Lard	Corn oil, sunflower oil	Olive oil, rapeseed oil	Flaxseed oil	Coconut oil, avocado oil
Cereals and Grains	White bread, pastries, biscuits, pasta	White rice, corn, oats	Rye bread, whole grain bread, brown rice, buckwheat, spelt	Amaranth, wild rice, quinoa, millet		
Meat	Beef, pork, veal, shellfish, canned tuna and sardines, pheasant	Turkey, chicken, lamb	Liver, oysters, venison, fish			
Eggs and Dairy	Processed cheese, margarine	Eggs, raw milk, hard cheeses, ice cream, whole milk, butter, cream	Yogurt, cottage cheese	Goat's milk, goat's cheese, buttermilk, whey	Breast milk, ghee	
Drinks	Beer, spirits, energy drinks	Wine, fizzy drinks, flavoured water, coffee	Tea, sparkling water	Ginger tea	Green tea	Herbal teas, lemon water, still mineral water
Sweeteners	Aspartame	White sugar, brown sugar, ketchup, mayo, mustard	Processed honey, molasses	Raw honey	Maple syrup, rice syrup, agave	Stevia
Other	Processed foods, sweets, cigarettes				Tofu	

doesn't apply solely to skin health or to autoimmune disease. Are you lacking in energy, with that sluggish, continual feeling of tiredness when you struggle to get out of bed in the morning? Suffer from sleep problems at night? Have you tried really hard to lose weight but found that no matter how much you exercise or how rigidly you try to stick to a diet the pounds just won't shift? Redressing your alkaline intake could be the single most important dietary change you make for your health.

Do you remember chemistry lessons at school when you were asked to test the pH of a certain liquid? You'd use those little yellow strips, dip them in the liquid, watch them turn orange or green or blue, then compare their colour change to a pH chart and note whether what you were testing was acid or alkaline. The acid/alkaline spectrum runs from 1 to 14, with 1 being super acidic and 14 being highly alkaline. Our blood has a very specific pH of 7.36, a figure that should not alter. As with body temperature, if our blood pH changed even slightly we would die. And again like body temperature, our system will do everything it can to maintain its delicate pH balance.

Modern living is putting so much pressure on maintaining this balance. A diet of high-grain, fast or processed foods, sugar and stimulants such as alcohol or caffeine is hugely acid promoting. Our emotions can have a strong, significant effect too. Stress, depression, worry and negativity contribute massively to internal acidity. It's important to understand that the problem is not so much a single food type or mood response, but rather the cumulative effect of an unhealthy, acid-rich, stressful lifestyle that is repeatedly bombarding the body over time. Our system needs to control its pH. The body will battle hard against everything we throw at it to maintain harmony.

There are other reasons for keeping our acid levels down. The outside of our red blood cells which carry oxygen around the body have a negative charge, which stops cells sticking together. Acidity strips and weakens that charge. When this happens, the cells begin to clump together, and consequently our energy goes through the floor. Eventually these cells weaken and die. When they die, they release

A NOTE ON MEAT

I have been a vegetarian for 25 years, and the recipes you will find in this book reflect that. Although I originally made the decision for ethical reasons, meat, especially red meat, is highly acidic and our bodies have to work hard to process it, so for me it now makes sense to avoid it for health reasons too. Tinned fish and seafood are also acidic. Fresh fish is less so, but there are the potentially high levels of mercury to consider. A well-balanced, plant-powered diet will successfully meet the nutrient requirements of almost everyone and wholly nourish the body and mind. I certainly recommend you follow the plan as laid out for the first 28 days. Thereafter, you may wish to experiment with reintroducing occasional meat and fish and seeing how it affects your skin and general health.

their own acids, compounding the problem. We're gradually depleting our alkaline reserves. The body, and our main organs of detoxification, including the skin, have to work immeasurably hard to battle this damaging environment. As a result we see disruption, which can eventually result in chronic inflammation and skin disease.

The chances are that you've been existing on an acid-rich lifestyle for a very long time. Here's the good news: altering your intake is possible instantly and the beneficial effects on your health, complexion and mental well-being can be seen very quickly. The heat in my skin, the redness and unbearable itching were all reduced within days, and healing began within weeks. I'm impatient by nature, so to see such rapid reversal results after years of fuelling my system so badly was remarkable, to say the least.

The methodology behind an alkaline diet is not to try raising the alkalinity of our blood, it's about reducing the strain, allowing the body to more easily maintain its healthy equilibrium. The intention is to fuel the system with nourishing, life-giving, alkaline foods. Far from the impossible task of changing our blood pH, we aim to counter the existing acidic environment and provide a calm, redefined, proportional platform for the body's own delicate balance.

So, where to begin? I find a morning green juice to be the fastest way to kick-start reversal. It's a great way of getting a ton of leafy, alkaline greens into the body, and it provides a better, longer-lasting energy injection than your morning coffee. Green, leafy vegetables and bright, vibrant fruit are the very best way to get the acid/alkaline balance redressed.

This isn't about an unmanageable, restrictive regime. It's simply about being aware. Take a look at the alkaline/acid chart and try to aim for an 80/20 balance in favour of alkaline foods. I naturally choose to eat salads, fresh vegetables and fruit because I know how good those foods make me feel and the subsequent effect they have on my skin. It's not about looking at a menu or supermarket shelf and feeling restricted. It's about wanting to fuel the body so that every part of it feels amazing. Upping our intake of green, leafy, natural foods to encourage the restoration of a health-promoting alkaline state is essential to the regeneration of bone health, immune function and overall well-being. It's vital for glowing skin, mental wellness and optimum weight.

PINK HIMALAYAN SALT

Sodium, the key ingredient in salt, is a crucial mineral also found in the human body. Vigorous exercise depletes our sodium levels and replacing this important electrolyte during or after training is crucial. Table salt is commercially refined and has often been stripped of all its minerals. It's chemically cleaned, bleached and heated at unnecessarily high temperatures. Himalayan salts on the other hand, are mineral packed pink crystals, sourced as you'd expect, from the Himalayan mountain range.

In addition to sodium chloride, Himalayan Salts contain the same 84 trace minerals and elements that are found in the human body including; sulphate, magnesium, calcium, potassium, bicarbonate, bromide, borate and strontium. As well as aiding nutrient absorption in our intestinal tract, these body strengthening minerals provide us with electrolytes which boost hydration, resulting in fresh and vibrant skin. Pink salts can reduce fluid retention to keep us looking radiant. They strengthen the immune system to make us more resistant to skin infections, and have been proven to alleviate allergies, heal skin disease and reduce toxins to promote a clear complexion. Pink salt is easily available online or at your local health food shop.

WATER AND SKIN

Of all the positive changes we can make for our health, consuming more water is the simplest and cheapest. We live in a part of the world where clean drinking water is readily available, but many people are still water deficient. Out of 30,000 people surveyed in 2014, fewer than 1 per cent said they drink the recommended eight glasses a day.

My daily intake of liquid used to consist of 50 per cent Diet Coke, 50 per cent red wine. I rarely drank water. On the odd occasion when I tried to be good, I would choose a bottle of sparkling mineral water over Diet Coke at the supermarket. The notion of eight glasses of still, plain water was completely alien to me. Water was boring; I didn't see the point.

My skin, which was red and sore at the best of times, was hugely dehydrated from the excessive amounts of red wine I was pumping through my liver and kidneys. Then I'd wake up the following morning and start my day with a bottle of Diet Coke. The diuretic effects of the caffeine it contains (see page 12) were simply adding to the dehydration.

Water is responsible for so many essential functions. Apart from quenching our thirst, it carries nutrients and oxygen to our cells and flushes toxins out of vital organs. It regulates our body temperature, detoxifies and moisturises the air in our lungs and plumps up our skin. If you suffer from skin problems, upping your water intake could be a really simple and effective way of reducing redness, relieving itchy skin and dramatically improving its appearance. Think of your skin as a bath sponge. When a sponge is dry, it's contracted, shrivelled and rigid. Run it under the tap and all of a sudden the sponge expands. Exactly like that sponge, our skin needs moisture to expand. A lack of internal hydration will often present itself as dryness, tightening and flaking on the skin's surface. Dry skin has less resilience and is more prone to wrinkles.

I often get asked how much water we should drink. There is no 'one size fits all' answer. The environment, temperature and physical exertion all affect consumption. As a broad guideline, if you're looking to improve or heal your skin, I would aim for 2–3 litres of water per day. Sparkling water can be slightly acidic and tap water can contain chemicals and metals, so still filtered or mineral water is best.

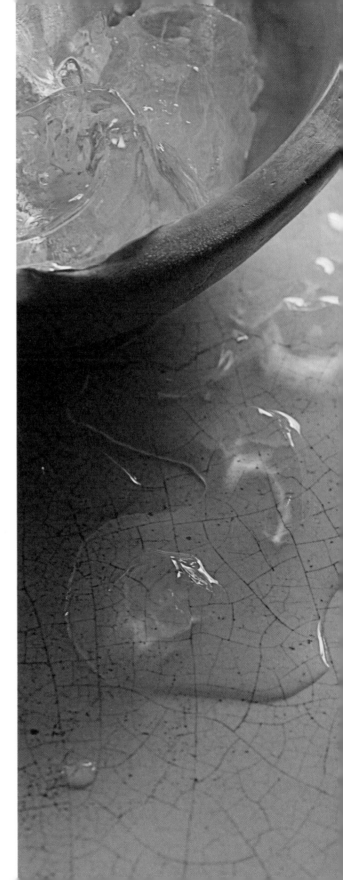

INTRO-JUICING THE JUICE CLEANSE

Whether you gradually transition to a cleaner way of eating to improve your complexion, or make immediate changes because you're struggling to cope with a serious skin problem, something I always recommend doing is a juice cleanse. My passion for juicing is no secret. I credit it for a complete reversal in my way of thinking about food and its true health benefits. It was a real catalyst for change and I miss my green juice if I go without it.

Giving your body a three-, five- or even seven-day break from digesting food, while pouring in a ton of nutrients, is a very effective way to cleanse your system. Within days of ditching my carb-heavy, sugar-rich diet for a juice cleanse and light salads, the redness and itching in my skin calmed completely. After less than a month I went out in short sleeves for the first time in years. Juicing works on a completely different level from an elimination diet alone. It offers the awesome benefits of food-as-medicine in a supercharged liquid form. It gives so much, yet makes absolutely no demands on the body in terms of digestion.

HOW JUICING WORKS

Juicing removes the insoluble fibre (the pulp) from fruit and vegetables. Don't get me wrong, fibre is good for you – it keeps your digestive tract healthy and it slows down the absorption of sugar. But in a short-term juice cleanse, the lack of insoluble fibre means your body absorbs 100 per cent of the available goodness. It's like a super-powerful injection of vitamins straight to your cells. The other awesome advantage of juicing is that it offers our digestive system a breather. In the absence of fibre, the digestive system doesn't have to work as hard to break down food and make the most of its nutritional benefits. Freshly pressed vegetable juices work so brilliantly in healing and detoxification plans because they are super-rich in nutrients and they nourish and restore the body at a cellular level.

I'm also a huge advocate of predominantly alkaline juice. I believe the acid/alkaline body balance is critical to optimum wellness, calming inflammation and healing damaged skin. As a general rule, green, leafy vegetables along with certain fruits are some of the most alkaline foods we can consume – so these are precisely what you want to put through your juicer. The energy, clarity and health benefits you will undoubtedly achieve from an alkaline-rich diet are amazing. Drink raw, green veg juice and your body barely has to make any effort to extract the vitamins and nutrients. You're giving the major organs of elimination a rest, and pouring all that goodness straight in. It's a shot of live, vibrant, plant-rich energy and I guarantee your skin will absolutely love you for it.

The other incredible benefit from juicing is the sheer quantity of plant-based goodness you're able to consume in one sitting! I'll often juice huge handfuls of spinach, broccoli stem, pears, cucumber, celery, kale... when you look at the mountain of greens you're pushing through the juicer, that's a ginormous stack of vitamins in a simple drink. You're combining that tower of goodness into a single, super-concentrated shot of nourishment. I'm fortunate in that I now enjoy my greens anyway – I like my side order of sautéed spinach and green beans when I eat out. But if you're not one for consuming as much veg as you possibly should, juicing is a superb way of upping your intake. Granted, the idea of starting your day with liquid spinach sounds less than appealing, but you won't believe how good it tastes! Okay, I'll concede that on its own it's not my drink of choice, but add a couple of apples, some lime and a little ginger to those breakfast juices and you will have absolutely no idea that you're drinking liquid veg! Sweeter ingredients such as carrots, beets, apples or pears make a green juice far more palatable and as you transition to a healthy, wholefood lifestyle you'll find yourself craving the sweetness less and less. I usually add an apple or pear to my juices but anything more and it's now too sweet for me.

The point of keeping the fruit ratio as low as possible is to reduce the sugar hit and insulin spikes which fibre-less juice can instigate. This is why many dedicated green juicers also like the nutri-machine or blended-juice concept. Blenders and nutri-machines pulverise the fruit and veg, instead of extracting the pulp. There are certainly benefits to both, but don't forget with a blended drink you are not going to get that instant nutrient hit that juicing offers and the body will still have to work a little at digesting the insoluble fibre. Personally, I also find the consistency of juice extracted from vegetables easier to drink than blended greens, which creates thicker smoothies.

In the West, our choices for breakfast quite possibly make it the very worst meal of the day! Your body deserves a more gentle, wholesome, energy injection after the night fast. By starting your day with a glass of greens you're making a commitment to yourself to set off on the right track. Forget caffeine; this juice is by far the best injection of energy you can give yourself. For me, my morning juice is also my psychological commitment to a good day. It's like saying, 'I'm going to start as I mean to go on', with an injection of energy, optimum health, well-being and vitamin goodness.

There are specific combinations of greens and herbs that work particularly well to heal skin. I'm going to share with you some of my favourites, but feel free to experiment with colours and flavours and, above all, have fun. Don't be afraid to try out your own ideas. Focusing on seasonal foods or less-expensive, locally sourced options may also be worth considering.

VITAL VITAMINS
VITAMIN A

It is widely acknowledged that vitamin A is one of the most important nutrients for healthy skin. It's essential for cell renewal and a lack of it can cause your skin to look dull and grey. Vitamin A thickens and stimulates the dermis (the middle layer of skin, where your collagen, elastin and blood vessels are) so it reduces wrinkles and increases blood flow to the surface of the skin. This increase in blood flow in turn slows the normal ageing breakdown of collagen and elastin.

Rough skin and lumps and bumps just under the skin's surface are a common sign of vitamin A deficiency. Acne, eczema, psoriasis and open wounds can all benefit greatly from increasing vitamin A in your diet.

Top food sources of vitamin A include: carrots,

pumpkins, sweet potatoes, butternut squash, mangoes, cantaloupe melons, dried apricots, leafy greens, spinach, kale and Swiss chard.

ZINC

According to the World Health Organization, 31.7 per cent of the world's population is deficient in this key mineral. Zinc is crucial for proper immune system function, triggering the generation of healthy white blood cells. Think of it as a 24/7 on-call skin doctor. Zinc helps to repair damaged tissues and heal wounds. It's also essential for regular cell growth and regeneration, carrying vitamin A to your skin and regulating your body's hormonal balance. While I'm against using steroid creams, applying a natural, zinc-based salve topically can help to prevent and alleviate the inflammation and scarring associated with acne. It's also an excellent natural sun protector.

Top food sources of zinc include: spinach, pumpkin seeds, cashew nuts, cacao powder, mushrooms, kidney beans, flaxseeds, garlic, egg yolks, chickpeas, salmon and sesame seeds.

SELENIUM

Selenium is essential for the efficient and effective operation of our immune system. Those of us with autoimmune illnesses such as psoriasis and rheumatoid arthritis could benefit greatly from eating foods naturally rich in selenium. Inadequate intake, and intestinal disorders that affect absorption can lead to deficiencies of selenium, and this can have consequences for our general health as well as that of our skin. Selenium has been found to optimise the immune system to fight bacterial and viral infections, the herpes virus, cold sores and shingles.

Top food sources of selenium include: Brazil nuts, chia seeds, tuna fish, shiitake mushrooms, sunflower, sesame and flaxseeds, broccoli, spinach, asparagus, brown rice, tofu, eggs and mustard seeds.

MILK THISTLE

Milk thistle, *Silybum marianum*, is a plant originating from the Mediterranean. It's a fantastic, natural preventative medicine and, to date, there is no synthetic pharmaceutical equivalent. Not only can it protect each cell of the liver from incoming toxins, it also encourages the liver to cleanse itself of damaging substances, such as alcohol, drugs, medications, mercury and other heavy metals.

The liver is our primary organ of detoxification, helping to remove toxins that can damage other internal systems, including the heart, eyes and skin, as well as our blood vessels. If our liver energy is stagnant, it struggles to cleanse the blood effectively. Toxic build-up can lead to fatigue, headaches, poor digestion, inflammation and even impaired immune function. This can result in skin problems including acne, psoriasis, eczema and dermatitis. Milk thistle is a powerful herb for supporting the liver to purify the blood and is one of the best-known herbs to help heal skin disorders. Its detoxifying, anti-inflammatory, antioxidant and demulcent properties can work to boost the immune system.

Milk thistle also has soothing properties that lubricate and help to heal inflamed, dry and cracked mucous membranes, calming irritation and inflammation of the kidneys and bladder. Taken internally, it also helps to soften and moisten the skin. Patients with skin problems ranging from acne to eczema have reported a clearing of skin impurities, healing of redness and inflammation and a dramatic improvement in dry, cracked skin.

Milk thistle can be taken as a supplement and you can buy it online or in health shops.

ACIDOPHILUS – THE GOOD BACTERIA

When we're healthy, trillions of micro-organisms flourish in our intestinal tract. Probiotics, also known as 'good bacteria', are living microorganisms similar to those that populate the human intestines. *Lactobacillus acidophilus*, commonly known as simply acidophilus, is a particular strain of probiotic. It helps us to digest and absorb food properly, but more importantly, it crowds out any harmful bacteria, preventing them from taking hold. There are lots of different probiotic strains, each of which affects the body in a variety of ways. Acidophilus is widely used, thanks to its effectiveness in successfully treating a variety of conditions.

A properly functioning intestinal tract is one of the body's first lines of defence against invaders, promoting a healthy immune system and, in turn, radiant skin. The microflora in the gut play an active role in a wide variety of diseases, and, naturally, it stands to reason they affect your health and skin throughout your life.

Taking acidophilus can replace beneficial bacteria lost by antibiotic use, poor dietary habits or other health conditions. Antibiotics are designed to wipe out nasty bacteria but they don't differentiate between good and bad, so it's crucial to replenish the good stuff – particularly after a course of antibiotics. Acidophilus also helps to fight inflammation in the gut by neutralising some toxins and helping to block out others. This anti-inflammatory effect can prove hugely beneficial for our skin.

Following the use of antibiotics or as a result of a bad, high-sugar diet, *Candida albicans*, a yeast that normally lives in harmony in your body, can begin to overgrow and cause infection. Chronic candidiasis can produce digestive disturbances, fatigue and allergies, and one of the first symptoms can often be a skin condition. Because they promote a healthy intestinal environment, acidophilus and other probiotics can help to halt candida overgrowth.

You've probably heard of pre- and probiotics, referring to those little pots of live-culture yogurt you can buy. Rather than getting your good bacteria from a yogurt, which is often crammed with sugar and other nasties, the better option would be to take a good-quality probiotic acidophilus supplement, purchased online or from any health store.

LECITHIN

Lecithin is a fat that plays an essential role in our body's cells; it regulates the nutrients that enter and exit the cells. Damaged cells reduce the body's ability to resist diseases and lecithin has a vital role in keeping the cells healthy and functioning.

Cosmetics companies include lecithin as an active ingredient in moisturisers because its essential fatty acid content helps to penetrate the skin and hydrate, replenish and repair our cells. Lecithin contains high levels of oleic and linoleic acid, which soften and moisturise the skin. It also attracts water to the skin, working to prevent dryness from deep within the skin tissues.

Medical uses for lecithin range from treating memory disorders such as Alzheimer's disease to lowering cholesterol levels and boosting the immune system. In foods, it's used as an emulsifier. It works by preventing water-hating (hydrophobic) and water-loving (hydrophilic) substances, such as oil and water, from separating – in mayonnaise, for example. Egg yolks are the best natural source of lecithin. If you want to avoid eating raw egg, though, maximum benefit is generally obtained when you eat the yolk lightly cooked (as in a soft-boiled or poached egg).

Probably the best way to significantly increase lecithin in your diet is to buy lecithin granules, which are made from soya beans – another natural source of this good fat. Simply add the granules to your juices and soups.

VITAMIN D3 – THE SUNSHINE VITAMIN

Vitamin D and its role in regulating our absorption of calcium and phosphorus has been documented for years. As new studies into its benefits are being conducted, there is overwhelming evidence that proves vitamin D to be a key player in our overall health. It seems it's essential for ensuring that our muscles, nerves and immune system function properly. Optimising vitamin D levels should be at the top of the list for most of us, as vitamin D deficiency has been linked to an astonishing array of common, chronic diseases.

Vitamin D is not simply a vitamin; it's actually a neuro-regulatory steroidal hormone that influences nearly 3,000 different genes in the human body. Receptors that respond to vitamin D have been found in almost every type of human cell, from our brain to our bones. Vitamin D has been proven to fight infections, as well as chronic inflammation. It helps to regulate antimicrobial proteins, which not only support the natural immunity of the skin but also help with the general repair of damaged tissue.

While vitamin D is naturally present in a wide variety of foods, including most fish and dairy products, the body is also capable of creating its own supply. When we're exposed to direct sunlight, our skin reacts to UVB rays by producing vitamin D.

With so many warnings about skin cancer over the past couple of decades, we've become paranoid about protecting our skin from the sun's rays by using SPF sprays, creams and lotions and, in some cases, staying out of the sun altogether. The liberal use of high-strength sunscreen has decreased the amount of sun exposure many people receive, resulting in a vitamin D deficiency being observed in some industrialised countries.

I'm not suggesting for a second that it's time to ditch the factor 30 in favour of burning your skin to a crisp, but for most people, between 10 and 15 minutes in the UK summer sun without sunscreen several times a week is probably a safe balance between adequate vitamin D levels and any risk of skin cancer. The advice comes from a group of seven British health organisations, which have issued a 'consensus statement' of their unified views. There are naturally a number of factors that can affect how vitamin D is made, such as your skin colour or how much skin you have exposed. You should always be very careful not to burn in the sun as over exposure will only result in damage to your skin.

Aside from sunshine, very few dietary sources naturally supply vitamin D: egg yolks, mushrooms and fatty fish such as salmon all contain small amounts. But when it comes to skin conditions I've found gentle exposure to sunshine can achieve some amazing results. It was winter in the UK when I first embarked on a natural regime to clear my eczema and psoriasis. Despite the cold, I put on a

sleeveless body warmer and took walks in the winter sun, exposing my arms to direct sunlight whenever possible. The result was incredible. If you're unable to get sunshine on your skin, during dark winter months, for example, adding a daily supplement to your diet can help maintain levels. Supplements can be bought online or from good health food stores.

SKIN SUPER FOODS
AVOCADO

The humble avocado is one of the few foods that contains every single vitamin and nutrient we need. Forget what you read about its high fat, high calorie count: its monounsaturated fats are brilliant for improving skin tone. These fats are great at maintaining adequate moisture levels in the epidermal layer of the skin, leaving it soft and healthy.

Avocados are high in fibre and low in sodium. They contain over 20 essential nutrients and are full of omega-3, which can help lower cholesterol and improve heart health. Packed full of vitamins, including A, B, C, D, E and K, eating avocado regularly does wonders for your complexion. Slice it into salads, mash it into a fresh guacamole, or blend it into a creamy, sweet mousse – there are so many delicious options. What's more, applying cool avocado directly to your face is a fantastic natural beauty treatment. It hydrates and nourishes without causing irritation. I hate using chemicals on my skin. Read the back of a standard face-mask packet and chances are there will be a long list of chemical ingredients you've never heard of. Making natural alternatives at home means you know exactly what's gone into them. An avocado face mask is one of my absolute favourites. A simple combination of avocado, raw honey and lime makes a lovely, hydrating treatment. Each ingredient adds unique properties that work together to provide nutrients and antioxidants directly to your skin. Suitable for all skin types, avocado face masks are particularly beneficial for dry and dehydrated skin. See page 178 – this little beauty will leave your face feeling smooth, nourished and soothed.

TURMERIC

Turmeric is that awesome, bright yellow little spice with a peppery taste and a pleasant aroma. It's a root, rather like ginger, and is sold fresh or powdered. Apart from being used in curries, turmeric has long been an important ingredient in traditional Indian medicine. Not only does it add a lovely flavour to food, but it also offers some fantastic health benefits for autoimmune disorders such as psoriasis.

The active ingredient in turmeric is curcumin. However, curcumin is not absorbed very well by the body, so it's important to use turmeric together with black pepper. Pepper contains a compound called piperine which increases our body's absorption of curcumin by an incredible 2,000 per cent.

Juice fresh turmeric root, create delicious puddings with turmeric milk (made by combining turmeric and almond milk) or add a pinch or two of the powder and a few grinds of black pepper to omelettes for a bright, peppery breakfast (see page 70).

SHIITAKE MUSHROOMS

Shiitake mushrooms have a long history of medicinal use, particularly in oriental traditions. No health benefit is better documented for shiitake mushrooms than their immune-regulating properties. There are plenty of studies that demonstrate the ability of whole shiitake mushrooms to help prevent excessive immune-system activity. What is fascinating is that there is just as much research highlighting their ability to help stimulate an immune-system response. In other words, from a dietary perspective, shiitake mushrooms appear to be able to regulate immune function in either direction, giving the system a boost when needed and quietening it when necessary. Widely referred to as 'medicinal mushrooms', these immune-regulating beauties are fantastic for those of us with autoimmune disorders.

BRAZIL NUTS

Brazil nuts are one of the best dietary sources of selenium (see pages 24–25). Snack on them, add them to smoothies or use them to create delicious super-rich chocolate truffles (see page 161).

RED CLOVER, NETTLE AND BURDOCK TEA

I've tried many herbal tea combinations to heal my skin over the years. Taken alone, without any changes to my diet, they never had much of an effect. In an effort to cleanse my liver and kidneys, as part of my juice detox, I combined red clover, nettle and burdock root to create a very bitter-tasting but highly effective blood purifier.

Red clover, *Trifolium pretense*, is a common member of the legume family. It is known to cleanse the bloodstream of toxins that can adversely affect the skin. It cleanses the liver, the primary organ responsible for blockages that can lead to a plethora of skin problems. Red clover acts as a diuretic, helping to produce urine whereby impurities such as uric acid can then be flushed out through the kidneys and bladder. It is also an anti-inflammatory and stimulates digestive fluids, helping to eliminate impurities, which in turn leads to healthier skin.

Nettle offers anti-inflammatory and analgesic effects, great for skin problems such as eczema or rashes. The high levels of chlorophyll in nettles gives them alkalising and detoxifying properties, making them an effective plant option for treating acne.

Burdock, *Arctium*, is another common plant.

The root of the burdock, like that of red clover, has blood-purifying properties. It helps skin problems by increasing circulation to the skin, detoxifying the epidermal tissues. Burdock root also has antibacterial and antifungal properties which have been shown to destroy bacteria and fungus cultures.

Skin-detox tea bags often contain one, or a combination of these herbs and can be bought online or from reputable health shops. The tea bags are much easier to use and far more convenient than loose tea, but I prefer loose tea for its strength and effectiveness. I recommend Red Clover, Nettle and Burdock Tea (see page 57) as part of my detox plan.

COCONUT OIL

To say I'm a little addicted to this stuff is an understatement. It really is my miracle find. After being given the cold shoulder for many years, thankfully coconut oil has recently been embraced by the health and wellness community for its seemingly endless body, mind and skin benefits.

Solid below 24°C, it looks like soft, white wax. Scrape a little out of the jar with your hands and it soon begins to melt with the warmth of your touch. Its uses and benefits are endless. It's my preferred moisturiser, cleanser, hair treatment, natural sunscreen, butter replacement and cooking oil.

Whether it's eaten or applied, the healing properties of this little miracle oil (when it's not the refined stuff) are quite staggering. Cold-pressed, virgin coconut oil acts as a moisturiser, multivitamin, multinutrient and antioxidant. Its unique combination of fatty acids – lauric, caprylic and capric – can have profound positive effects on health. These acids contain antifungal, antibacterial and antiviral properties.

Coconut oil has been used extensively in tropical regions for thousands of years. It was popular in Western countries, too, back in the seventies, until it got a bad press for containing lots of saturated fat. In fact, coconut oil is 100 per cent fat. However, the structure of its fat differs from the saturated fat often found in animal products such as meat and cheese.

Coconut oil contains medium chain triglycerides (MCTs), which are metabolised differently to the long chain saturated fats that are found in animal products. MCTs are easily absorbed into the small intestine with other nutrients, which prevents MCTs from being deposited into the body as fat. They've been shown to have therapeutic effects on cognitive and brain disorders such as Alzheimer's and, far from causing us to gain weight, coconut oil has also proven successful in aiding fat loss.

Coconut oil also strengthens the immune system, as the lauric acid it contains gets converted to a biologically active molecule named monolaurin in the body. Research has shown monolaurin to be an effective way of dealing with the viruses and bacteria responsible for diseases such as herpes and influenza. Monolaurin is a potent germ and fungus killer and coconut oil is a fantastic source.

I am absolutely convinced that my skin problems were at least in part a symptom of candida overgrowth (see page 26). Other common indicators include urinary-tract and bladder infections, stomach and intestinal problems, ear-, nose- and throat-related issues and itchy, dry skin. Inflammations in internal organs and patchy, red or peeling skin (particularly on the scalp), are common signs of an excessive and uncontrolled growth of yeast called *Candida albicans* in the gut. Coconut has been shown to prevent and even cure candida. It provides relief from the inflammation caused by candida, both externally and internally.

COCONUT OIL FOR HAIR CARE AND SKIN CARE

Coconut oil makes a fantastic, intensive hair conditioner. In summer I'll set a little pot outside to melt, then rub it in my hands and run my hands through my hair. Not only does it add moisture and shine, but it also provides the essential proteins required for nourishing and healing dry or damaged hair. If you suffer from scalp psoriasis, dandruff or dry skin around your hairline, applying coconut oil to your face and scalp can reduce and prevent chronic dryness. I like to apply it in the evening, wrap my hair in a towel, leave the coconut oil to work its magic and wash it out the following morning. Depending on how problematic your scalp psoriasis is, this process can be repeated daily or at least twice weekly to ease symptoms.

I also use coconut oil as my preferred moisturiser every single day. It's my post-shower body lotion and face cream. Virgin coconut oil contains the same fatty acids as those naturally occurring in our skin. There is, therefore, a remarkable compatibility between its inherent structure and that of our skin's surface. It's absorbed better than other oils, allowing it to penetrate much more quickly and deeply, strengthening the underlying connective tissue. In skin diseases such as psoriasis, skin cells grow too rapidly and erratically, creating plaque layers of red, flaky skin. Coconut oil replenishes our skin cells' fatty acids with its more stable ones. This can repair the damage and encourage cells to regrow correctly. Aside from its effectiveness in targeting specific skin problems, coconut oil has antioxidant properties which benefit the skin by restoring its radiance. Its combination of fatty acids and vitamins K and E also works to prevent scarring from acne, psoriasis and surface damage to the skin. Another awesome thing about coconut oil is that it absorbs nicely into your skin without leaving it feeling oily or greasy.

There are endless ways to incorporate coconut oil into your everyday diet and skin-care regime. Use it in raw desserts, add it to baked recipes in place of butter, include a spoonful in your smoothie and begin using it as your preferred cooking oil. I find the best time to apply it to my skin is immediately after a bath or shower and often before bed to give it time to absorb overnight. Do read the label: avoid refined or hydrogenated versions and look instead for organic, cold-pressed, virgin coconut oil.

TOPICALS

Topical treatments are products such as creams, ointments, oils, tars, emollients and gels that are applied directly onto the skin. Medicated creams, designed to slow down or normalise the excessive cell production associated with psoriasis and to reduce inflammation and itching in eczema, are often prescribed by doctors or available over the counter. These can sometimes be a tempting 'quick fix' solution, but they aren't guaranteed to work and are not usually intended as a longterm solution. In addition, there are other chemicals that we might use on a daily basis, such as makeup and cleansing products, that also impact on the health of our skin.

SODIUM LAURYL SULFATE (SLS)

You might think that the chemicals in the makeup, shampoos, soaps and shower gels we use can't really cause us any serious health problems. In fact, what we apply topically can have a more harmful effect than the foods we consume. When we eat something, the enzymes in our saliva and stomach help to break it down and flush toxins from the body. When we put chemicals on to our skin through applying makeup, using shower gel or brushing our teeth, they get absorbed straight into the bloodstream without filtering of any kind.

Read the back of your shampoo bottle or body wash and chances are you'll see an ingredient called sodium lauryl sulfate. SLS is a widely used and inexpensive chemical found in many mainstream personal hygiene products. Its purpose is to create 'foam' when you use it. Ironically it's also widely known to be a skin irritant.

In 2014 the *International Journal of Toxicology* ran a study on the harmful side effects of SLS. The results show a direct correlation between the level of SLS in a product and skin irritation. As a result of these findings, it is recommended that SLS concentrations in products intended for prolonged contact with skin should not exceed 1 per cent. Worryingly, many household cleaning products contain levels as high as 20 per cent. Aside from skin irritation, there are studies that have found residual levels of SLS in the brain, lungs, liver and heart. It can stay in our system for days after use, so while it may be considered safe to use at 1 per cent, over time the amount absorbed by the bloodstream can mean accumulated concentrations in the body are much higher. It's these gradual, cumulative effects of repeated exposure that are of real concern.

SLS isn't the only cause for concern. Preservatives such as parabens and formaldehyde, for example, are used in cosmetics to prevent the growth of bacteria, mould and yeast. Both have been known to cause allergic skin reactions and may also be harmful to our immune system. Synthetic fragrance ingredients can trigger irritation, causing skin rashes as well as headaches, coughing, wheezing and other respiratory problems.

Not enough is really known about long-term

exposure to SLS and these other, potentially harmful, contaminants. We ought to give our skin the same thoughtful care we give to our diet, because so much of what goes on our skin is absorbed by it. If you're struggling with an existing skin condition the best advice is to avoid them and avoid the risk altogether. Switch to a product range that matches your skin's natural pH and has no irritants, so that the chemicals won't be absorbed into your body.

SALTS AND ESSENTIAL OILS

Rather than add synthetic foams to your bath, use pure Dead Sea salts and a combination of simple essential oils. The salts contain natural minerals that have antiseptic and antifungal properties to alleviate dry skin problems, and essential oils can work wonders to relieve stress, reduce inflammation and encourage your skin to retain moisture.

I'm often asked if there's anything that can be done about the little white patches left on the skin after clearing psoriasis, acne or eczema. These patches can be highly visible – I'd often joke that after clearing psoriasis I looked like a dalmatian! It can takes weeks or months for skin to regain its normal colour after skin inflammation has cleared.

Scientists believe two immune-system proteins are responsible for preventing the release of melanin (the stuff that colours our skin) until inflammation settles down. Then the build-up of melanin is released, and the skin can show hyper-pigmentation — dark spots. The good news is there are some natural products that can help to even skin tone and colouration.

Having struggled with a variety of skin conditions over the years, I've found specific essential oils to be incredibly beneficial in treating both the problems and subsequent scarring. Using topical treatments on your skin is no substitute for healing from within, but we're taking a holistic approach, replacing chemically laden shower gels and moisturisers with a much gentler, natural alternative. I recommend:

LAVENDER OIL

Lavender oil is one of my favourites. Not only does its soft, floral scent remind me of the bright purple patch of flowering blooms at my grandad's house, but it also has some terrific benefits for the skin. Lavender oil has antiseptic, antibacterial, antifungal, and anti-inflammatory properties. Applied directly it helps to regenerate skin cells so it's perfect for mature skin, sun spots and scarring. It is moisturising, calming and smells amazing, which means it can help you to relax and unwind. Pure lavender oil is relatively inexpensive and I would highly recommend adding a few drops to a warm bath for all skin types and needs.

ROSEHIP OIL

Rosehip oil is particularly brilliant at improving the appearance of scarred skin, repairing UV damage and regenerating healthy skin tissue. Studies have shown that even old scars can benefit from topical applications of rosehip oil. I first began using it to improve the appearance of facial scars that remained as a result of teenage acne. In later years I also used it on the little white patches left behind by my psoriasis. Rosehip oil contains retinol (Vitamin A)and has a high fatty acid content, which may explain its ability to restore skin colour by reducing hyper-pigmentation and redness. Massage it gently into the affected area twice a day. Depending on the severity of your scars, it may take a few weeks to see significant results.

FRANKINCENSE OIL

Frankincense oil has long been revered in the Middle East where it's a popular ingredient in cosmetics. Aside from its fantastic moisturising properties, I absolutely love the smell. Frankincense oil promotes healthy cell regeneration and keeps existing cells and tissues healthy. This is particularly useful for treating psoriasis where overproduction of skin cells can be a real problem. Frankincense induces calmness, serenity and relaxation. It's the perfect addition to your moisturiser as a day or night cream. Alternatively try adding one or two drops to a bowl of hot water and, with a towel over your head, allow the steam to create a refreshing, relaxing facial.

*Frankincense is considered an emmenagogue (a herb that stimulates blood flow in the pelvic area and uterus) and an astringent (causes body tissue to tighten) and it is therefore not recommended for use during pregnancy.

GERANIUM OIL

Like lavender, geranium oil can lift your mood, lessen fatigue and promote emotional wellness. Its antiseptic properties can help speed up the healing of wounds and treat a variety of skin problems. Topical application can also assist with insect bites and stop itching. It can help to eliminate the appearance of scars and dark spots by improving blood circulation just below the surface of the skin and promoting an equal distribution of melanin.

*Since it influences certain hormone secretions, geranium essential oil is not recommended for use by pregnant women or for those who are breast-feeding.

JOJOBA OIL

Jojoba oil is not actually an oil, but a liquid wax obtained from the seeds of the jojoba plant. It's the only oil that closely resembles human sebum – an oily substance naturally produced by the oil glands below the skin's surface. You can use jojoba oil head-to-toe as a body or face moisturiser. Massaging a few drops into your skin straight after a bath or shower locks in moisture, keeping your skin soft and smooth. It has anti-inflammatory properties that help to reduce inflammation caused by skin dryness. Jojoba oil can also be used as an intensive conditioner, to tame frizz or soothe an irritated scalp. It's one of the best oils for dry, damaged hair and other problems such as scalp psoriasis, dandruff and hair loss.

IMPORTANT

When using oils, always do a skin patch test first. Although these are deemed as safe to use on the skin, some people can be allergic to nuts and seeds or sensitive to certain oils which can cause dermatitis or allergic reactions. Be sensible and always test new ingredients out before incorporating them into any kind of skincare regime. The inner forearm is a great place to do a test since the skin is delicate, similar to facial skin. Essential oils should always be diluted in a carrier oil, such as almond oil, to a maximum of 5 per cent.

Additionally, certain essential oils should be avoided by pregnant women, young children and babies, so be sure to do your homework beforehand.

EXERCISE AND SKIN

One of the first things you'll notice as you up your water intake and eat lots more fresh, alkaline greens is a desire to move. Moving is so important for our well-being and in a world where many of us spend much of the day sitting at a screen and evenings in front of the television, it's vital to build exercise into our routine. A combination of gentle, intermittent movement and more vigorous workouts is vital for optimal health, beauty and skin.

When we do move, all our biological systems are able to function correctly and efficiently. Regular exercise is not just great for improving our general well-being; anything that promotes healthy circulation also helps keep our skin beautifully vibrant and glowing.

When we move we increase blood flow around the body, which in turn helps to nourish skin cells. Blood transports oxygen and nutrients to working cells and channels away waste products. By increasing our blood flow through exercise, we're helping the heart to pump cellular debris out of our system.

Exercise also ups the production of mood-boosting hormones (endorphins) in the brain. These feel-good transmitters not only combat the negative effects of stress, but they can also regulate our appetite and enhance our immune-system response. It really is the shortest route to an instant feeling of well-being and a healthy physical glow.

My psoriasis often looked worse immediately after exercise. With blood pumping and skin sweating, the patches appeared redder and more angry. Don't let that deter you. Pick something that works for you. If your skin is dry, it's probably worth steering clear of chlorine for the time being, so avoid public swimming pools. You may, in any case, be reluctant to bare your skin, but remember that gentle exposure to fresh air and sunlight can be a real benefit.

If you don't exercise at all at the moment, start slowly. My journey began with a 20-minute walk each morning and evening. That eventually turned into half an hour's jogging. Within a year I was competing in triathlons. Now I Thai-box,

EXERCISE REALLY *is* THE SHORTEST ROUTE TO AN INSTANT FEELING OF WELL-BEING.

I wakeboard, I lift weights, I run, I swim, I cycle. I don't feel as though any of it is a chore. I genuinely love the sports I do and that's the important part. Exercise needn't be complicated or expensive. Complaining about the cost of gym membership and fitness gear is your mind's way of making excuses. Stop it. Pick something enjoyable and manageable so that it becomes a simple, fun part of your daily routine.

THE LYMPHATIC SYSTEM

Our lymphatic system also plays a vital role in our body's ability to detoxify, nourish and regenerate tissue. It filters our metabolic waste, reduces pain and swelling, and helps us maintain a healthy immune response. Think of it as an inbuilt drainage channel. Congestion of the lymph can overburden the body. Unlike our heart, the lymphatic system does not have its own pump and relies solely on the movement of our muscles and diaphragm to circulate. Acne, especially along the jawline, near the ears, or down the sides of the mouth and chin (this is where lymph vessels run close to the surface), is a sign you may have a sluggish lymphatic system.

Lymphatic Exercise

Exercise is key to getting the lymph moving and detoxifying our system. Yoga, because of the rhythmic breathing and intense muscular contractions involved, is particularly good for lymph circulation.

Lymphatic Massage

Massage, especially gentle, lymphatic massage, works wonders to stimulate lymph flow. This kind of massage is based on light, rhythmic and constant movements, gently manipulating the skin, while applying very little pressure. Massage encourages the lymph to move freely, resulting in clearer, healthier skin and eliminating the buildup of toxins and fluids. If you struggle with puffiness, dull skin, under-eye circles or water retention, or feel tenderness and swelling around your lymph nodes, a massage can be the ideal way to restore healthy lymph flow and rev up your internal detox.

Dry Body Brushing

Body brushing is excellent for reducing cellulite, stimulating the immune system and generally waking up lymphatic circulation. Use a natural body brush to gently slough away dead skin cells before you bathe or shower. It's important to brush using long, even strokes, starting at your feet and always moving towards your heart – that's the direction in which the lymph flows. Focus on problem areas such as the back of your thighs to dissolve cellulite and brush lightly on more sensitive areas or where skin is thinner. If you're struggling with conditions such as psoriasis or eczema, avoid directly dry brushing areas where the skin's surface is broken.

REFERENCES

I'm not a doctor, and the information and suggestions I've shared here are based on my own personal research and experiences. If you would like to find out more or do your own further reading, you can find a full list of the references I used at www.mygoodnessrecipes.com/radiant-references

BEFORE AND AFTER

The important thing to remember, when it comes to skin problems, is that we all differ a little. The speed with which long-term conditions such as psoriasis, eczema and rosacea begin to clear can depend on so many factors. Healing varies greatly from person to person. I've known a change in diet begin to yield results within just a few days, while for others it may take weeks or even months to see a noticable difference on the skin's surface. Rest assured, by focusing on a healthy, clean, plant-based diet you are creating the very best internal environment for your body to begin getting well again. Below are some before and after photos from my own journey, and on the following pages you'll find a selection of before and after photos and testimonials from some of my online followers* who have followed my programme and had great results.

* Some names have been changed

MY SKIN – BEFORE

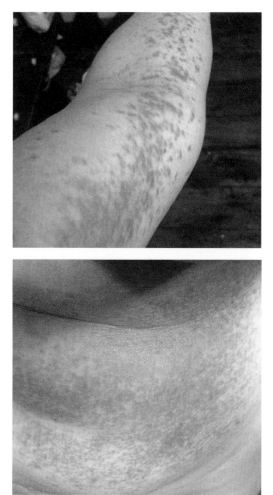

MY SKIN – NOW

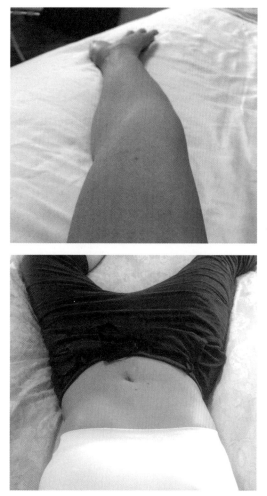

WARDA — BEFORE

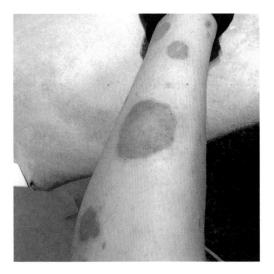

WARDA — NOW

Dear Hanna,

I healed completely over a year ago and I love the change and magic you bring to peoples lives. You're such a huge inspiration!

The day I decided to follow your path and truly engage in a more natural, clean lifestyle and diet was such a huge day for me. Being able to control my own health and future empowered me in a way I didn't know was possible. I was so happy and joyful engaging in the journey and thriving toward the vision of a healthy future. The journey itself is hard, it takes patience and persistence, even so that was the time I felt the happiest! I didn't look back, not even once!

The journey is amazing, not only when you see results (cause we all know that takes a while) but just because getting your body into balance is such a huge feeling.

Today, I try to make clean food as often as I can and try to juice several times a week.

I cant keep it 100 per cent strict all the time but I have followed your advice on discovering what works for me and try to keep it as healthy as possible. I am still clear and so lucky to be!

Thank you for your amazing work, for being my guide and star in this journey.

Warda

It's been 2 weeks now and I can see my psoriasis patches are improving visibly. Also, I've dropped a lot of extra weight. I want to thank you once again.

Testimonial 2

Hanna, [my transformation] is thanks to you. Keep up the fantastic work you do.

Testimonial 3

ALICE – BEFORE

ALICE – NOW

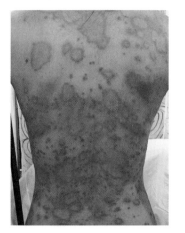

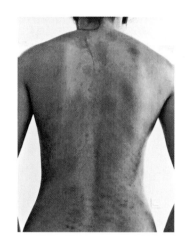

AMY – BEFORE

AMY – NOW

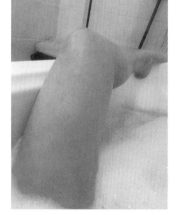

As well as Amy's remarkable before and after photos, the centre image shows an important part of her healing process. Her skin had cleared, but was still missing pigment where the psoriasis patches had been. Her skin colour eventually returned (right).

> *I can't begin to tell you how helpful you and your website have been – especially in those times when it all seems too hard and I'm ready to throw in the towel. Keep up the good work.*

Testimonial 4

> *After I gave birth, I spent months eating whatever I wanted to get through the day. Food was my best friend, but I soon realised that I wasn't losing any baby weight and had in fact put on more! With Hanna's support, recipes and advice, I'm now 15kg lighter and feel better than I have done in years! Best of all, this healthy lifestyle is so simple and I never feel as though I'm missing out on anything.*
> Rachel

THE SKIN PLAN

←——————————————→

HOW TO USE THIS PLAN

If you're looking to improve your overall health and complexion, the juices and recipes in this book are all skin friendly and designed to do just that. If, however, you're struggling with a more serious, long-term skin condition such as eczema or psoriasis, I would highly recommend completing my juice cleanse and switching to a natural skincare regime, followed by a gradual reintroduction of light, alkaline foods.

A juice fast will give your body a complete break from solid food, and so your body will suddenly have a lot more free strength to focus on things such as removing built-up toxins and healing old wounds.

My plan and recipes are designed not only to heal your skin, but to do so properly, not to suppress the symptoms as so many prescription medications do, but to truly heal from the inside out. Not only will your skin look different, it will feel different too. You will feel different. This isn't about suppressing the immune system to stop it attacking itself, this is about resetting and replenishing your body for good.

WHAT'S THE PLAN?

Your mission, when it comes to a diet tailored to clearing your skin, is two fold. First to eliminate the foods that are potentially causing or inflaming the problem and second to begin introducing foods which will play an active part in healing.

Juicing and reverting to a predominantly plant-powered, high-alkaline lifestyle might be a completely alien concept to you. Don't panic, you're not going to starve! This isn't about a prohibitive, unmanageable, fad diet. It's about a complete lifestyle change that's going to improve your energy, health and skin.

EXCUSES, EXCUSES

The mind is a wonderful thing, but it's also a sneaky little liar and often tries to convince us not to take certain actions we know are good for us. We're ultimately afraid of discomfort and change and tend to avoid them at any cost – including our own long-term health and happiness. I'm going to make things as easy as possible for you by including a daily step-by-step guide. Stick with me: the visible results will speak for themselves and be the only incentive you need. I want you to feel excited rather than daunted.

'I Just Love Food'

You're preaching to the converted here. I absolutely adore food. I find it impossible to focus on food solely as an energy source; to me it's so much more than that. It's comfort, it's nourishment, it's art and creativity, it's time spent with friends relaxing over a lazy Sunday lunch. Yes, my emotional attachment to food is real. That's not something I can relinquish and neither should we have to.

We are no longer the hunter-gatherers we once were. Food is not merely fuel for survival. As evolved human beings, food has become an integral part of our social lives. I don't want you to stop enjoying it! And that's the reason I want to talk you through a process that's sustainable. This is not about temporary, tasteless powdered shakes or counting calories. It's about enjoying an abundance of wholesome, nutritious foods. But the right foods. The foods that are going to make your skin look and feel so good you'll be craving even more of them.

'I Can't Cook'

I appreciate that the enjoyment of cooking isn't for everyone. It's become a passion for me, so I'll happily spend hours in the kitchen. But even if you don't enjoy it to that extreme, there's still a definite sense of fulfilment that comes from preparing a meal.

In our culture of 'now' we've become so used to having everything done for us in an instant that quite often we assume we can't accomplish something before we've even tried. My aim is to guide you through effortless, practical recipes and meal plans that will make this lifestyle change super easy. You don't need to shop at a fancy, big-city food market to source the ingredients. The food you prepare doesn't have to look elaborate. What's important is that you know exactly what's gone into it and that it's going to fulfil you with a sense of satisfaction from making it and eating it because you understand the benefits to your body.

'I Don't Have Time'

Preparing food from scratch each day can seem like a lot of hard work. But think of it this way: one of the advantages of making fresh food at home, aside from knowing exactly what's gone into it, is the sheer quantity of inexpensive, easy meals you can produce by spending an hour in the kitchen. Making soups and stews in bulk will give you a freezer full of the very best, wholesome, nutritious 'ready' meals with an absolute ton of health benefits at a fraction of the cost of shop-bought junk. If your weekdays are hectic, set aside a couple of hours one evening or some time at the weekend and prep your wholesome meals in bulk. You can freeze them in individual portion sizes that quickly defrost when you need them. That's what 'ready meals' should mean!

PREPPING YOUR CLEAN KITCHEN

Setting yourself up with the right tools is not only going to make things physically easier, it will also help you stay mentally focused on your healthy lifestyle. My toaster and microwave used to get used daily. I've long since ditched both. On the very rare occasions when I eat spelt bread or warm fruit bread, I'll toast it for a minute or two under the grill.

These days it's my juicer, steamer and food processor that get the most use. It's essential to keep your healthy gadgets to hand. Prominence and pride of place on the kitchen worktop are the key. It makes things easy and serves as a good reminder.

JUICER

I am a huge fan of juicing and talk about it a lot throughout the book. Suffice to say I won't bore you too much here! My juicer has become my favourite

kitchen gadget. I drink a green juice each morning when I'm at home and really miss it when I'm travelling. I own two juicers and while the benefits of slow juicing can't be denied, it's without doubt my centrifugal, whole-fruit juicer that gets the most use. I'm all for quality food and nutrients but for me that has to be balanced with convenience. I simply would not have time each morning to wash, chop and slow juice all my veg. Chucking in handfuls of spinach, large chunks of broccoli and whole apples works brilliantly for me. On days off and at weekends I tend to have a little more time and there's no denying the quality of juice I get from my slow juicer is fantastic. Whichever you invest in, it really will make an undeniable difference to your health.

FOOD PROCESSOR/BLENDER

There are a million and one blenders, food processors and nutri machines available on the market. Knowing where to begin can seem like a bit of a minefield. It's often tempting to go for a cheap option with lots of accessories, blades and blending bowls, but in truth it's more worthwhile spending a little extra money on something that will cover the basics very, very well. I use my food processor to chop veg, purée fruit, blend soups and smoothies, knead dough, mill grains, create nut butters, emulsify dressings, mix batter, whip cream, crush ice, grind herbs and so much more. It's not necessary to have a million and one attachments, but it's important that the quality is there. Yes, there are cheaper food processors on the market, but I found myself replacing regular £30 blenders every few months because they simply weren't up to the job. Recipes such as cashew cream can be blitzed super smooth without any grainy bits when you've got the right kitchen equipment. Trust me, it's most definitely worth the investment.

GLASS JARS

I also keep lots of airtight, glass storage jars handy in the kitchen. These are brilliant for preserving the stuff that doesn't need refrigerating. It also means I can buy in bulk (saving money) and split dried foods into storable, dry containers. They're fab for storing homemade cookies (if you can keep them that long!)

and for recipes such as avocado pesto, chia jam or pear and maple chutney. Tall glass bottles with a pouring stopper make the perfect salad dressing servers. Plus, if you'd like to try sprouting your own seeds, simply reuse screwtop jars for this.

BAMBOO STEAMER

Steaming food is simple, economical, fast, healthy and versatile. But the thing I love about it most is that it retains so much of the food's nutritional value. It preserves 90 per cent of antioxidants in fresh vegetables and much of the water-soluble vitamins B and C. For example, broccoli, when steamed, retains 81 per cent of its vitamin C, and when cooked in water, only 30 per cent. Steamed broccoli loses only 11 per cent of its flavonoids (plant-based compounds with powerful antioxidant properties found in many fruits and vegetables). Cooked in water, broccoli loses 66 per cent of these flavonoids, and done in the microwave, it loses 97 per cent. Steaming also allows food to retain its colour, flavour, shape and texture.

You don't need to go out and buy a fancy electric steamer. I use a tiered bamboo version that I've had for over ten years and it's brilliant. I use it most for steaming broccoli and ginger or asparagus spears. It keeps the greens tender, so you don't end up with overcooked, sloppy veg.

MINI CHOPPER

Successfully sticking to a clean diet is all about keeping things simple. Those bottled sauces, full of added salt, sugar and flavourings, are so convenient for us. The alternative has to be equally as attractive, and while homemade sauces may taste much nicer and fresher, they're no good if you haven't got the time or the energy to make them. Hummus and pesto are great examples. I can make a superfast hummus using tinned chickpeas, tahini, a garlic clove and fresh lemon. It tastes delicious. But realistically it's only going to keep well for a few days, so the process of making it fresh has to be quick and simple to compete with the lure of picking up a tub next time I'm out shopping. And that's why I love my mini chopper! If I need just a small quantity of something fresh without the faff of washing up the food mixer,

my chopper is superb. You can usually pick one up for under £20 and you'll love it for chopping nuts, blitzing sauces, puréeing fruit and more.

ICE-CREAM MAKER

It was my mother who bought me my first ice-cream maker a few years ago when I was still eating dairy. Back then I'd pour tubs of full-fat double cream and mountains of refined sugar into it to create sickly sweet (but admittedly quite delicious!) homemade ice cream. These days, though, I use to it to combine coconut milk and banana into a gorgeous coco-nana ice cream. You can make ice cream without one but using an ice-cream maker involves less fuss and less patience! Non-essential but a lovely luxury.

SPIRALISER

My first experience of spiralised veg was at a little vegan cafe in Dubrovnik, Croatia. It had been months since I'd eaten pasta but they served the most amazing sweet potato spaghetti. I was hooked and immediately bought a spiraliser when I got home. These clever little things enable you to fashion a whole variety of veg into delicious raw spaghetti spirals. Trust me, you might think eating uncooked courgette sounds odd, but once you've tried courgetti and pesto you will fall in love. The ability to slice and shred a range of vegetables into ribbons has always been possible with a julienne peeler, and in truth I'll still use a peeler at times to save on washing-up, but the technique has been made easier, fuss-free and far more appealing with the arrival of this nifty gadget .

Courgettes, carrots, pumpkins and so many more vegetables can be transformed into tasty spirals. Think curly cucumber ringlets or fresh apple coleslaw or how about sweet potato and parsnip root pasta instead of wheat spaghetti (see page 135).

SALAD SPINNER

There's only one thing worse than soggy salad leaves and that's lettuce covered in pesticides. To ensure you're removing all the chemicals from the shop-bought stuff, it's a good idea to rinse it well, then whizz it through a salad spinner to dry the leaves. Yes, this little gadget is going to take up some cupboard space, but it also doubles up as a salad bowl. Fresh, homegrown leaves are just brilliant. If you have any room in your garden or yard, sprinkle a packet of cut-and-come-again salad seeds into a pot of fine soil and within weeks you will have an endless supply of summer salad.

STORE-CUPBOARD STAPLES

The one thing I've found essential to staying on the right track food-wise, is making sure I have the right ingredients to hand to create quick, healthy, nutritious meals. How easy is it to come home from work, look through the cupboards and conjure up an excuse to order takeout? Keep these store-cupboard staples to hand and pop goes the cop-out.

SEEDS

Sprinkled on salads, stirred through granola or blended into creamy nut smoothies, seeds offer a simple, nutritious boost to so many meals. My favourites are sunflower, pumpkin, chia and flaxseeds. Their healthy omega content is fantastic and a handful of these ensures you're getting all the essential oils your skin needs.

DRIED FRUIT AND NUTS

Nuts are a brilliant 'good fat' snack food. I always keep a bag of whole, unsalted, unsugared almonds in the cupboard. I'm also a huge fan of ground almonds, which make a superb replacement for wheat flour in baking. Sealed packets of almond meal last for ages (once opened store them in the fridge). Chopped dates are another favourite: they replace butter and sugar brilliantly in baking and offer an easy snack option if you have a sweet tooth.

GRAINS

Before quitting gluten, my cupboards used to be stocked full of wheat pasta. My replacement these days is brown rice pasta, which offers the same simplicity without that sluggish, lethargic feeling.

DRIED HERBS

I love using fresh herbs and spices in recipes. They're such a simple way to add a ton of flavour and always stop me from overusing salt in food. I have a little kitchen garden pot in the back yard and find certain herbs such as rosemary grow well all year round. It's not always possible to use fresh herbs and spices, so keep a shelf stocked full of dried alternatives.

OILS

I've already waxed lyrical about the incredibly versatile benefits of coconut oil. As well as slathering it on my skin, I cook and bake with it. It's great as a butter substitute when you're baking, and is my favourite oil for frying. It keeps for an age unopened and, once opened, if you avoid cross-contaminating it with other food bits on your knife or spoon, it will store well for a good few months.

THE PLAN
HOW WILL YOU FEEL?

If this is the first time you've embarked on a juice detox, you're in for some new feelings. This way of clearing your skin is probably very different from the medicines and creams you've tried in the past: this is clearance from the inside out. As such, you might experience a variety of changes in your body you weren't expecting. So, let me prepare you for those.

First – and this is not going to be easy to hear – there is a good chance your skin could get worse. This is not the case for everyone; we all vary in our range and rate of clearance. I was mid-flare when I began my detox and my skin DID get worse for the first two weeks. As I've explained, the skin is essentially an organ of detoxification. So whatever is happening on the inside has got to come out.

Second, expect some other side effects, such as tiredness, headaches, nausea and strong cravings.

Any headaches and nausea you might experience, alongside cravings for specific foods, are merely symptoms of 'withdrawal' from certain foods and drinks like caffeine and sugar. Whatever you do, stick with it. Remember that, although in full it lasts 28 days, the toughest part of the plan only takes the first three days. The tiredness is something you can work with. Plenty of rest is vitally important on the plan. Take a break from work, cancel your regular commitments, do whatever it takes to give yourself the best possible environment for completing the plan.

Taking salt baths and using natural oils make up an important part of your new routine. Combine these treatments with restful early nights. Your body carries out essential repair and maintenance work while you're sleeping. Give it a real chance to do so.

ALTERED DIET – NORMAL LIFE

When I first made the transition from my regular diet, the thought of completely transforming my lifestyle was overwhelming. My starting point was zero exercise, a diet made up predominantly of refined carbohydrates, wine every week day (more alcohol at weekends!) and a social life that revolved around restaurants and bars. This wasn't just a case of eliminating gluten for a week or going dry for a month; this was a whole combination of life-changing factors, which had to work for me long term. The prospect was daunting, although not half as daunting as being put on chemotherapy medication, or having to live with a skin condition for the rest of my life.

As far as my skin was concerned I'd hit rock bottom; the severity of my psoriasis meant something had to change drastically. I've since learned that we're all different in terms of what we're able to cope with. What may appear to me to be a tiny blemish on someone's arm might be considered an unbearably visible skin disease for the person having to live with it. Conversely, a happy, outgoing, confident person might be far less affected by a skin condition as noticeable or painful as mine. Guys often said to me that it must be so much more difficult for a girl – though I don't believe that's necessarily true either. I really think it comes down to the individual, male or female, we all have different coping strategies and pain thresholds.

The reason I refer to severity is that when something is causing us too much mental and physical pain to be ignored, there's obviously a greater incentive to resolve it. During times when I was able to hide my patches of psoriasis from the world and cover my spots with makeup, there was far less incentive to solve the underlying problem. Change is daunting, but I can't even begin to tell you how incredible the rewards are, and not just in terms of clear skin, because the mental strength and clarity that come with it are pretty incredible too.

It would be unrealistic for me to tell you your lifestyle is not going to change. Long term that change will undoubtedly be for the better, but meanwhile it's the short-term sacrifices you'll have to persevere with. Believe me, there are ways to make it easier on yourself. Please don't envisage sitting indoors miserably sipping a cocktail of green vegetables while slathered in coconut oil, ignoring texts from your friends asking you to come out. There will be a transition and initially you may have to alter your social life a little, but I go to restaurants and bars a lot these days. For me it's as much about socialising and company as it is about food and drink. I'd always been a bit of a party girl and I remember the first time I went out with friends after beginning this new lifestyle I got a fair bit of stick for ordering water! At some point that evening they'd started on shots, and to make sure I didn't feel left out they ordered seven sambuccas and a shot glass of water for me! I realised then, tough as it was, that an evening out was much more about being in the company of good friends than what I was pouring down my neck. As the weeks and months went by, my change in diet and alcohol abstinence simply became my chosen lifestyle. I can honestly say I rarely think about drinking these days and the feeling of never having a hangover is pure bliss.

Admittedly, choice of restaurant venue may take a little more forethought when you start the plan, but restaurants are fast adapting to a growing desire to eat well. Most understand the importance of preparing fresh food to cater for specific dietary requirements. Lots offer gluten-free options along with herbal teas and juices. It's not so much about never eating out again, just changing what you order. I used to love big plates of pasta and doughy garlic bread at Italian restaurants, whereas now I stick to soups and superfood salads. It might not be the easiest transition to make and it doesn't have to be forever, but if a lot of your social life revolves around dining out, there has to be a compromise that will work for you in the long run.

Keep it simple. It's easy to check if a meal is gluten or dairy free. When I order salad I ask them to ensure that mine comes without tomatoes or peppers, and if a meal includes chips on the side, I ask for sweet potatoes or extra green veg instead.

Being invited to dinner parties was something else which worried me a little at the start. I was really conscious when receiving an invite not to reply with a full list of dietary demands! I think there's a balance to be struck between eating well to look after your skin and enjoying the company of friends who have taken time to prepare food for you. I explained the reasons for changing my diet to my friends from the beginning. Most had absolutely no idea my skin was so bad – I hid it well – and were really understanding and keen to help. They've also been amazed at some of the incredible raw desserts I've made for them and many have been inspired to change the way they think about food.

For me, the key is preparation. Take a little time out from your regular social scene if you need to. Refocus that energy on healing yourself. Have a look online at restaurant menus to see what options are available; give friends plenty of notice if they're planning to have you round for dinner and there's something you really can't eat. Keep healthy, skin-friendly snacks handy so that you don't feel like the odd one out when everyone's tucking into chocolate biscuits at work. Just small things that will help you to stay focused, determined and on the right track.

It's important to remember that this is not forever. You are not consigned to a life of lettuce leaves! Eliminating a skin problem is the hardest part. Once you've got clear skin, maintaining it is much easier. Reducing internal inflammation and realigning the immune system is key. Once you've achieved that, it's much easier to be flexible in what you eat and drink and strike a workable, comfortable balance.

FALLING OFF THE PLAN

If you struggle to stick to the plan, don't get stressed. Yes, it is simple, but that's not to say it's easy. I've been there. I've done it. I live by it.

I understand the commitment required to start and stick to it. Don't get disheartened if you fall off the detox wagon, but do think about why you struggled to commit to it. Then begin again. Picture life with clear skin, imagine waking up in the morning full of life and energy, think about how good it would feel to lose weight without even trying – then focus on those end goals. Don't be upset if the changes are not immediate. We're trying to undo years of poor fuelling here, so it's bound to take a little time to clear the system. But have faith: you will get there.

SKIN CLEANSE – STAGE ONE, DAY ONE

Key points to remember:

» Take some 'BEFORE' pictures. You might not feel like it, but in future you'll be so happy to look back at just how far you've come.

» This is not forever! The first few days are tough, but you will eat again!

» Drink your water. If you're not used to 2 litres a day, at first it can feel like an awful lot.

First thing

Good morning, welcome to the first moment of a life-changing day! Start your day with a cup of hot water with a large chunk of fresh lemon in it. Or preferably a mug of Red Clover, Nettle and Burdock tea (see page 57).

Start the day

Exercise. No excuses about needing to get to work or not having the time. If you're struggling to fit it in, rise and shine a little earlier. At this time of day 20–30 minutes is perfect, whether it's a walk, jog, swim or cycle. Whatever you feel comfortable doing, simply move!

Shower time

Take a shower using Dead Sea salt to exfoliate your skin. Avoid all harsh chemicals during the plan. That includes regular shower gels. Use Dead Sea salt to clean your skin and add a few drops of calming pure lavender oil if you prefer a fragrance.

Breakfast time

High 5 Juice – Gimme Some Skin (see page 54). Time for your breakfast juice. This is also the time to take your minerals and vitamins – zinc, selenium, D3 and a probiotic acidophilus supplement are all important to the healing process. Make sure you take one of each straight after your juice.

Mid-morning

If you're starting your working day, don't forget to keep your bottled water handy. You will need to drink at least 2 litres of still mineral or filtered tap water over the course of the day, so it's important to start as you mean to go on. Add fresh lemon or lime to your water if you find drinking it a little boring.

Lunch time

High 5 Juice – Gimme Some Skin. It's time for lunch. While the first three days of the plan will feel a little dull and repetitive, remind yourself: IT'S ONLY THREE DAYS. You can do this. You're alkalising your body using the power of this little green juice. Stick with it.

Mid-afternoon

If you're able to take a little exercise, try to get some fresh air, even if it's only a ten-minute walk. Relax and breathe. Your body is going to go through some major changes over the coming days. Take some time to think about and enjoy it.

Late afternoon

Just checking in to make sure you're still sipping that water.

Early evening

Enjoy some outdoor exercise. Whether it's walking home from work, jogging in the local park or hiking along a path. Try to expose your skin to some sunshine.

Dinner time

High 5 Juice – Gimme Some Skin. Dinner time. This is always the hardest part of the day for me when I'm juicing. I'm so used to sitting down to an evening meal. Remember: you've almost completed Day One. Think about how awesome you're going to feel in the morning. Just two more tough days to go.

Evening

Enjoy a long, relaxing, Dead Sea salt bath. Add a few drops of calming lavender oil to your bath water, light some candles – do whatever it takes to truly unwind. Think about all you've achieved today and the great things that lie ahead.

Gently towel dry your skin and apply plenty of coconut oil. The feeling may be a little strange at first as it's fairly oily, but I guarantee you will wake up with lovely soft skin. I still use coconut oil on my own skin daily and often have nights where I moisturise with it and throw on some old PJs to sleep in. When my skin was particularly bad, I put oil on and wrapped clingfilm around the worst parts to hold the moisture against my skin. If it's not too uncomfortable for you, I would certainly recommend it.

Bedtime

CONGRATULATIONS on completing Day One! It may seem like very early stages to you, but I know just how it feels to get this far. The commitment you've made to clearing your skin is phenomenal. You're amazing. Get an early night and enjoy your rest.

SKIN CLEANSE – STAGE ONE, DAY TWO

Key points to remember:

» You have the strength to do this. You did it yesterday, so you CAN do this again today!

» Feeling tired is normal, and there is even the possibility your skin may get worse before it gets better. This is a true detox. Do not let it deter you. It's all part of the healing process.

» Don't cheat; don't skip parts of the plan. Drink your tea, enjoy your water.

First thing

Good morning, welcome to Day Two. Start as you mean to go on, with strength and commitment. Relax and try to enjoy your cup of Red Clover, Nettle and Burdock Tea (see page 57). I appreciate it's an acquired taste and not to everyone's liking. But remember the good it's doing.

Start the day

Exercise. If this isn't a usual part of your daily routine, it may feel a little forced to begin with. Making time for 20–30 minutes of exercise if you have a busy schedule can feel tough, but I guarantee that over the next few weeks you will actually miss this if you DON'T do it! Choose something you enjoy, whether it's a morning yoga session or a rebound session on a mini trampoline.

Shower time

Take a shower using Dead Sea salt to exfoliate your skin. Avoid all harsh chemicals during the plan. That includes regular shower gels. Use Dead Sea salt to clean your skin and add a few drops of calming lavender oil if you prefer a fragrance.

Breakfast time

High 5 Juice – Gimme Some Skin (see page 54) and take those vitamins. Your breakfast juice and vitamins are an important start to the day. Even though I'm fully clear of psoriasis and eczema, I'll often reboot with a three-day detox from time to time. It makes my skin feel even better and reminds me to be grateful for the foods I AM able to eat!

Mid-morning

If you're not used to drinking so much water during the day, this concept might still feel a little alien to you. Just remember to keep that large bottle of water with you at all times and drink from it even if you don't feel particularly thirsty. We quite often mistake thirst for hunger. So, next time you feel hungry, try sipping a little water.

Lunch time

High 5 Juice – Gimme Some Skin. Incredibly you're already over half way through the toughest part of the plan! Remember what you've achieved so far. If you're struggling to enjoy this little green juice, just look at how far you've come. You're alkalising your body and the changes you're experiencing are as a direct result of what YOU are putting in. That puts YOU in control. And that feels a little bit amazing.

Mid-afternoon

If you're able to take a little exercise, try to get some fresh air, even if it's only a ten-minute walk. Relax and breathe. Take some time to think about what you've achieved so far. It may only be Day Two, but I'm fully aware of how tough this first part can be. Congratulate yourself on taking this one big step on a whole new journey.

Early evening

For most people the plan needs to be tailored around a regular nine-to-five routine, and exercise has possibly not been top of your priority list when you get in from work. But remember: this is a whole lifestyle change, so whether you walk, run, skip or bounce, take 30 minutes out of your day to fill your lungs with air and cleanse the blood.

Dinner time

High 5 Juice – Gimme Some Skin. If you're in a family environment, the rest of the clan enjoying home-cooked food while you're sipping on juice might feel tough and unfair. Talk to your family about what you're doing and why. And, if necessary, take a little time out of that environment for yourself. Watch the Jonny Kennedy documentary about a man who really could not change his skin condition or Jason Vale's *Super Juice Me* to inspire you to persevere.

Evening

Enjoy a long, relaxing, Dead Sea salt bath. Add a few drops of calming lavender oil to your bath water, apply your coconut oil and relax.

Bedtime

CONGRATULATIONS on completing Day Two! You're over half way through the most restrictive part of the plan. Enjoy some rest. You deserve it.

SKIN CLEANSE – STAGE ONE, DAY THREE

Key points to remember:

» This is Day Three of the toughest part of the plan. You're well over half way. CONGRATULATIONS!

» Today can often feel the hardest in terms of tiredness. Your body has experienced some fairly dramatic changes these past two days. Go with it and get plenty of rest.

» Listen to what your body is asking. This concept can feel a little strange at first but in the absence of stimulants (sugar, caffeine, alcohol, etc.) comes true energy. If you're tired – sleep. If you have energy – exercise.

First thing

Red Clover, Nettle and Burdock Tea time (see page 57). While tomorrow we're looking at varying the juices and introducing some foods, this little tea will be with us a while longer!

Start the day

Exercise. Day Three can feel very different for some than it does for others. I often feel content and dreamily sleepy on Day Three of a detox but at the same time any bloating or carb lethargy disappears. Make sure you exercise, preferably in the fresh air – even if it's only a 30-minute walk.

Shower time

Take a shower using Dead Sea salt to exfoliate your skin. Avoid all harsh chemicals during the plan. That includes regular shower gels. Use Dead Sea salt to clean your skin and add a few drops of calming lavender oil if you prefer a fragrance.

Breakfast time

High 5 Juice – Gimme Some Skin (see page 54) and take those vitamins. Your breakfast juice and vitamins are vital. I'm fully aware that this is the seventh 'meal' this week, which consists only of green juice! Drink, enjoy and look forward to tomorrow's change.

Mid-morning

Your body should be a little more used to you hydrating it by now! That in turn should slow down the endless trips to the loo that you may have made as a result of increased water intake over the past couple of days! Fear not, this is your body's favourite way of expelling toxins.

Lunch time

High 5 Juice – Gimme Some Skin. Green juice. I'm all too aware that this may begin to feel a little like Groundhog Day!

Mid-afternoon

Whether it's a walk in the park, kicking a football about with the kids in the garden or a lunch-time swim, try to break up your day with some mid-afternoon exercise.

Late afternoon

Drinking 2 litres of water will hopefully have become second nature by Day Three. If you're still struggling to remember despite having that big bottle in front of you, it might be worth buying four 500ml bottles and making sure you drink two in the morning and two in the afternoon. Whatever makes it simple until it becomes second nature.

Dinner time

High 5 Juice – Gimme Some Skin. Your final juice of Days One to Three. AMAZING, YOU DID IT! You should be incredibly proud of making this huge lifestyle change. Whether your skin is getting better, getting worse or not changing just yet, you should certainly feel some internal difference and mentally a huge sense of accomplishment.

Evening

Enjoy a long, relaxing, Dead Sea salt bath. Add a few drops of calming lavender oil to your bath water, apply your coconut oil and relax.

Bed time

CONGRATULATIONS on completing Day Three! Tomorrow we'll introduce some new juices, soups and 'clean' foods. I know how tough this has been for you and how keen you are to see results on the outside. Be aware that the internal changes you are making WILL begin to show.

SKIN CLEANSE – STAGE TWO

Days 4 to 11 of the plan

Days 4 to 7 allow for a little more flexibility. I'm not talking about reverting to your previous unhealthy lifestyle, but after three very strict days of green juice, tea and water I hope your taste buds will be salivating at the thought of fresh salads and soups.

We're still being cautious at this stage, though, so please don't worry that this is it for life! We're just carefully building on what we've achieved so far without fear of aggravating anything. If you're ever in doubt as to whether something is 'allowed' at the start of the plan, it's best to double-check or to leave it out. It's not worth undoing all the groundwork.

Just know that in one month from now things will be very different. You will learn to love your new skin, your new body and your new lifestyle.

You should begin to feel your natural strength and energy over the next few days, but don't worry if your body is still asking you to rest and relax.

The flexibility of this week will also allow for a social life! It's often difficult when you're on a juice detox, and admittedly not every restaurant serves soups and salads. But with a little careful planning there should be no reason why you can't enjoy meals out and social time with friends.

SKIN CLEANSE – DAYS 4 TO 11

Remember:

» Be grateful for the foods you can eat.

» You're still detoxing. You will continue to feel your body change. It's normal.

» While the plan is much more flexible than Days One to Three, it's still really important you stick to all elements of it.

First thing

As per the first three days, a cup of Red Clover, Nettle and Burdock Tea (see page 57) is preferable but feel free to mix it up a little! Go crazy and treat yourself to chamomile or a hot water with lemon instead.

Start the day

Exercise. It's still really important to keep moving. Chose something you enjoy. Exercise ought to be a permanent habit for all of us. When we do not exercise, it leads to accumulation of toxic substances and waste materials inside our body.

Shower time

Using a Dead Sea salt scrub during your morning shower should also become second nature. I still use Dead Sea salts and natural oils in my showers and baths on a daily basis.

Breakfast time

High 5 Juice – Gimme Some Skin (see page 54). Time for your breakfast juice. I know, I know you've lived off this juice for the past three days! I'd prefer you to stick to it for breakfast over the next few days, but if you're really struggling, opt for steamed spinach and a poached egg instead. This is also the time to take your vitamins. Make sure you take one of each. This is essential during the 28-day plan.

Mid-morning

I'm sure I don't need to remind you how essential water consumption is. We cannot live without it for more than about 100 hours, whereas other nutrients may be neglected for weeks or months.

Lunch time

Lunch time and you can ACTUALLY EAT! Choose from one of the soups or salads in the recipe section (see pages 72–89). Eat slowly, chew properly and be grateful for every bite! If you'd prefer to stick to a juice, you're more than welcome to do so. Simply pick one of the juicy skin recipes instead.

Mid-afternoon

Whether it's a walk in the park, kicking a football about with the kids in the garden or a lunch-time swim, try to break up your day with some mid-afternoon exercise.

Late afternoon

Drinking 2 litres of water will hopefully have become second nature by now. Whatever makes it simple until it becomes habit.

Dinner time

Dinner time. Again, feel free to choose a soup, salad or juice from the recipe section. If you're eating out at any point during the first week, order a salad, minus the nightshades (see pages 14–15). I eat out lots and I've never had a problem yet.

I'm often in situations where friends pick a dessert from the menu after a meal. So that I don't feel I'm missing out, I ask for a peppermint or chamomile tea instead. If you're eating at home you can vary this with a hot water and lemon drink or some Red Clover, Nettle and Burdock Tea if you prefer.

Evening

Enjoy a long, relaxing, Dead Sea Salt bath. Add a few drops of calming lavender oil to your bath water, apply your coconut oil and relax.

Bed time

Continue to get a good night's rest during the first few weeks of the plan. Your body is still adapting. Take time to relax and give it chance to repair.

SKIN CLEANSE – DAYS 12 TO 28

Almost two weeks into the plan. This was the point at which I first saw a small but noticeable improvement in the appearance of my skin. That's not to say this will be the case for you, so please do not be disheartened if your progress differs. There is also the chance your skin has already begun to show signs of improvement very early on. We're all different and I've seen dramatic changes happen in as few as three days and I've also known people persevere for a month or more with slow and gradual recovery.

Now what?

I haven't created a specific daily timeline for days 12 to 28 because by now you should have a good understanding of what your body needs from you. I'd also encourage a little flexibility to ensure the plan complements your lifestyle. There may be days, for example, when it's easier to eat at breakfast time and grab a green juice in the evening. That's absolutely fine. Just stick to the principles you've learnt over the past few days. Follow these few simple rules and you can't go far wrong!

» Drink your Red Clover, Nettle and Burdock Tea (or hot water with lemon)

» Exercise at least twice daily – preferably outdoors

» Drink 2 litres of water every day

» Substitute at least one meal a day with a skin juice recipe (see pages 54–56)

» Take Dead Sea salt baths/scrubs

» Use coconut oil to moisturise your skin

» Take your vitamins

» Get lots of rest

KEEP IT SIMPLE

Keep things really simple over the next couple of weeks. Even if you're seeing an improvement, don't be tempted to deviate too quickly from the plan. Once you've completed the initial 28 days, we can begin to get a little more creative. We can add variety and extra elements to see how your skin reacts.

SKIN CLEANSE – DAY 29+

So, what now? There are some basic rules to stick to but aside from those this is the part of the plan that allows you to begin experimenting with new foods and recipes. If you've seen a noticeable improvement in your skin, you may want to begin reintroducing certain foods to watch for a reaction.

Whatever you do, DO NOT be tempted to revert to your pre-cleanse lifestyle. It's all too easy to do. One of my Twitter followers, Sarah, emailed me to say: 'Over the last six weeks I have fallen off the diet (in a big way – eating rubbish!) and my skin and scalp have got bad again.'

I'm not saying you can never enjoy some of the foods you loved pre-cleanse. I'm saying, take it easy! Once in a while is fine, but just because you don't see an instant reaction don't be tempted to go back to bad habits. The good news is that Sarah has all the tools she needs to clear again. Having that level of control is an awesome and empowering feeling.

Keep in mind the NEVER EVER list

This includes the nightshade foods, the strawberries, oranges and fizzy drinks. Think seriously about whether you want to reintroduce alcohol. If you do, try to limit it to the occasional glass of wine.

Keep it Alkaline

Focus on your acid/alkaline balance. Ideally, regardless of skin condition, we need to keep to 80/20 – that's a diet made up of 80 per cent alkaline foods and 20 per cent acidic.

Keep Juicing

Juicing has become a huge part of my life. In fact, I can't recall a single day over the past six months when I haven't had at least one juice! I also make sure that I follow a simple three-day green juice detox at least once every couple of months. It makes my skin feel incredible afterwards and it reminds me to be eternally grateful for the foods I CAN eat.

Keep Drinking your Herbal Teas

I always choose jasmine, chamomile or peppermint tea, and I still drink Red Clover, Nettle and and Burdock tea at home from time to time.

Keep up the Water Consumption

Aside from herbal tea, I no longer drink anything but water. I always make sure I have a fridge full of bottled, still mineral water. I've learnt to love it and what it does for my body and skin. I still drink 2–3 litres a day and sometimes more.

Keep Moving

Exercise is vital and should be considered an important part of any skincare regime. It increases blood flow to the skin and allows the sweat glands to improve their function to rid the body of toxins. Increased blood flow carries more oxygen to the skin and also helps carry away waste products, including free radicals, from working cells. It also provides an excellent form of stress relief. Find something you enjoy doing and keep doing it.

Keep Applying the Dead Sea Salt and Coconut Oil

Bathing in Dead Sea minerals has become the norm for me. I also dry body-brush and exfoliate with Dead Sea salt often. As I've said, coconut oil has become my preferred cooking and baking oil, and I apply it to my skin as a moisturiser and cleanser. (I keep cooking and moisturising jars separate!)

Keep Taking your Minerals and Vitamins

I no longer take every single vitamin and mineral every single day, but I do ensure that I keep my selenium levels up by eating plenty of Brazil nuts, and take zinc if I'm having a week where my diet isn't as clean as I'd like it to be, vitamin D3 if the sunshine is a little absent, and acidophilus to promote good bacteria in my gut. I no longer take milk thistle because I don't drink alcohol and so my liver functions better than ever.

Keep Relaxing

Occasionally 'life' takes over and it's difficult to avoid stressful situations. However, the way we respond to them IS up to us. Detoxing gave me new skin, a new body and new clarity: I see life from a very different perspective these days. I'm much calmer, much more tolerant, much more relaxed and I find stressful situations far easier to deal with. Continuing with a clean diet and exercise regime will give you the power to do the same. You may discover your new-found strength to commit to this plan gives you the emotional drive to change other aspects of your life, such as a stressful work or relationship situation.

Keep Talking. Keep Sharing

I love hearing inspirational stories and I'm always intrigued by people's life journeys. Sharing your thoughts and feelings helps me to help others:
www.mygoodnessrecipes.com
@mygoodnessrecipes (Instagram)
@HannaSillitoe (Twitter)

DRINKS

High Five – Gimme Some Skin

← ⟶

makes 1 glass

A perfect little skin cleanser that combines five cooling, alkaline fruit and veg, each providing a powerful vitamin boost. With magnesium in spinach to promote healthy sleep, the power of celery, cucumber and avocado to help prevent unwanted inflammation and the pectin in apples to coat your gut, this all-round cooling juice will alkalise your body, calm internal heat and reduce skin redness and itching.

½ cucumber
2 celery sticks
3 apples
Handful of spinach
½ avocado, stoned and flesh scooped out
1 tablespoon lecithin granules
4–6 ice cubes

Wash the ingredients. Run the cucumber, celery, apples and spinach through the juicer. I find it helps to juice the spinach leaves between harder ingredients such as apples to squeeze the most juice out of them.

Add to your blender with the avocado, lecithin granules and some ice. Blend until smooth and drink immediately.

♥ *Lecithin softens, tones and moisturises skin. It also restores the barrier function of the skin, helping cells retain water to hydrate deeper layers. It's also a powerful antioxidant, which helps protect cells from free-radical damage. Lecithin granules are available online or from good health-food shops.*

Liquorice All Sorts

← ⟶

makes 1 glass

The awesome additional health benefits of juicing herbs cannot be overstated. Whether you're looking to improve skin, sleep better, reduce blood pressure or relieve the pain of arthritis or IBS, there's a herb out there for you. The use of herbs as medicine is scarcely new – these incredible plants have been used to heal for thousands of years. I love the warm, spicy, aniseed flavour created by juicing fennel, ginger and tarragon. If you are fond of liquorice you're going to adore this one.

2 pears
Small handful of tarragon
Chunk of fennel
½ cucumber
Chunk of broccoli stem
½ lime
Chunk of ginger
4–6 ice cubes, to serve

Wash the ingredients. Put one pear into the juicer chute, top with the other ingredients, then add the second pear. This ensures the smaller leaves are well juiced.

Serve in a glass with ice.

♥ *Cucumber is hugely hydrating and cooling. It flushes out toxins and keeps skin glowing and fresh. Tarragon is rich in vitamin C, which boosts the immune system, strengthens defences and helps to regenerate skin and mucous membranes.*

A Proper Skinful

←——————————————→

makes 1 glass

This juice contains so many amazing ingredients to repair skin from the inside out. Apples are anti-everything! Antiviral, anti-inflammatory, antioxidant and anti-allergy. Lemons have immune boosting powers and are excellent as a digestive aid and liver cleanser. Underlying liver issues can manifest as problem skin conditions, and it's important to target the underlying cause rather than solely focus on the skin symptoms. Asparagus contains high levels of the amino acid asparagine, which acts as a natural diuretic. Increased urination not only releases fluid but also helps rid the body of excess salts. Celery, with its high water content, will continue to hydrate your body while mint acts as an excellent skin cleanser and helps to cure infections.

6 small asparagus spears
2 celery sticks
2 apples
A few sprigs of mint
Small chunk of lemon
4–6 ice cubes, to serve

Wash all the ingredients. To squeeze the most out of herbs such as mint, I find it helps if you load them into the juicer between solid ingredients such as the two apples in this recipe.

Run everything through your juicer. Serve in a glass with ice.

♥ *Mint contains antioxidant vitamins A and C, which ease swelling and inflammation. It also contains the B vitamins riboflavin and folate, which can help to brighten skin. In addition mint can soothe sore skin, reduce redness and relieve itching.*

Just Beet It

←——————————————→

makes 1 glass

I had a huge problem with spots as a teenager and in recent years I started suffering from jawline acne outbreaks, which are more commonly associated with hormonal changes. Drinking beetroot juice regularly may be beneficial in the prevention and cure of skin inflammation like acne. In fact, it would be easier to list the things beetroot doesn't do for our overall health and wellness. Not only is it great for boosting stamina and making our muscles work harder, but beetroot's high nitrate content also makes it brilliant at keeping our blood vessels open, in turn allowing more oxygen to flow and lowering blood pressure. It also contains potassium, an essential stress-busting nutrient, plus magnesium, iron, vitamins A, B6 and C and folic acid... phew! Coriander calms the mood and aids sleep – this clever plant is full of zinc and binds to heavy metals in the body, helping to expel them as toxins.

1 small beetroot
2 celery sticks
2 red apples
A few sprigs of coriander
Small chunk of lemon
4–6 ice cubes, to serve

Wash the ingredients. Run everything through your juicer. Serve in a glass with ice.

♥ *The chemical compound quercetin is especially prevalent in red apples, mostly in their skins. Quercetin is able to block the immune cells that are capable of triggering allergic reactions and mistaken inflammatory responses in autoimmune disease, which is why these sweet little additions are perfect for regulating autoimmune disorders.*

Red Clover, Nettle *and* Burdock Tea

←—————————————————→

makes 1 cup

This skin-supportive combination is designed to nourish, cleanse and revitalise the body. Its positive effect on our digestive system can help to ease stress and in turn heal the skin.

I won't lie and promise you it's going to taste amazing. This tea is very bitter and has an acquired flavour. But it's so very good for skin conditions that I can't recommend it highly enough.

Dried red clover, nettle and burdock root can all be bought individually as loose tea from good herbal or health-food stores and online. Simply use a gauze infuser and allow hot water to absorb the goodness. There are lots of different tea infusers available, from gauze tea balls to tea infuser sacs and basket infusers. There is no right or wrong infuser, simply go for the one which makes it easiest for you. I find it's best to drink this first thing in the morning on an empty stomach.

1 teaspoon dried red clover
1 teaspoon dried nettle
1 teaspoon dried burdock root

Combine all the ingredients and place into a tea infuser. Allow to infuse in boiled water for 7–10 minutes. Remove the infuser and drink the tea warm.

♥ *Red clover is known for cleansing the blood and is a powerful healer of both the digestive and immune systems. It's also a diaphoretic, which stimulates sweating to remove toxins through the skin, and is often used to treat skin conditions such as acne, eczema and psoriasis. Nettle is known for cleansing the kidneys, whilst burdock root's anti-bacterial and antifungal properties can detoxify the epidermal tissues in our skin.*

Mulled Winter Punch

←—————————————————→

makes 1 pitcher

People often ask me if I miss alcohol. In truth, I rarely think about it these days. When I first quit the booze, a little over two years ago, I found it really difficult at times of celebration, such as Christmas. Drinking is deeply ingrained in Western culture and non-alcoholic alternatives can be so dull. This warming combination of winter spices makes a delicious alternative to mulled wine and is certainly much better for your liver!

500ml red grape juice
250ml pomegranate juice
250ml apple juice
5 whole cloves
3 cardamon pods
1 star anise
2 cinnamon sticks
Pinch of grated nutmeg
1 tablespoon manuka honey
Zest and juice of 1 lemon

Warm the juices gently together in a saucepan over a low heat for 5 minutes.

Add the spices, honey and lemon zest and juice and simmer for 20–30 minutes, allowing the flavours to infuse.

Strain the juice and discard the leftover spices. Serve warm in mugs.

♥ *Pomegranate juice is rich in antioxidants, which not only nourish the skin but also prevent damage caused by free radicals. Free radicals are tiny chemical particles, the bits leftover from cellular damage. Left to their own devices, free radicals can go on to damage otherwise healthy cells in a process called oxidation. They're one of the main culprits involved in rapid ageing of the skin. Think of it as the same process that turns a healthy apple brown.*

Summer Raspberry Spritzer

←———————————→

makes 1 pitcher

This is a wonderful zingy and fresh alternative to sugar-filled or artificially sweetened fizzy lemonade. It's really simple to make and perfect to serve over ice at summer parties.

4 Golden Delicious apples
2 lemons
Small chunk of ginger
200g raspberries
1 litre sparkling water

TO SERVE
8–10 ice cubes
Lemon slices
A few extra raspberries

Wash the apples, lemons, ginger and raspberries gently under running water.

Run the fruit through a juicer.

There should be no need to strain once juiced. Just pour into a large glass jug with the sparkling water.

Stir well and serve with ice, fresh lemon slices and fresh raspberries.

♥ *Not only is this lemonade free from refined sugar, it's also wonderful for cleansing the system, especially the liver and kidneys. Raspberries prevent damage to the cell membranes, reducing fungal and bacterial growth in the body. They can also reduce allergic reactions, thanks to their antihistaminic effect.*

Pineapple Mint Mojito

←———————————→

makes 1 pitcher

Sweet pineapple, spicy ginger, fresh mint and sour lime are just the best combination. This super-simple mocktail is really easy to make, tastes amazing and looks brilliantly impressive at summer parties. Whilst sparkling water is not as alkalising as still, I was a real fizzy-drink addict and homemade cocktails such as this one are naturally a much better party alternative than alcohol or bottled pop.

½ pineapple
2 limes
Large chunk of ginger
1 litre sparkling water

TO SERVE
8–10 ice cubes
A few extra pineapple chunks
15 mint leaves, chopped

Wash the pineapple, limes and ginger under running water.

Run the fruit through a juicer – most wide-chute juicers can handle pineapple with the skin left on.

Pour into a large glass jug with the sparkling water.

Stir well and serve with ice, chunks of fresh pineapple and chopped mint leaves.

♥ *Pineapple is full of vitamin C. This vitamin has long been considered highly effective for those of us with sensitive or inflamed skin and acne. Pineapple also contains bromelain and antioxidants, which can prove extremely beneficial in the treatment and prevention of spots, fine lines, sun damage and uneven skin tone.*

Water Infusions

Since our body is around 60 per cent water, it's really important for our complexion to stay well hydrated throughout the day. We all know the best way to do this is to drink plenty of still, filtered, natural water, but in truth most of us naively rely on sugar-filled fizzy drinks, squash and endless cups of tea or coffee to make up that daily liquid consumption.

In truth, water is flavourless and boring, and if you're not used to drinking the recommended 2 litres a day, that can actually feel like quite a daunting quantity to get through, not to mention the endless trips to the loo! So many of us are completely unaware that walking around in a dehydrated state can actually make us feel really lethargic, irritated and headachy. When it comes to healthy skin, it's crucial to maintain adequate fluid levels and drinking water is most definitely the very best way to do that.

Try to monitor your intake by carrying a bottle around with you so that you know exactly how much you've drunk. Don't be tempted by those pre-bottled flavoured waters either – most contain sugar or sweeteners and lots are made using artificial flavourings.

Infusing water yourself using fresh fruit, herbs and veg is the perfect way to make plain water so much more interesting. Infused waters are free from refined sugars and have no added artificial colours or flavourings. They also come with a wide range of benefits and taste really delicious.

I make my infused water by washing, then slicing the fruits, vegetables and herbs. I put them in a large, glass jar, add ice and fill the jar with water. It usually takes 30 minutes to an hour for the flavours to develop and I find most combinations can be kept in the fridge for up to a couple of days.

Here are some infusion ideas with specific benefits for healthy skin. But be brave and don't be afraid to experiment with your own combinations.

Watermelon, cucumber *and* mint

¼ watermelon, sliced
½ cucumber, sliced
10 mint leaves

Put the ingredients in a large glass jar, add ice and fill the jar with filtered water. Store the jar in the fridge for a day or two.

♥ *Both watermelon and cucumber are superbly hydrating and wonderful for radiant skin. Mint is a good antiseptic and an excellent skin cleanser.*

Cucumber, raspberry *and* basil

½ cucumber, sliced
10 raspberries
10 basil leaves

Put the ingredients in a large glass jar, add ice and fill the jar with filtered water. Store the jar in the fridge for a day or two.

♥ *Cucumber is very hydrating, it flushes out toxins and keeps skin moisturised. Raspberries have anti-inflammatory properties, and basil helps prevent outbreaks of acne by acting as a blood purifier.*

Rosemary, apple *and* blackberries

3 rosemary sprigs
1 apple, sliced
10 blackberries

Put the ingredients in a large glass jar, add ice and fill the jar with filtered water. Store the jar in the fridge for a day or two.

♥ *The nutrients in rosemary can help protect skin cells from sun damage and free radicals. Apples are full of vitamin C, which benefits skin and hair. Blackberries help to detox the body and assist in maintaining the elasticity of the skin.*

Lemon, ginger *and* manuka honey

2 lemons, sliced
Large chunk of ginger, sliced
1 tablespoon manuka honey

Put the ingredients in a large glass jar, add ice and fill the jar with filtered water. Store the jar in the fridge for a day or two.

♥ *Lemons are extremely alkalising and wonderful cleansers. Ginger boosts the immune system and manuka honey can help to heal wounds and infections.*

Rhubarb, pear *and* cinnamon

2 rhubarb sticks
1 pear, sliced
1 cinnamon stick

Put the ingredients in a large glass jar, add ice and fill the jar with filtered water. Store the jar in the fridge for a day or two.

♥ *Rhubarb contains a compound called lutein, which is essential for the health of the skin and eyes. Apples contain skin-friendly nutrients, including vitamin C and copper, and cinnamon helps to tighten pores and keep your complexion clear and smooth.*

BREAKFAST

←————→

Bright Green Breakfast Bowl

←——————————→

Makes 2 bowls

I love my morning green juices and blended avocado smoothies, but this bright green breakfast bowl takes things to a whole new level. It's so delicious, takes just minutes to make and because it's served in a bowl as opposed to a glass, you can top it with nuts, seeds and berries for a myriad of additional textures, flavours and skin health benefits.

1 ripe avocado, halved and stoned
2 ripe bananas, peeled
100ml almond milk
Handful of spinach
Juice of 1 lime
2 tablespoons manuka honey
5 basil leaves
5 ice cubes

OPTIONAL TOPPINGS
Pumpkin, sunflower or chia seeds
Almonds, walnuts or pecans
Homemade granola (see page 66)
Shredded coconut
Fresh berries

Scoop the flesh from the avocado into a blender. Add the bananas, milk, spinach, lime juice, honey and basil.

Blitz until smooth, add the ice cubes and purée again until smooth.

Divide between two bowls and top with seeds, nuts, granola and/or berries of your choice.

♥ *One of the main skin benefits from eating avocados comes from their high oleic acid content. This monounsaturated fatty acid maintains moisture in the epidermal layer of your skin, helping to keep it soft and hydrated.*

Chia Berry Bottom

←——————————→

Makes 2

This is my favourite, healthy alternative to 'fruit at the bottom' yogurt. I often make it the evening before and pop it in the fridge ready for a quick breakfast the following morning.

100g raspberries
1 teaspoon manuka honey
100ml almond milk
2 pitted dates
½ teaspoon vanilla extract
2 tablespoons chia seeds

Blend the raspberries and honey to create a smooth, thick, fruity sauce.

Divide between two glasses or clean jam jars and pop in the fridge.

Blend the almond milk, dates and vanilla extract. Spoon the chia seeds into the milk and stir continuously for 2–3 minutes. Leave to stand for 5 minutes to thicken, then stir again.

Pour the chia mixture over your set berry bottom and allow to set for at least an hour in the fridge or overnight if you prefer.

♥ *Chia seeds are one of the richest plant-based sources of omega oils and therefore a great alternative to fish oil for vegans. Omega oils can help reduce inflammation, enhance cognitive performance and reduce high cholesterol.*

Creamy Quinoa Breakfast Porridge

←—————————————→

Makes 2 bowls

Quinoa makes such a delicious alternative to porridge oats for breakfast. When I need something warming and sustaining to start the day, this is my go-to favourite for instant comfort and nourishment.

100g quinoa
500ml almond milk
2 pears, grated
2 tablespoons manuka honey
1 teaspoon ground cinnamon
1 star anise
1 vanilla pod
2 tablespoons flaked almonds

TO SERVE
1 banana, peeled and sliced
2 teaspoons almond butter
Cinnamon powder

Rinse the quinoa and put in a saucepan. Pour in half the almond milk, the grated pears and the honey. Gently bring the milk to the boil and then lower the heat and simmer for 10 minutes.

Add the rest of the milk, the cinnamon, star anise and vanilla pod. Cook for a further 5 minutes, then remove from the heat, throw in the flaked almonds and stir well.

Divide between two bowls and top each with sliced banana, a teaspoon of almond butter and a sprinkling of cinnamon.

♥ *Quinoa is loaded with complete protein and is naturally gluten-free. The ample collagen in quinoa rejuvenates your skin and reduces wrinkles.*

Five-spice Pecan Granola

←—————————————→

Makes 10–14 servings

The great thing about making granola yourself is being able to add nuts, seeds and spices to your own taste. Chinese five-spice powder is an oriental blend of five fragrant (and healthy) spices – fennel seeds, cinnamon, star anise, cloves and Sichuan pepper.

450g gluten-free jumbo oats
100g almonds
100g pecans
100g sunflower seeds
½ teaspoon sea salt
1 teaspoon Chinese five-spice powder
1 teaspoon ground cinnamon
1 teaspoon ground ginger
100ml melted coconut oil
200ml maple syrup or honey
1 teaspoon vanilla extract
200g dried mixed fruit or raisins

Preheat the oven to 160°C/fan 140°C/gas mark 3.

Mix together all the ingredients except the dried fruit in a large mixing bowl. Use your hands or a wooden spoon to combine everything well.

Spread out the mixture on a large baking tray and bake in the oven for 20 minutes.

Remove from the oven and shake to redistribute the granola evenly. Return to the oven for a further 10–20 minutes, checking regularly.

Once it's baked, allow the granola to cool, then mix in the dried fruit. Store in an airtight container for up to a month.

♥ *Cloves contain significant amounts of a substance called eugenol which numerous studies suggest has a powerful anti-inflammatory effect on the body.*

Almond *and* Coconut Flour Cinnamon Pancakes

Makes a stack for 2

There are many things the Dutch excel at: telling it like it is, riding bicycles and making pancakes – to name but a few. The pancakes in Holland are huge, served on enormous Delft blue plates with a choice of hundreds of toppings. As we are half Dutch, pancake day was always a big deal when my sister and I were kids. Mum would cook an entire stack and we'd power our way through them until we literally could not eat any more! When I cut gluten from my diet I stopped eating pancakes for a long time, until I discovered the combination of ground almonds and coconut flour make a great substitute for wheat flour. These pancakes are thick and fluffy, perfect as an indulgent breakfast or delicious dessert.

75g ground almonds

75g coconut flour

½ teaspoon baking powder

Pinch of pink Himalayan salt

½ teaspoon ground cinnamon

3 tablespoons melted coconut oil, plus extra for frying

1 tablespoon manuka honey

2 free-range eggs

120ml almond milk

½ teaspoon vanilla extract

Maple syrup, to serve

Combine the ground almonds, coconut flour, baking powder, salt and cinnamon in a small bowl. Set aside.

In a second bowl, stir together the coconut oil and honey. Whisk in the eggs, almond milk and vanilla extract.

Fold the dry ingredients into the batter using a spatula and mix gently until just combined. Don't overwork the batter, otherwise the pancakes won't be as fluffy.

Heat a tablespoon of coconut oil in a heavy-based frying pan over a medium heat.

Use a ladle to spoon a little batter carefully into the pan and cook for about 2–3 minutes on the first side. Check the underside and flip when golden brown. Cook for a further couple of minutes on the other side.

Continue this process until all of the batter has been used, adding more coconut oil to the pan as needed.

Serve with a generous drizzle of maple syrup.

♥ *There are lots of reasons to love all that coconut flour has to offer. It's high in nutrients, low in calories and has a low score on the glycaemic index. Unlike grain flours, coconut flour very rarely causes any digestive or autoimmune responses.*

Sweet Potato Rosti *and* Poached Egg

Serves 2

The bright orange colour of sweet potatoes is the very thing that makes them so healthy. They're packed full of beta-carotene, the precursor to vitamin A, which is essential for vision and a healthy immune system. This recipe not only looks bright and beautiful, it also tastes delicious and makes the perfect Sunday brunch.

1 medium sweet potato
1 large onion
3 free-range eggs
3 tablespoons melted coconut oil
Drop of white wine vinegar
Salt and pepper
Thyme leaves, to garnish

Preheat the oven to 200°C/fan 180°C/gas mark 6.

Peel the sweet potato and onion, then grate them into a bowl. Squeeze any excess moisture from the mixture.

Beat one of the eggs with a fork, stir it into the potato and onion mix and season with salt and pepper.

Spoon half the mixture into a circular pancake ring or cookie cutter. Use your fingers to compress everything and gently push out the formed rosti.

Heat the coconut oil in a heavy-based frying pan, and use a fish slice to slide the rosti carefully into the hot oil.

Fry for a couple of minutes until the underside is golden brown. Carefully turn and repeat on the second side. Repeat with the remaining mixture.

Place both rostis on a baking tray and pop into the oven until baked through: this usually takes 20–30 minutes. The outside will be golden brown and they should be piping hot all the way through.

Towards the end of the cooking time, fill a small pan just over one-third full with cold water and bring it to the boil. Add the vinegar and turn down to simmer.

Crack the remaining eggs, one at a time, into a small bowl and carefully slide into the simmering water. Lightly poach for 3–4 minutes, then remove the eggs with a slotted spoon and drain on kitchen paper.

Place an egg onto each baked rosti and serve with an extra twist of salt and pepper and the thyme leaves.

♥ *Sweet potato is considered as an excellent source of natural, health-promoting compounds known as beta-carotene and anthocyanins. Anthocyanins are potent antioxidants and highly effective anti-inflammatories; they also prevent free radicals from damaging your skin tissue, helping to reduce excessive pigmentation.*

Shiitake *and* Spinach Turmeric Omelette

←——————————————————→

Makes 1

This is one of my favourite breakfasts. Turmeric and shiitake mushrooms are two of the best immune-regulating foods on the planet. The clever thing about these two amazing ingredients is that they don't just boost the immune system, they're also brilliant at preventing excessive immune-system activity. It's this clever balance that makes them so unique.

1 teaspoon melted coconut oil

4 shiitake mushrooms, roughly chopped

2 large free-range eggs

1 teaspoon ground turmeric

Handful of fresh spinach

Pinch of ground nutmeg

Salt and pepper

Heat the coconut oil in a frying pan and add the shiitake mushrooms with a pinch of salt and pepper. Fry until golden, then turn the heat down.

Crack the eggs into a mixing bowl with the turmeric and a pinch of salt and pepper. Beat well with a fork.

Add the egg mixture to the pan and move the pan around to spread the egg evenly over the mushrooms. When the omelette begins to cook and firm up, but still has a little raw egg on top, add the spinach leaves and pinch of nutmeg.

Using a spatula or fish slice, ease around the edges of the omelette, then fold it in half. When it starts to turn golden brown underneath, remove the pan from the heat and slide the omelette on to a plate.

♥ *Shiitake mushrooms are one of the very few foods which have the amazing ability to regulate our immune system. That's not solely to boost it or suppress it, but to do both to bring it back into line. Not only are they delicious, but these immune-regulating beauties are also fantastic for those of us with autoimmune skin problems.*

SOUPS *and* SALADS

Homemade Vegetable Stock

←――――――――――――→

Makes 1 litre

There's no hard-and-fast rule when it comes to stock. Provided you have a fairy decent selection of root vegetables and herbs, pretty much anything goes. Making stock at home is ridiculously easy and, once you're done, you can freeze it to use in soups, casseroles and sauces for weeks to come.

2 tablespoons olive oil
2 onions, roughly chopped
3 carrots, roughly chopped
1 leek, roughly chopped
6 celery sticks, roughly chopped
4 garlic cloves
4–5 thyme sprigs
2 rosemary sprigs
2 bay leaves
Small bunch of parsley
A few black peppercorns
Optional extras: fennel, mushrooms, parsnips, sage

Heat the oil in a large pan over a medium heat and tip in all the vegetables, garlic, herbs and peppercorns. Sauté, stirring constantly, for about 5 minutes until the veg begin to soften slightly.

Boil a kettleful of water, carefully pour the boiling water over the vegetables in the pan, then cover the pan with a lid and simmer over a very low heat for 50 minutes to an hour.

Strain the stock and use straight away, or cool and refrigerate or freeze.

♥ *Shop-bought stock cubes often contain lots of salt, sugar, flavourings, colours and palm oil, all of which can wreak havoc with problem skin. Making your own stock ensures you know exactly what has gone into it and allows you to control the level of salt so that you can season dishes more delicately.*

Spiced Red Lentil *and* Carrot Soup

←――――――――――――→

Serves 4

This spicy, hearty soup is thick and nutritious, perfect as a winter meal. I love red lentils because they store well and don't require time-consuming overnight soaking.

2 tablespoons olive oil
3 carrots, diced
2 celery sticks, chopped
2 garlic cloves, crushed
1 small onion, diced
1.5 litres Homemade Vegetable Stock (see left)
150g red lentils
400g can cannellini beans, drained and rinsed
2 bay leaves
Juice of 1 lemon
2 teaspoons ground cumin
1 teaspoon garam masala
Cumin seeds, to serve
Salt and pepper

Heat the olive oil in a large, heavy-based saucepan. Add the carrots, celery, garlic and onion and sauté for about 15 minutes, stirring occasionally, until the carrots begin to soften.

Add the stock to the pan along with the lentils, cannellini beans, bay leaves, lemon juice and spices.

Bring the soup just to the boil, then lower the heat and gently simmer for 30–40 minutes until the lentils are soft.

Blitz the soup with a stick blender or in a blender until smooth – or leave it chunky if you prefer.

Season with salt and pepper and serve sprinkled with cumin seeds.

♥ *Lentils are part of the legume family and are an excellent source of plant protein. The insoluble dietary fibre found in red lentils helps prevent constipation and other digestive disorders such as IBS.*

Squash *and* Root Cumin Soup

Serves 4

This is a lovely, warming winter soup. Although it takes a while to prepare, it doesn't involve too much work and it freezes beautifully, ready to be reheated on those cold, winter evenings.

1 butternut squash
½ swede
1 sweet potato
2 parsnips
2 garlic cloves, peeled but whole
3 tablespoons melted coconut oil
1 teaspoon manuka honey
2 teaspoons ground cumin
1 leek, chopped
2 onions, chopped
1 tablespoon organic gluten-free
  bouillon powder
2 carrots
2 celery sticks
2 teaspoons cumin seeds, to serve
Salt and pepper

Preheat the oven to 180°C/fan 160°C/gas mark 4.

Slice the squash in half and scoop out the seeds with a spoon. Cut the root off the swede and peel it along with the sweet potato and parsnips. Chop into chunks and place in a roasting tray with the garlic cloves.

Spoon 2 tablespoons of the coconut oil over the veg, add a drizzle of honey and sprinkle with a teaspoon of the ground cumin.

Transfer to the oven to roast for 1–1½ hours, turning the vegetables occasionally to ensure they roast and soften evenly.

Meanwhile, warm the remaining coconut oil in a large, heavy-based saucepan and gently sauté the leek and onions for 5–10 minutes until softened.

Add 1 litre water, the bouillon powder, carrots and celery to the saucepan. Continue to simmer gently for 20–30 minutes.

Scoop the flesh away from the skin of the squash, discard the skin and add the flesh along with the other roast root vegetables to the pan, mixing well. Allow to cool, then ladle carefully into a food processor or blender. You may need to do this in two batches.

Blitz until smooth and return to the pan to warm gently. Season with the remaining ground cumin, some salt and pepper and serve with a sprinkling of cumin seeds.

♥ *The essential oils present in cumin have disinfectant and anti-fungal properties. Vitamin E, also present in cumin, combats the free radicals that attack the skin and result in signs of premature ageing such as wrinkles, age spots and sagging.*

Immunity Ramen

Serves 2

I make my own veggie stock using a wide variety of whatever's in the fridge. It usually consists of veg that needs using up. Homemade stock freezes well, so you can always have a ready supply. If, however, you need a quick, convenient substitute, always buy an organic, gluten-free bouillon powder which contains no artificial preservatives, colourings or flavourings.

700ml Homemade Vegetable Stock
   (see page 74) or 2 tablespoons
   organic, gluten-free bouillon
   powder dissolved in 1 litre water
2 servings buckwheat noodles
   (usually sold in packets divided
   into servings)
6 tenderstem broccoli
2 baby pak choi
4 baby leeks
3 spring onions
6 shiitake mushrooms
2 garlic cloves
Small chunk of ginger, peeled
Juice of 1 lime
4 star anise
Salt and pepper

TO SERVE
Sesame seeds
Handful of fresh coriander

Heat the 700ml homemade stock, if using, with an extra 300ml water in a large saucepan. (You may wish to change the ratio depending on how strong-tasting your stock is.) If you're using a powder stock, there is obviously no need to add extra water as you already have the appropriate volume. Allow the stock to simmer gently.

Add the buckwheat noodles to the stock and simmer for 1–2 minutes. Add the veg and all the other ingredients and simmer for a further 5–7 minutes. The noodles should soften and the vegetables should stay bright green and crunchy, retaining all their wonderful vitamins.

Season with salt and pepper and serve in two large soup bowls, sprinkled with sesame seeds and coriander.

♥ *This soup is packed full of healthy, seasonal greens, immune-regulating shiitake mushrooms and deliciously fragrant, healing spices. The combination of vitamins, antioxidants and powerful spices makes it a wonderful, immune-system-healing broth.*

Beet *and* Bramley Apple Borscht

Serves 4

Borscht is a variety of soup based on beetroot, and thought to originate from Russia and the Ukraine. Popular among many nations of Eastern and Central Europe, this is a beautiful, deep pink soup that tastes as gorgeous as it looks.

5 raw beetroot, halved
1 small sweet potato, roughly chopped
1 red onion, chopped
2 shallots, coarsely chopped
6 thyme sprigs
2 bay leaves
2 tablespoons olive oil
2 carrots, chopped
2 celery sticks, chopped
6 garlic cloves, chopped
2 Bramley apples
1.5 litres Homemade Vegetable Stock (see page 74)
2 tablespoons red wine vinegar
1 tablespoon honey
Salt and pepper
Chopped fresh chives, to serve

Preheat the oven to 180°C/fan 160°C/gas mark 4.

Put the beetroot, sweet potato, red onion, shallots, thyme and bay leaves in a large roasting tin, drizzle with a tablespoon of the olive oil and toss everything together. Season with salt and pepper. Roast in the oven for 35–45 minutes or until the beets and potatoes are just about cooked through.

Heat the remaining oil in a large, heavy-based saucepan over a low heat. Add the carrots, celery, garlic and a splash of water, cover and sweat for 10–15 minutes, stirring occasionally, until the celery and carrots soften a little. Remove from the heat.

Pick out the bay leaves and thyme stalks from the roasting pan, then add the roasted veg to the saucepan. Core and roughly chop the apples and add these too.

Pour in the stock and bring to the boil, then lower the heat and simmer, uncovered, for about 15 minutes.

Cool the soup, stir in the red wine vinegar and honey, season with salt and pepper, then carefully ladle into a blender (you might need to blend in batches). Blend until smooth.

Reheat gently before serving, check and adjust the seasoning if needed and serve with freshly chopped chives.

♥ *One of the major benefits of beetroot lies in its colour pigment, a substance called betalain. This is a powerful antioxidant and anti-inflammatory, which can help detox the body and in turn lead to a glowing complexion.*

Coconut *and* Cardamom Sweet Potato Soup

⟵――――――――――――――――⟶

Serves 4

I love this recipe because it's so simple to throw together yet tastes incredibly creamy and delicious. The addition of ground cardamom and fresh ginger gives this soup a fragrant, refreshing, sweet and peppery flavour.

2 tablespoons melted coconut oil

1 red onion, chopped

Chunk of ginger, peeled and finely sliced

2 garlic cloves, crushed

2 large sweet potatoes, chopped

1 teaspoon ground cardamom

400ml can coconut milk

750ml Homemade Vegetable Stock (see page 74)

Salt and pepper

TO SERVE

Juice of ½ lime

Toasted coconut flakes

Fresh coriander

Heat the oil in a large pan over a low heat. Add the onion, ginger and garlic and cook for 10 minutes to soften, stirring often.

Stir in the sweet potatoes and ground cardamom. Cook for 2 minutes, then pour in the coconut milk.

Let the soup simmer for 2 minutes, then mix in the vegetable stock. Cover the pan with a lid and simmer gently for 15 minutes.

Blitz the soup with a stick blender until smooth or allow to cool and blitz in a blender, in batches if necessary.

Gently reheat to serve, season to taste and stir in the lime juice. Serve with a sprinkling of toasted coconut flakes and coriander leaves.

♥ *Cardamom can have a great stress-relieving effect on the body, regulating blood pressure, stimulating the metabolism and improving digestion.*

Honey-roast Parsnip *and* Rosemary Soup

←——————————→

Serves 4

Roasting parsnips in manuka honey really brings out their sweet, earthy flavour. Combined with cannellini beans and rosemary, they make a deliciously thick and wonderfully aromatic soup.

4 large parsnips, halved
4 tablespoons olive oil
1 tablespoon manuka honey
1 onion
400g can cannellini beans, drained and rinsed
1.5 litres Homemade Vegetable Stock (see page 74)
1 bay leaf
1 tablespoon dried rosemary
Salt and pepper

Preheat the oven to 190°C/fan 170°C/gas mark 5.

Place the parsnips in a roasting tin. Toss in 1 tablespoon of the olive oil and the honey. Roast in the oven for 15–20 minutes until soft.

Heat the rest of the oil in a large, heavy-based saucepan over a medium heat. Cook the onion, stirring occasionally, for 10 minutes until it begins to soften. Add the cannellini beans to the pan.

Pour in the stock, add the bay leaf, roast parsnips and dried rosemary and simmer for 15 minutes.

Remove and discard the bay leaf, then blitz the soup with a stick blender or allow it to cool slightly and blitz in a blender until smooth.

Gently reheat to serve and season to taste with salt and black pepper.

♥ *Parsnips can improve the digestive processes, strengthen the immune system and lower blood pressure. They are also packed full of water-soluble antioxidants, which help the human body maintain healthy connective tissue, teeth and gums.*

Hydrating Watermelon Salad

←——————————→

Serves 2

This is such a perfect summer salad, wonderfully hydrating, thanks to possibly two of the most water-rich foods on the planet – watermelon and cucumber. I love the beautiful colour contrast between red and green but I'm aware that, despite supermarkets seemingly catering for our every need all year round, watermelon still tends to be fairly seasonal. If you can, look for the seeded sort. Honeydew or cantaloupe melon would work well as an alternative when watermelon is not available.

½ watermelon, cut into triangles
½ red onion, finely sliced
½ cucumber sliced
50g pitted black olives, sliced
1 tablespoon olive oil
Juice of ½ lime
1 teaspoon manuka honey
Handful of mint leaves, chopped
Black pepper
Pinch of pink Himalayan salt

Mix the watermelon, red onion, cucumber and olives together in a salad bowl.

Drizzle with the olive oil, lime juice and manuka honey.

Stir in the chopped mint leaves and add a few twists of black pepper and a pinch of pink Himalayan salt.

♥ *With a pH level of 9.0 and containing 92 per cent water, watermelon is incredibly alkaline. Besides being extremely delicious, the fruit quenches our thirst as well as boosting the body with antioxidant lycopene and vitamin A.*

Fig _and_ Pear Salad

⟵――――――――――――――――――⟶

Serves 2

I adore fresh figs; they're so sweet and luscious, with a delicate aroma and divine flavour. On the downside their season is super-short, so you'll need to grab them when you can. Fresh figs are available in the UK from August through to early October. You'll often find that Asian supermarkets are the first to stock them from mid-summer onwards.
Figs are very delicate and need gentle handling. They also have a fairly short shelf life, so pop them in the fridge and use them as soon as possible. As they have more flavour at room temperature, remember to remove them from the fridge an hour or two before preparing this salad.

6 fresh figs
2 pears, sliced
75g rocket leaves
75g watercress
40g walnut halves
Handful of flaked almonds

FOR THE DRESSING
1 teaspoon maple syrup
2 tablespoons lemon juice
5 tablespoons olive oil
½ teaspoon wholegrain mustard
1 teaspoon balsamic vinegar
Salt and pepper

Gently wipe the fig skins with a damp cloth, trim off the stems if they're hard and slice into quarters.

Toss the figs and pears in a salad bowl with the rocket and watercress.

Combine the dressing ingredients in a jar, close the lid and shake well.

Pour the dressing over the salad and mix in the walnuts and flaked almonds. Serve at room temperature.

♥ *Figs are a rich source of skin-friendly minerals and vitamins, including copper, phosphorus and vitamins A, C and E, which help to rejuvenate and refresh the skin.*

Beautifully Bright Rainbow Slaw

⟵—————————⟶

Serves 4

This fresh, light, beautiful, bright rainbow combination not only looks wonderfully appetising, but it also tastes delicious either on its own or spooned into jacket sweet potatoes.

½ green cabbage, thinly sliced
½ red cabbage, thinly sliced
2 carrots, grated
1 apple, coarsely grated
3 celery sticks, sliced
5 radishes, thinly sliced
1 small red onion, finely sliced

FOR THE DRESSING
1 tablespoon wholegrain mustard
Juice of ½ lime
1 teaspoon manuka honey
1 teaspoon apple cider vinegar
1 tablespoon olive oil
Pinch of salt

Combine the sliced and grated salad ingredients in a large mixing bowl.

Whisk together the dressing ingredients in a separate bowl.

Pour the dressing over the rainbow slaw vegetables, toss well and chill until ready to serve.

♥ *The high levels of vitamin A in cabbage are good not only for your skin, but also for your eyes. Vitamin A helps to prevent macular degeneration and cataract formation.*

Sprouted Gado-gado Salad

←————————————————→

Serves 2

Literally translated, the word gado-gado means 'pot-pourri' or 'medley' and it's the perfect description for this mixed vegetable salad, which is hugely popular across Indonesia. Gado-gado variations are served everywhere, from five-star restaurants to humble street stalls. The ingredients vary slightly according to the season and depending on what's locally available. Most versions include egg, tofu and potatoes alongside some raw and steamed greens. The nutty gado-gado sauce is essential and brings the dish together beautifully. This sprouted version is really tasty, bright and colourful. The sprouted seeds give it a true pot-pourri look and add so many health benefits. Remember that gado-gado varies depending on what's available seasonally and locally, so feel free to mix it up.

6 radishes, sliced

¼ cucumber, sliced lengthways

3 carrots, thinly sliced

Handful of alfalfa sprouts

50g tofu, cubed

½ sweet potato, chopped into
    small cubes

2 free-range eggs

10 asparagus spears

50g green beans

Juice of ½ lime

Sesame seeds, to serve

FOR THE SAUCE

1 teaspoon melted coconut oil

2 shallots, chopped

Chunk of ginger, grated

1 garlic clove, finely chopped

Juice of ½ lime

200ml coconut milk

3 tablespoons almond butter

Pinch of sea salt

1 teaspoon maple syrup

Divide the prepared radishes, cucumber and carrots between two bowls, then add the alfalfa sprouts and cubes of tofu to each bowl, arranging them neatly around the centre.

Choose a saucepan that is the right size for your bamboo steamer to sit on top. Add some water to the pan and bring to the boil, then add the sweet potato cubes and lower the heat to a simmer.

After 10 minutes add the eggs to the boiling water and place the bamboo steamer on top, with the asparagus spears and green beans in it. Simmer gently for a further 7 minutes before removing from the heat.

Drain the sweet potatoes and eggs. Cool the eggs under cold running water so that you can easily peel them. Peel them and cut in half. Divide the sweet potatoes between the two bowls and top with the halved eggs and the asparagus and beans. The steamed greens should still be crunchy and bright green. Squeeze fresh lime juice over the salads.

To make the sauce, gently heat the coconut oil in a pan. Add the shallots, grated ginger, chopped garlic and a squeeze of lime juice. Cook for 10 minutes to soften.

Pour in the coconut milk and keep the sauce over a low heat. Add the almond butter, salt and maple syrup. Keep stirring the sauce to ensure the flavours mix well.

Once everything has melted nicely and combined, turn the heat off and allow the sauce to cool. I like to serve it warm but not hot. Simply drizzle this delicious, nutty dressing over the two portions of salad, sprinkle with some sesame seeds and enjoy.

♥ *The proteins in tofu help improve the elasticity of skin and tone facial muscles, making your skin youthful and supple. Alfalfa sprouts are rich in alfalfa chlorophyll. The vitamins B1 and B6 found in this great plant are essential for healthy hair and skin cells.*

Quinoa Tabbouleh

← →

Serves 2

I love this Middle Eastern salad, typically made with bulgar wheat, but here it becomes super-healthy because I use quinoa instead. Many versions include cherry tomatoes, but nightshades can be really problematic for immune-related skin conditions, so I've omitted them from this recipe. Loaded with plant-powered protein, this is a dish that makes both a delicious veggie main course and a lovely summer side option.

200g quinoa
Juice of 1 lemon
1 garlic clove, crushed
3 tablespoons extra-virgin olive oil
½ cucumber
½ red onion
Handful of flat-leaf parsley
Handful of mint leaves
2 spring onions
Salt and pepper

Rinse the quinoa well and put it in a pan with about double its volume of water. Bring to the boil, cover, lower the heat and gently simmer for 10–15 minutes.

Turn off the heat and leave to cool, then drain off any remaining water.

Mix together most of the lemon juice, the garlic and olive oil in a bowl. Season to taste.

Peel and deseed the cucumber and chop into small pieces, then very finely chop the red onion, parsley, mint and spring onions.

Stir everything together and season with the remaining lemon juice, and more salt and pepper if necessary.

♥ *Parsley contains the immune-enhancing vitamins C and A and is a powerful antioxidant. In fact vitamin C not only nourishes the skin, it also reduces scars and blemishes and stimulates the production of collagen, which is the key to cell reproduction and repair.*

Almond Manuka Satay

⟵─────────────⟶

Makes 400ml

Almonds are one of the most alkaline nuts you can eat. My skin seems absolutely to hate peanut butter, which is a shame because I love it! Fortunately almond butter is the perfect replacement spread on rice cakes and used in recipes. Make sure you look for a brand with no added nasties such as extra salt and sugar. You just want beautifully smooth or crunchy almonds, depending on which version you prefer. Here is my almond and manuka version of a typical satay sauce. This nutty, sweet satay is absolutely delicious as a salad dressing, pad Thai sauce or marinade for mushroom skewers.

2 tablespoons melted coconut oil
2 shallots, chopped
1 garlic clove, crushed
Chunk of ginger, grated
200ml coconut milk
150g almond butter
1 tablespoon manuka honey
1 tablespoon tamari (gluten-free soy sauce)
Juice of ½ lime
Salt

Gently warm the coconut oil in a saucepan. Add the shallots, garlic and ginger and gently cook for 5–10 minutes until soft.

Add the coconut milk to the pan and stir in the almond butter, manuka honey and tamari sauce. Warm for a further 10 minutes until all the ingredients have melted and combined.

Finally squeeze in the lime juice and season with a little salt if needed.

Store in a glass jar with a tight-fitting lid in the fridge for up to 1 week.

Raspberry Salad Dressing

⟵─────────────⟶

Makes 150ml

I love this bright, fruity, summer dressing. It's such a quick and easy vinaigrette to make with a lovely, tangy taste.

100g raspberries
4 tablespoons light olive oil
2 tablespoons balsamic vinegar
1 tablespoon manuka honey
Small pinch of salt

Gently rinse the raspberries under cold water. Add everything to your food processor and blitz for a lovely, fruity salad dressing.

Store in a glass jar in the fridge for up to 2 weeks.

Classic French Dressing

← →

Makes 150ml

Once you've made this simple salad dressing you will never be tempted by shop-bought again. Perfect for livening up salads without all the added salt and sugar you'll often find in bottled versions.

½ garlic clove, crushed
2 tablespoons finely chopped shallot
2 tablespoons white wine vinegar
2 teaspoons Dijon mustard
5 tablespoons extra-virgin olive oil
1 teaspoon lemon juice
Pinch each of salt and pepper

Put the garlic, shallot, vinegar, salt and pepper in a glass jar. Pop the lid on and shake well. Pour into a small bowl, whisk in the mustard, then very slowly add the oil in a thin, steady stream, whisking constantly until the dressing is emulsified.

Add the lemon juice and whisk again.

Return to the glass jar and store in the fridge for up to 2 weeks.

Caper Ranch Dressing

← →

Makes 400ml

I love this ranch dressing. Creamy without being over-heavy and made using a delicious combination of fresh herbs and garlic, this wonderfully tasty dressing is perfect for drizzling generously over salads.

2 free-range egg yolks, at room temperature
1 teaspoon Dijon mustard
200ml light olive oil
2 tablespoons white wine vinegar
Pinch of salt
100ml almond milk
Juice of ½ lemon
1 garlic clove, crushed
1 tablespoon capers
3 mini gherkins, chopped
Sprinkling of chopped chives
Sprinkling of chopped parsley

Whisk the egg yolks on high speed. Add the mustard and whisk again.

Very slowly pour the oil into the mix, whisking constantly on high speed as you very gradually add the oil. The mixture should quickly begin to thicken.

Add the vinegar and salt and keep whisking. The mixture should be of a thick, mayonnaise consistency.

Slowly add the almond milk and lemon juice to thin down the mayo into a dressing.

Add the crushed garlic, capers, gherkins and herbs.

Transfer to a glass jar and store in the fridge for up to 2 weeks.

DIPS *and* SAUCES

←——————→

Tomato-less Sauce

⟵─────────────────⟶

Makes 750ml

So, why would anyone want a tomato-free sauce? Surely tomatoes are healthy? The truth is, for most people, they are, but for anyone struggling with a skin problem such as psoriasis or another autoimmune disorder like arthritis, tomatoes can pose a real problem. Tomatoes, along with potatoes, peppers and chillies, form part of the nightshade family. Nightshades can be problematic because of their lectin, saponin and capsaicin content.
I decide to create this amazing tomato substitute after craving Italian tomato-based pasta dishes and my favourite rogan josh curry. This sauce not only looks tomatoey, it actually tastes good enough to pass for tomato sauce. Believe me, I tried it on my friends and they absolutely fell for it! I love it with rice pasta. Lemon juice is crucial to getting the acidity just right, so make sure you have at least one fresh lemon to hand so that you can adjust the flavour accordingly.

2 tablespoons olive oil
3 white onions, roughly chopped
4 celery sticks, chopped
2 raw beetroot, chopped
2 carrots, chopped
2 garlic cloves, chopped
Handful of curly-leaf parsley
1 tablespoon organic vegetable
   stock powder
1 teaspoon dried oregano
Juice of 1 lemon
Drop of balsamic vinegar (optional)
Basil leaves (optional)
Salt and pepper

Heat the olive oil in a large saucepan and sauté the onions and celery for 5–10 minutes until they begin to soften.

Stir the beetroot and carrots into the onions along with the garlic and parsley. Simmer over a gentle heat for 5 minutes.

Add enough water to the saucepan to just about cover the vegetables. Stir in the vegetable stock powder, oregano and a little salt and pepper. Cover the pan and gently simmer for 45–60 minutes until the beetroot and carrots soften.

Allow to cool, then pour into a food processor and blitz. The beets and carrots will mean the sauce will taste fairly sweet, so add lemon juice and keep blitzing until you get the flavour just right. You may wish to add a touch of balsamic vinegar too and, depending on what you'd like to use your sauce for, some fresh basil.

Store in a jar in the fridge for up to 5 days. The sauce may turn a little more pink as the colour of the beets comes out!

♥ *Inflammation is often a sign that our immune system is acting up. Symptoms, which include redness, swelling and pain, can cause a lot of discomfort. Beetroot contains betalains and these have anti-inflammatory properties that can reduce inflammation and skin redness.*

Cheese-less Cheese Sauce

⟵——————————⟶

Makes 400ml

When it came to cutting out dairy, the one thing I missed like crazy was cheese. Nutritional yeast is my magic ingredient here. This sauce is fabulous served cold as a dip for corn chips and works brilliantly stirred into warm pasta and risotto dishes.

1 large sweet potato
1 large carrot
½ white onion
1 garlic clove
4 heaped tablespoons nutritional yeast
2 tablespoons olive oil
Juice of ½ lemon
50ml water
Pinch of celery salt
Salt and pepper

Peel and roughly chop the sweet potato, carrot, onion and garlic. Add to a pan of water and boil for 30–40 minutes until soft.

Drain and allow to cool a little, then tip the boiled veg into a blender or food processor and blitz until soft.

Add the nutritional yeast, olive oil, lemon juice, water, celery salt and some salt and pepper.

Blitz everything again until it forms a smooth, creamy, thick sauce. You may want to add a little more water if the sauce is too thick. Taste and add more seasoning if required.

Serve as a dipping sauce or stir into pasta and risotto dishes in place of cheese.

♥ *Nutritional yeast is a brilliant vegetarian source of vitamin B12, which is a really important nutrient for the body. It's crucial for the production of red blood cells. Most sources of vitamin B12 are animal-based, so nutritional yeast is a major player in the health of vegans and vegetarians.*

Sweet *or* Savoury Cashew Cream

⟵―――――――――――――――――⟶

Makes 1 jar

The great thing about this cashew cream recipe is its versatility. Once you've made the cream base you can add maple syrup and cinnamon to sweeten it or use nutritional yeast and a drop or two of white wine vinegar to create a delicious savoury 'cheese' sauce. I use it to make my Dauphinoise Sweet Potatoes (see page 108) and it's also perfect for adding to soups, veg and pasta dishes or, in the case of the sweet version, pouring over hot crumbles and puddings.

This is one of the few recipes where the tools you use really do matter. Making cashew cream in a standard food processor might result in a grainy, spoonable mixture and what you're really after is the velvety-smooth blend you get when using a superior extraction machine. If you're going to make dairy-free cashew cream or nut butters on a regular basis, I would definitely recommend investing in a high-quality food processor.

200g cashew nuts, soaked in warm water for 1–2 hours
400ml can coconut milk
1 teaspoon melted coconut oil

FOR THE SWEET VERSION
1 tablespoon maple syrup
A few drops of vanilla extract
1 teaspoon ground cinnamon (optional)

FOR THE SAVOURY VERSION
1 teaspoon white wine vinegar
2 heaped tablespoons nutritional yeast
Pinch of sea salt

Soaking the cashew nuts will help achieve a smooth blend. If your food processor isn't great, soak the nuts for 4 hours.

Drain the nuts and add to your food processor along with the coconut milk and coconut oil.

Blitz on the highest setting for 1 minute. The finished cream should be of a perfectly smooth consistency.

For sweet cashew cream, simply add the maple syrup, a little vanilla extract and cinnamon (if you wish).

For a savoury, 'cheese'-style sauce, add the white wine vinegar, nutritional yeast and sea salt.

Once you've added your sweet or savoury options, blitz the cream again to create a velvety-smooth sauce.

♥ *The copper and iron in cashews work together to help the body generate red blood cells to keep the blood vessels, nerves, immune system and bones healthy and functioning properly.*

Garlic *and* Herb Butter Bean Dip

←—————————————→

Serves 4

I absolutely love this creamy, buttery dip. I actually discovered it by accident after running out of canned chickpeas and needing a last-minute substitute for hummus! It has a softer, more mellow flavour than the chickpea version and adding a combination of fresh herbs gives it a lovely, fresh, summery taste.

400g can butter beans, drained and rinsed
2 garlic cloves
Juice of 1 lemon
2 tablespoons olive oil
1 tablespoon water
2 tablespoons roughly chopped dill
2 tablespoons roughly chopped mint
1 tablespoon roughly chopped flat-leaf parsley
Salt and pepper

Put the butter beans, garlic, lemon juice, oil, water and chopped herbs in a food processor and process until smooth.

Season with salt and pepper to taste.

♥ *Butter beans have a smooth, delicate flavour and a creamy, buttery texture. In addition to providing slow-burning complex carbohydrates, butter beans can increase energy levels by helping to replenish the body's iron and magnesium stores.*

Brazil Nut Pesto

←—————————————→

Serves 4

Traditionally made using crushed garlic, fresh basil and pine nuts blended with Parmesan cheese and olive oil, pesto originates from Liguria in north Italy. Ligurians are very proud of their pesto and fiercely defend their traditional recipe, so much so that they have very strict rules and regulations about ingredients and preparation methods. My pesto recipes are far less stringent! I've tried different herb, leaf and nut combinations, but the thing I love most about this version is how rich and creamy it tastes. Nutritional yeast makes a perfect, dairy-free substitute for Parmesan. Not only does the pesto taste terrific, it's also a complete breeze to make.

Handful of flat-leaf parsley
Handful of basil leaves, stalks removed
150g Brazil nuts
1 garlic clove
Juice of 1 lemon
2 tablespoons olive oil
1 tablespoon nutritional yeast
Salt and pepper

Simply place all the ingredients in a food processor and blend for a couple of minutes to create a smooth, creamy pesto.

The addition of fresh lemon juice will help naturally preserve your pesto. Store in the fridge and use over 5–7 days.

♥ *Brazil nuts are the very best natural source of selenium, an essential trace mineral required by the body. We need selenium for the normal functioning of our immune system and thyroid gland. Selenium can also help lower the risk of joint inflammation and plays a very important role both in terms of your body functioning properly and as part of your skincare regime.*

Pink Peppercorn Hummus

⟵————————⟶

Serves 4

Hummus is one of my favourite quick-blitz dips. It's delicious on sweet potatoes, served with rice crackers or alongside a summer salad. Pink peppercorns make this version taste zesty and light. In fact, they are not true peppercorns but aromatic berries. Pink peppercorns have a citrus flavour and are much more fragrant than black pepper.

2 x 400g cans chickpeas
1 tablespoon tahini
1 garlic clove, crushed
1 teaspoon pink peppercorns, plus extra to garnish
Pinch of pink Himalyan salt
Juice of 1 lemon
½ teaspoon ground cumin
100ml extra-virgin olive oil

Drain the chickpeas and rinse under cold water.

Add these to a food processor with the rest of the ingredients and blitz until smooth.

Spoon the hummus into a bowl and drizzle over a little olive oil.

Garnish with crushed pink peppercorns to serve.

❤ *Chickpeas contain the key mineral manganese, which helps protect skin against damage from ultraviolet light. Other nutrients such as folate and vitamin B are super-important for healthy skin cells. Tahini is a thick paste made from ground sesame seeds. Sesame seeds are a good source of amino acids, vitamin E, B vitamins, trace minerals and fatty acids, all of which help with skin-cell rejuvenation and prevent early signs of ageing.*

Guacamole

⟵————————⟶

Serves 4

I am a little addicted to avocados. They are so delicious, incredibly nutritious and full of omega-9 fatty acids. I love making guacamole dip, avocado mousse or simply eating them straight from their skin with a teaspoon! With over 25 nutrients and an infinite list of benefits for your skin, hair and health, they're a brilliant addition to a skin-friendly diet.

3 ripe avocados, halved and stoned
Juice of 1 lime
Handful of fresh coriander, chopped, plus extra to garnish
½ red onion, finely chopped
Pinch of pink Himalayan salt

Use a spoon to scoop out the avocado flesh into a bowl. Add the lime juice, coriander, chopped red onion and salt and use the back of a fork to mash everything together.

Garnish with chopped coriander leaves.

❤ *One of the main skin benefits of eating avocados comes from their high oleic acid content. This monounsaturated fatty acid maintains moisture in the epidermal layer of your skin, helping to keep it soft and hydrated. An omega-9 fat, oleic acid is also involved in regenerating damaged skin cells and reducing facial redness and irritation. If you suffer from skin irritation and dryness, try eating more avocado for skin health and hydration.*

Aioli – Garlic Mayo

← →

Makes 400ml

There are a few tricks to making mayonnaise. Ensure your bowl and whisk are super-clean, use an electric whisk and use eggs at room temperature – that way there's far less risk of your mayonnaise splitting. Extra-virgin olive oil has too strong a flavour for this recipe, so find a light version with very little flavour. Use a good-quality vinegar, preferably white wine vinegar. This will give the mayo a more delicate flavour.

2 free-range egg yolks, at room temperature
1 heaped teaspoon Dijon mustard
350ml light olive oil
Juice of ½ lemon
1 tablespoon white wine vinegar
1 garlic clove, crushed
Salt and pepper

Whisk the egg yolks and mustard in a mixing bowl at high speed.

Still whisking, very, very slowly begin to pour half the olive oil into the mixture. It's essential to do this really slowly and to whisk the mixture constantly as you pour. My trick is to pour the oil carefully down the side of the bowl so that it slowly trickles into the mixture. Gradually, the mixture will begin to emulsify, becoming thick, velvety and smooth.

Add the lemon juice, vinegar, crushed garlic and a pinch of salt and continue to whisk. When it's all incorporated, add the remaining oil, taste and season with a little more salt and some pepper if needed.

Store in a sterilised jar in the fridge for up to a week.

💙 *Garlic contains a large amount of allicin, which has antifungal, anti-ageing and skin-smoothing benefits. Sulphur present in garlic prevents infections and helps to reduce inflammation. It also enhances blood flow, giving the skin a natural glow.*

Fragrant Mango Chutney

← →

Makes 400ml

This mango chutney recipe is incredibly fragrant, sweet and spicy, delicious either as a spread, a dip, or used in cooking a variety of Indian dishes.

2 tablespoons melted coconut oil
1 red onion, finely sliced
Chunk of ginger, grated
2 garlic cloves, crushed
1 teaspoon ground cumin
2 teaspoons ground coriander
1 teaspoon ground turmeric
1 teaspoon ground cloves
1 teaspoon ground cinnamon
2 ripe mangoes, peeled, stoned and diced
3 tablespoons maple syrup
350ml white wine vinegar
Juice of ½ lemon
Pinch of salt

Heat the oil in a saucepan over a medium heat. Throw in the red onion, ginger and garlic and sauté for a couple of minutes. Add the spices and sauté for 3–5 minutes until the onion begins to soften.

Add the mangoes, maple syrup, vinegar and a pinch of salt to the pan and stir to combine. Bring the mixture to the boil, then lower the heat. Stir in lemon juice and leave to simmer for 1 hour. Remove from the heat and allow to cool.

I like my mango chunky but if you prefer a smoother blend simply pulse the chutney in a food processor once it's cooled down. Store in a sterilised airtight jar. Unopened chutney will keep well for months. Once opened, it should be stored in the fridge and used within 3 weeks.

💙 *The vitamin A in mangoes helps to rejuvenate dull, tired skin.*

Indian Coconut Raita Dip

⟵————————⟶

Serves 4

This cool, creamy condiment is a must with spicy Indian dishes. The mint, coriander and lime give it a lovely fresh flavour. It's perfect served as a poppadom dip.

400g natural coconut yogurt
Large handful of mint
Large handful of coriander
Juice of 1 lime
2 tablespoons manuka honey
½ teaspoon salt

Spoon the yogurt into a bowl. Strip the mint leaves from their stalks and chop finely; discard the stalks. Chop the fresh coriander leaves and stalks. Stir the fresh herbs into the yogurt.

Add the lime juice, manuka honey and salt and combine well.

Place in the fridge to chill before serving.

♥ *Coconut yogurt is a good source of bone-building calcium. It contains vitamin B12, crucial for red blood cell production, and vitamin D, vital for calcium absorption.*

Kachumber Coriander Lime Salad

⟵————————⟶

Serves 4

Kachumber is a small side salad that usually comprises onion, cucumber and sometimes fresh tomato. My version has no tomato and the light, fresh flavours beautifully balance rich Indian dips and curries. Delicious served with poppadoms or Indian roti breads and a generous helping of mango chutney (see page 101) or cooling coconut raita (see left).

1 red onion, finely chopped
½ cucumber, finely diced
Handful of coriander, finely chopped
10 mint leaves, finely chopped
Pinch of ground cumin
Juice of ½ lime
1 teaspoon manuka honey
Pinch of salt

Mix together the onion, cucumber and chopped coriander and mint. Add the cumin and a pinch of salt. Stir in the lime juice and honey and chill in the fridge until ready to serve.

This salad is best eaten within a few hours or on the day it's made.

♥ *Eating raw onions can be very helpful in promoting skin health. The anti-inflammatory and antibacterial properties of red onions, which are less fiery than their white or yellow counterparts, can help a great deal in improving skin conditions such as acne.*

GREENS, SNACKS
and SIDES

Sautéed Spinach *with* Caramelised Figs *and* Almonds

←——————————————→

Serves 2

If you've always thought of spinach as a little boring and uninspiring, this recipe is guaranteed to change your mind. Figs are such a wonderful ingredient, and I just love the blend of sweet and savoury with that sharp little kick from the lemon juice.

2 tablespoons olive oil
2 garlic cloves, thinly sliced
½ red onion, finely sliced
2 tablespoons maple syrup
6 dried plump figs, sliced
200ml Homemade Vegetable Stock (see page 74)
200g baby spinach
50g flaked almonds
Squeeze of lemon juice
Salt and pepper

Heat the olive oil in a saucepan over a medium heat. Once it's hot, lower the heat, add the garlic, onion and a tablespoon of the maple syrup. Cook for 2–3 minutes until the onion begins to soften.

Add the figs and vegetable stock and simmer for another couple of minutes until the stock is almost completely reduced, then add the rest of the maple syrup and gently warm for 30 seconds.

Drop in the spinach, a handful at a time, and cook while stirring, until it has wilted.

Add the flaked almonds and a squeeze of lemon juice, stir and serve seasoned with salt and pepper.

♥ *Figs are rich in vitamins B and C, phosphorus, potassium, calcium and magnesium. The high omega-3 fatty acids in figs keep the skin well moisturised and conditioned from within.*

Mangetout *with* Maple *and* Mustard Seeds

←——————————————→

Serves 4

This is one of my favourite vegetable side dishes. It works so well served as an accompaniment of greens or tossed into rice or noodles. The trick with greens is to keep them bright and crunchy, so be careful not to overcook them.

400g French beans
3 tablespoons sesame oil
3 tablespoons mustard seeds
1 garlic clove, crushed
2 tablespoons maple syrup
2 tablespoons apple cider vinegar
400g mangetout
Coarse sea salt and black pepper

Bring a large saucepan of water to the boil. Drop in the green beans and cook for 2–3 minutes until tender but still crisp. Drain.

Warm the sesame oil in a heavy-based pan. Toast the mustard seeds in the oil over a low heat just until they pop (about 1 minute), stirring to prevent them from burning.

Add the garlic, maple syrup and vinegar to the pan and warm for a further couple of minutes. Then throw in the green beans and mangetout, so that they heat through but don't overcook, and toss to coat well. Season with salt and pepper and serve.

♥ *Both mangetout and French beans are packed with vitamin C. Adequate vitamin C intake not only improves the immune system, but it can also create and maintain collagen, an important protein found in hair and skin.*

Dauphinoise Sweet Potatoes

←―――――――――――――――→

Serves 4–6

Creamy, comforting side dishes such as this one are perfect winter food. When it's cold outside there's nothing nicer than a bowl of rich, healthy carbs to make you feel all warm and nourished.

3 large sweet potatoes
400ml Savoury Cashew Cream (see page 97)
1 garlic clove, crushed
1 teaspoon dried thyme
Pinch of grated nutmeg
Salt and pepper

Preheat the oven to 180°C/fan 160°C/gas mark 4.

Peel the potatoes and slice them thinly, either with a sharp knife or a mandolin.

Put the cashew cream sauce, garlic, thyme and nutmeg into a large saucepan and gently warm. Add the potatoes to the cream and simmer for 3–5 minutes until they just begin to soften. Keep gently stirring to stop the potatoes sticking to the bottom of the pan.

Use a slotted spoon to lift out the sweet potato slices and layer them into an ovenproof dish, overlapping the slices and sprinkling each layer with a little salt and pepper. Pour the remaining cashew cream over the potatoes and bake in the oven for 30–40 minutes until they're tender and the top turns golden.

Leave to stand for 5 minutes before serving.

♥ *Sweet potatoes contain choline, a very important and versatile nutrient that aids sleep. Choline also helps to maintain the structure of cellular membranes, assists in the transmission of nerve impulses and in the absorption of fat, and it also reduces chronic inflammation.*

Whole Stem Broccoli *with* Lemon *and* Garlic

Serves 2

The one thing that often disappoints me with vegetable side dishes served in restaurants is how bland, overcooked and uninspiring they can be. When it comes to broccoli there's nothing more unappetising than a soggy bowl of overdone florets. Having followed a predominantly vegetarian diet for over twenty years, I've learned to make fresh, creative vegetable combinations. I must admit, until last year I'd never really given much thought to eating broccoli stems before. For years I've chopped the florets off with a kitchen knife and used the stalks in my morning green juice. Broccoli stalks have a wonderful, mild sweet flavour and are much higher in fibre than the florets. Not only do garlic and lemon taste delicious together, this recipe also makes use of every part of the broccoli, creating a fresh, crunchy dish.

1 full head of broccoli
3 tablespoons olive oil
3 garlic cloves, crushed
Juice of 1 lemon and zest of
½ lemon
Salt and pepper
Lemon wedges, to serve

Wash and dry the whole broccoli and chop only a few millimetres off the base of the stem. Next use a knife to slice the broccoli into long lengths from the base of the stem right through to the florets, using every part of the vegetable.

Heat the olive oil in a wok, throw in the sliced broccoli and stir-fry for 2–3 minutes.

Add the garlic, lemon juice and zest and stir-fry for a further 5 minutes, tossing the broccoli constantly until it's bright green and tender.

Season with salt and pepper and serve with lemon wedges for squeezing.

♥ *Well-cooked broccoli stems are juicy and more satisfying than the frilly florets. Like other green vegetables, broccoli can do wonders for your skin because it's full of dietary fibre, vitamins, minerals and antioxidants. Rich in vitamins C and E, which stimulate collagen production, broccoli keeps your skin healthy, while its vitamin A content protects your cell membranes and can prevent ultraviolet radiation damage.*

Cumin *and* Coriander Kale Crisps

⟵⟶

Serves 2–4

Kale crisps are a fantastic alternative to regular potato crisps. Even if you're not a fan of kale you have to give these a try. They're simple to make but you do need to be on hand to check the oven at regular intervals. Remember, the goal is obviously to crisp the kale, not scorch it to smithereens. Keep a watchful eye on it and move the leaves around so that you're not left with kale that's soggy in some places and charred to ash in others.

200g curly kale
1 tablespoon melted coconut oil
Juice of ½ lemon
1 tablespoon sesame seeds
½ teaspoon ground cumin
½ teaspoon ground coriander
1 teaspoon sea salt

Preheat the oven to 150°C/fan 130°C/gas mark 2.

Strip the kale leaves from the stalks, and tear the leaves, taking care to keep them in large pieces, ideally a few centimetres across.

Put the kale leaves in a large mixing bowl and toss with the other ingredients. Spread out on a large oven tray and bake for 10–15 minutes, tossing them every 5 minutes to ensure they roast evenly on all sides without burning.

♥ *Kale comes packed with skin-friendly copper. This mineral boosts the synthesis of melanin, the pigment that protects our skin from the sun. Kale is also high in vitamin C, which helps us to make the collagen needed for skin strength.*

Beet Crisps

⟵⟶

Serves 2

These beet crisps are so quick and easy to make, and they're a delicious savoury snack. Supermarkets all tend to sell the traditional red beetroot, but if you have a local grocer or organic shop close by, check them out for alternative varieties, such as the bright yellow Boldor beetroot, to add a little colour to your snack bowl.

2 large raw beetroot (I like to use different varieties to create lovely colourful crisps)
2 tablespoons melted coconut oil
1 teaspoon dried thyme
Pinch of sea salt and sprinkling of pepper

Preheat the oven to 180°C/fan 160°C/gas mark 4.

Scrub the beets so that the skin is clean and mud free. Slice them super, super finely using a sharp knife or a mandolin.

Toss the beet slices in a bowl with the melted coconut oil, dried thyme and a pinch of sea salt. Make sure you rub the oil into the slices well to ensure they're evenly coated.

Lay the slices on a baking sheet, ensuring they don't overlap. Bake in the oven for 15 minutes, then turn the slices and bake for a further 5–10 minutes until crisp and brown around the edges.

Allow to cool and serve sprinkled with salt and pepper.

♥ *High in folate, beets stimulate the production and repair of cells, which helps protect against premature ageing.*

Cumin-spiced Sweet Potato Wedges

←————————————→

Serves 4

These sweet potato chips make such an amazing alternative to regular chips. They're really easy to make, too. Just cut them into wedges, toss with some olive oil, fresh lemon and spices and bake at a high temperature so that they're lightly crispy on the outside and soft in the middle. I love to serve them with garlic mayo (see page 101).

3 large sweet potatoes
Juice of 1 lemon
3 tablespoons olive oil
2 teaspoons ground cumin
1 teaspoon ground coriander
1 teaspoon garlic powder
Salt and pepper

Preheat the oven to 200°C/fan 180°C/gas mark 6.

Wash and scrub the potatoes – there's no need to peel them. Cut each one in half, then cut each half into quarters so that you have 8 chunky wedges from each potato.

Stir together the lemon juice, oil and spices in a large mixing bowl. Add the potatoes and toss together, using your fingers to rub in the oil and spices.

Arrange the potatoes, skin-side down, on a baking tray and bake in the oven for 30–40 minutes until soft on the inside and crispy on the outside.

♥ *Cumin has a high vitamin E content, which keeps your skin healthy and glowing. It also has disinfectant and anti-fungal properties which can protect you from fungal and microbial infections.*

Plant-powered 'Parmesan'

←————————————→

Makes 180g

Of all the things I eliminated from my diet to rescue my skin, dairy was the last to go. While it never did my skin any favours, it was tough to give it up; I had a serious love of cheese!

The brilliant thing about this dairy-free Parmesan substitute is its versatility and it's so simple to make. I love to keep a jar of it handy and use it as a delicious savoury addition sprinkled on anything from pizza and pasta dishes to soups and salads.

150g whole almonds
2 tablespoons nutritional yeast
1 teaspoon garlic powder
½ teaspoon sea salt

Put all the ingredients in a food processor and pulse until the almonds resemble fine breadcrumbs.

Store in an airtight glass jar in the fridge. It will easily last a couple of months.

♥ *Omega-3 fatty acids help regulate blood sugars, reduce blood pressure, support the immune system and increase energy levels and skin radiance. Your body can't make these essential fatty acids but almonds are a fantastic source. They're also crammed full of vitamin E. The vitamin E in almonds can help nourish your skin and protect it from the sun's damaging ultraviolet rays.*

Super-seed Quinoa Loaf

Makes 1 450g loaf

The thing I love most about this recipe is its simplicity. When it comes to baking traditional loaves there's often a lot of waiting involved. This super seed beauty requires zero active baking yeast, so there's no need to cover bowls with warm tea towels or wait for dough to rise. It's simply a case of mixing everything in a food processor and stirring the seeds through the mix. What you get in return for your (minimal) efforts is a lovely, dense, nutty loaf, packed full of healthy oils, vitamins and nutrients.

Melted coconut oil, for greasing
200g quinoa
500ml water
1 free-range egg
50g gluten-free rolled oats
1 tablespoon nutritional yeast
    (flakes or powder)
1 teaspoon baking powder
60g sunflower seeds
60g pumpkin seeds
Salt

Preheat the oven to 180°C/fan 160°C/gas mark 4. Grease a sheet of baking paper with coconut oil and place it, oiled-side up, in a 450g loaf tin.

Rinse the quinoa and cover with 400ml of the water. Bring to the boil, then simmer gently, covered, for around 15 minutes until it's tender or the water has been completely absorbed. Allow to cool.

Combine the egg and water in a food processor and blitz together. Add the cooked quinoa, oats, nutritional yeast and baking powder and pulse to combine.

Finally stir in the sunflower and pumpkin seeds and season with a little salt.

Scoop the bread mix into the prepared loaf tin and level the surface.

Bake in the oven for 20 minutes, then remove and carefully lift the loaf out of its tin using the baking paper.

Peel off the baking paper and place the loaf on a tray. Cook for a further 30 minutes until it is evenly browned all over.

Transfer the loaf to a cooling rack and allow to cool. Then slice it and enjoy topped with mashed avocado or nut butter.

♥ *Quinoa is a super seed, a great source of fibre, full of protein and it contains all nine essential amino acids. Sunflower seeds give your skin an additional glow, thanks to a healthy dose of vitamin E.*

Buckwheat, Banana *and* Brazil Nut Vitamin B Bread

Makes 1 450g loaf

Buckwheat is such a nutritious superfood and works so well in this recipe. You can find the groats – they are triangular seeds, not grains – in health stores. The name buckwheat is a little deceiving, though, because it actually contains no wheat whatsoever: it's completely gluten-free. The banana and cinnamon give this loaf a lovely, naturally sweet flavour. It's just perfect topped with nut butter.

150g buckwheat groats

1 tablespoon melted coconut oil, plus extra for greasing

2 large ripe bananas

100g pitted dates, chopped

50g Brazil nuts

50g raisins

100g gluten-free rolled oats

Pinch of cinnamon

Pinch of salt

30g sunflower seeds

30g pumpkin seeds

Salt

Preheat the oven to 170°C/fan 150°C/gas mark 3. Grease a sheet of baking paper with coconut oil and use it to line a 450g loaf tin.

Put the buckwheat groats in a medium saucepan with enough water to cover. Add the coconut oil and ½ teaspoon salt. Bring to a simmer, then cover with a tight-fitting lid and simmer on low for a further 18–20 minutes. Drain and set aside to cool.

Blitz the bananas in a food processor. Add the buckwheat, dates, Brazil nuts, raisins, oats, cinnamon and a pinch of salt to the blitzed bananas and pulse to create a sticky but coarse mix. Lastly stir in the seeds.

Spoon the mixture into the prepared loaf tin and bake in the oven for 40 minutes.

Remove from the oven and allow to cool slightly. Place a lightly greased baking tray on top of the loaf tin. Carefully tip it upside down and peel away the baking paper from the bread. Return the baking tray to the oven and bake the bread for a further 10–15 minutes to firm up the outside.

Transfer the loaf to a cooling rack and allow to cool.

♥ *Brazil nuts are an excellent source of the B-complex group of vitamins, which help promote healthy hair and skin. They also contain exceptionally high levels of selenium, which is essential for a healthy immune system.*

Italian Besan Bread Sticks

⟵─────────────────⟶

Serves 4

This flour seems to have the widest variety of alternative names in the world! Besan flour, garbanzo flour, chickpea flour, gram flour... it's all essentially the same thing: a pulse flour made from ground chickpeas, so it's gluten-free. It's really popular in India where it's used to make everything from breads to bhajis and even desserts, but it's also used in Spanish tortillas and Italian breads.
These Italian breadsticks are a little like polenta in texture. They're really easy to make and require hardly any additional ingredients, just a little patience while the batter rests. I love to serve them with pesto (see page 98) and olive tapenade dips.

200g gram flour
200ml water
1 free-range egg
1 tablespoon Italian seasoning
3 tablespoons olive oil
Salt and pepper

Tip the flour into a mixing bowl. Add the water and whisk until smooth. Crack in the egg and whisk again. Stir in the Italian seasoning and salt and pepper to taste.

Leave the mixture on the worktop for a couple of hours. Gently skim off any froth that forms on the surface of the mixture with a slotted spoon.

Preheat the oven to 220°C/fan 200°C/gas mark 7. Pour the olive oil into a shallow baking tray and pop into the oven until it's hot.

Remove the tray and carefully pour in the batter. Return the tray to the oven and bake for 15–20 minutes, just until the edges of the bread begin to brown.

Remove the bread from the tray and cut into long sticks. Serve while warm.

♥ *Gram flour is higher in protein and folate than regular wheat flour. It also delivers a boost of iron, magnesium and phosphorus.*

Stuffed Savoury Chickpea Wraps

Makes 4

These simple, vegan, gluten-free, dairy-free, spiced breads make the perfect accompaniment to curry. With the addition of mixed beans and guacamole to create savoury wraps, they offer a wonderfully filling alternative to sandwiches and are a meal in themselves. It's well worth keeping a bag of gram flour in your store cupboard: made from chickpeas, it has a nutty flavour and is a great source of protein.

200g gram flour
200ml water
½ teaspoon ground turmeric
½ teaspoon ground cumin
½ teaspoon garam masala
½ teaspoon garlic powder
Melted coconut oil, for frying
Salt and pepper

TO SERVE
400g can mixed beans in water,
    drained and rinsed
Guacamole (see page 100)
Handful of fresh coriander

Combine the flour, water, spices and some seasoning in a bowl. Whisk until smooth.

Leave the batter to rest for 5 minutes.

Heat a heavy-based pan over a medium heat and add a teaspoon of coconut oil.

When the oil is hot, turn the heat down and ladle a spoonful of batter into the pan, gently tilting in all directions to thin out the mixture evenly.

Cook for 4–6 minutes or until you can lift the edges with a fish slice and the underside has turned golden brown. Flip and cook for a further couple of minutes. Lift on to a plate and cover with a clean tea towel to keep warm. Repeat the process with the remaining batter, using more coconut oil as needed.

Serve topped with mixed beans, guacamole and fresh coriander.

♥ *Chickpeas are an excellent natural source of zinc and copper, two minerals that are essential for the development and function of the immune cells.*

Sesame-seed Rice Snaps

⟵──────────────────⟶

Serves 4

These delicious, golden, sesame-seed snaps make a wonderful alternative to wheat crackers. They're herby and crisp, just perfect for serving with dips and nut butters.

150g white rice flour
1 teaspoon garlic powder
½ teaspoon salt
1 teaspoon dried thyme
1 teaspoon dried rosemary
3 tablespoons extra-virgin olive oil
100ml water
1 tablespoon sesame oil, for
   greasing
30g sesame seeds

Preheat the oven to 200°C/fan 180°C/gas mark 6.

Put the flour, garlic powder, salt and herbs in a bowl and mix well with a fork. Pour in the olive oil and mix through. Now pour in the water a little at a time and use a fork to continue combining the ingredients. You want the mixture to come together to form a kneadable dough.

Grease two sheets of baking paper with the sesame oil. Place the dough ball in the centre of one sheet and roll out the dough with a rolling pin until it's about 0.5 centimetre thick.

Liberally sprinkle the sesame seeds evenly over the dough. Lay the second sheet of greased baking paper on top of the dough, oiled-side down. Use the rolling pin to apply pressure evenly by gently rolling over the greaseproof paper, allowing the sesame seeds to be pressed into the dough. Remove the paper to reveal the dough, which should now be just a couple of millimetres thick.

Bake in the oven for 10–15 minutes until toasted and golden brown.

Allow to cool and break apart to serve with dips or nut butters.

♥ *Sesame seeds are an excellent source of copper, a very good source of manganese, and are full of magnesium, zinc and selenium, all of which promote glowing skin.*

MAINS

Risotto Primavera

⟵——————————⟶

Serves 4

This is a classic spring vegetable risotto, beautiful and vibrant. Arborio rice, widely available in supermarkets, is grown in northern Italy, and it's the best variety to use for this risotto dish. The key to make this easy on yourself is to have all your ingredients ready to add as you go. Make sure you don't overcook the dish; you want the rice to remain tender and the veg to be bright green and crunchy.

2 tablespoons olive oil
4 medium shallots, finely chopped
1 small leek, finely sliced
1 garlic clove, crushed
350g arborio risotto rice
1.5 litres Homemade Vegetable
  Stock (see page 74)
100g frozen peas
100g frozen broad beans
250g fresh asparagus, chopped
Zest and juice of ½ lemon
Small handful of chopped parsley
Small handful of chopped mint
  leaves
Salt and pepper
Plant-powered 'Parmesan', to serve
  (see page 112; optional)

Heat the olive oil in a large saucepan and sauté the shallots and leek for 5–7 minutes, until soft. Add the garlic and rice and cook, stirring, for 2 minutes, until the rice turns translucent at the edges.

Warm the stock in a separate saucepan and add a ladleful to the rice. Cook gently, stirring frequently, until the stock has been absorbed. Then repeat with another ladleful. Continue to add hot stock and stir in this way for 20–25 minutes, until the rice is almost tender and all the stock has been added.

Add the peas, broad beans and asparagus and cook for a further 5–10 minutes. By now the rice should be tender and cooked through.

Remove from the heat, stir in the lemon zest and juice and the fresh herbs. Season with salt and pepper and serve, adding some 'Parmesan' if you wish.

♥ *Asparagus, being packed with antioxidants, is one of the best vegetables for neutralising cell-damaging free radicals, which in turn may help slow the ageing process.*

Garden Pea Frittata

⟵————————————————————⟶

Serves 2

Frittatas make the perfect lazy brunch. They're also a brilliant way of using up any roast vegetables left over from Sunday lunch, but you can throw pretty much any veg into the mix. I make this with frozen peas and sweet potatoes, but adding some cooked sweetcorn and carrots works particularly well too. If you haven't got any leftovers, it's just as easy to make this recipe from scratch using frozen veg and a few chestnut mushrooms.

1 small sweet potato (or leftover roasted sweet potato, sliced)
2 tablespoons melted coconut oil
1 red onion, thinly sliced
4 chestnut mushrooms, sliced
100g frozen peas
4 large free-range eggs
1 teaspoon dried thyme
1 teaspoon dried rosemary
Juice of ½ lemon
Salt and pepper

TO SERVE
Rocket, spinach and watercress
Handful of parsley, finely chopped
Lemon wedges
2 teaspoons wholegrain mustard (optional)

If you don't have any leftover roast sweet potato, peel and thickly slice a raw sweet potato and pop the slices into a pan of boiling water for 7–10 minutes until the slices begin to soften. Drain and set aside.

Preheat the grill to medium-high.

Heat the coconut oil in a large, non-stick frying pan over a medium heat. Add the red onion and sliced sweet potato, and gently fry for 5 minutes. Add the mushrooms and peas and cook for a further 2 minutes.

Whisk together the eggs, add the dried thyme and rosemary, and season with salt and pepper. Pour the beaten eggs into the frying pan and mix gently but quickly with the veg. Lower the heat and continue to cook for 6–8 minutes. Once the top side has almost set, pop under the grill for 2–3 minutes or until firm and golden. You may need to protect the handle of the pan by covering it with foil if it is not heatproof.

Slide the frittata out of the pan, cut in two and serve each portion with fresh salad leaves, parsley, a drizzle of lemon juice and some wholegrain mustard if you wish.

♥ *The skin-friendly nutrients present in garden peas include vitamins B6 and C and folate. Frozen peas retain these nutrients, which work to combat inflammation and damage by free radicals to help ensure your skin doesn't lose its collagen and elastin proteins, thereby keeping it smooth and supple.*

Sweet Potato Italian 'Cheese' Crust

⟵—————————————⟶

Makes 2 bases

I've played with lots of different pizza base recipes using everything from cauliflower to quinoa. There are so many surprisingly delicious alternatives to wheat flour, all of which work far better than you would expect! The thing I love about this combination – its simplicity aside – is its wonderful, cheesy herb flavour and the soft, doughy texture. There's nothing more disappointing than a tasteless, cardboard-like, bland pizza base: fortunately this is just the opposite!

300g sweet potato

3 tablespoons nutritional yeast

150g gluten-free flour

½ teaspoon baking powder

2 teaspoons dried oregano

Squeeze of lemon juice

Pinch of salt

Toppings of your choice, such as olives, artichoke, fresh rocket, caramelised red onion, pineapple chunks

Preheat the oven to 180°C/fan 160°C/gas mark 4.

Cut the sweet potato in half and bake in the oven for 45 minutes. Allow to cool, scoop out the flesh and discard the skin.

Put the sweet potato flesh into a food processor along with the nutritional yeast, 120g of the flour, the baking powder, oregano, squeeze of lemon juice and salt and blitz. The mixture should begin to form a dough; gradually add more flour until it forms a complete dough ball.

Flour your worktop with the remaining flour and split the dough in two. Use a rolling pin to roll the dough into two round, flat bases, about 0.5 centimetre thick.

Pop the pizza bases into the oven on a preheated pizza stone or flat baking tray and bake for 20–30 minutes until the edges begin to crisp a little.

Remove the crusts from the oven, add the desired toppings and return to the oven for 5 minutes. Serve warm.

♥ *Oregano is rich in vitamins A and C, hence it acts as a protective scavenger against free radicals that play a role in ageing and various skin diseases.*

Layered Courgette Lasagne

← →

Serves 6–8

When I gave up tomatoes, dairy and gluten I honestly did not think I'd ever be eating lasagne again. Since tomatoes, cheese sauce and pasta sheets are the primary ingredients of regular lasagne I wasn't sure how an alternative would be possible. Well, it is, using my skin-friendly sauces and courgettes in place of pasta sheets, which give it a lovely, fresh, light flavour. Thinly sliced courgette doesn't need too long in the oven, so I prefer to prepare the spinach and mushrooms in advance and bake the lasagne just long enough to warm everything through and soften the courgette.

1 tablespoon olive oil

300g chestnut mushrooms, chopped

2 garlic cloves, crushed

200g spinach

Pinch of grated nutmeg

200ml Cheese-less Cheese Sauce (see page 96)

3 courgettes

200ml Tomato-less Sauce (see page 94)

Plant-powered Parmesan (see page 112), for sprinkling

Salt and pepper

Basil leaves, to serve

Preheat the oven to 160°C/fan 140°C/gas mark 3.

Heat the olive oil in a frying pan, add the chopped mushrooms, garlic and a little salt and sauté until the mushrooms begin to soften.

Bring a pan of water to the boil, then lower the heat to a simmer. Add the spinach and cook for 2–4 minutes until it's just wilted. Drain thoroughly and season with a pinch of nutmeg.

Put half the mushrooms in a ceramic lasagne dish (approx. 23cm square) and top with a half the Cheese-less Sauce.

Thinly slice the courgettes lengthways and use 6 to 8 long strips exactly as you would lasagne sheets to form a layer over the mushrooms and sauce.

Next layer the spinach and half the Tomato-less Sauce.

Add a second layer of courgette slices and spoon over the remaining Tomato-less Sauce. Layer the rest of the mushrooms on top, followed by a final layer of Cheese-less Cheese Sauce, and sprinkle over some 'Parmesan'.

Place in the oven and bake for 15–20 minutes until the lasagne begins to bubble.

Season with black pepper and serve scattered with basil leaves.

♥ *Courgette has a high water content which hydrates the skin. Water flushes out toxins from your system and helps restore moisture. Courgette is also is a good source of vitamins A and C, both powerful antioxidants that help to fight harmful free radicals.*

Sweet Potato Gnocchi

Serves 2

I do adore pasta. Quick to cook, filling and easy to prepare. Wheat pasta was always my go-to simple dinner. I loved it; my body hated it! I'd eat a giant bowl of the stuff and feel awful afterwards. Those of us with gluten intolerance are highly affected by gluten. It leads to what is known as 'leaky gut', causing food particles to float around the body where they don't belong and in turn setting off problematic immune responses.

So what's the solution? Something that's gluten free, just as quick and easy to make and equally filling. Sweet potato gnocchi... and it's delicious! What's more, these gorgeous little potato pasta dumplings freeze brilliantly. So make lots, pop them into a freezer bag and you've got a quick-cook option for those evenings when you just don't feel like preparing fresh food. They cook straight from frozen, so you don't even have to remember to defrost.

300g sweet potato
150g rice flour, plus extra
   for dusting
1 teaspoon dried sage
1 teaspoon dried rosemary
Pinch or two of salt

TO SERVE
Lightly cooked vegetables, pesto
   or pasta sauce and sage or
   thyme leaves

Preheat the oven to 160°C/fan 140°C/gas mark 3.

Cut the sweet potato in half and bake in the oven for 45 minutes until soft. Allow to cool, scoop out the flesh and discard the skin.

Using the dough blade attachment in your food processor, blitz the baked sweet potato and the rest of the ingredients together to form a smooth, soft dough – you may need to add a little more rice flour depending on the moisture content of your sweet potato. (If you don't have a food processor, use a masher to mash the potato until soft and smooth, then stir in the flour with a wooden spoon until you're able to knead the dough with your hands.)

Roll the dough between your hands to create a long sausage. Place on a lightly floured surface and cut into 1cm pieces.

Use the back of a fork to press the gnocchi pieces lightly into discs. Creating little grooves with the back of a fork helps pesto or sauce stick to the gnocchi better.

Bring a pan of water to the boil and lower the heat to allow it to simmer. Add the gnocchi to the pan. They will sink at first but float when they are ready. They should take 3–4 minutes to cook. Remove from the pan using a slotted spoon. Serve with fresh veg, your favourite pesto or pasta sauce and fresh sage or thyme leaves.

♥ *Its high levels of beta-carotene make sweet potato a skin superfood. Beta-carotene is an antioxidant that is converted to vitamin A inside the body. It helps repair skin tissue and protects against the sun's harsh rays.*

Root Pasta *with* Pesto *and* Artichoke Hearts

⟵──────────────────────⟶

Serves 2

I've been lucky enough to spend a little time in Croatia. If you've never been and you get the opportunity to go, you really should – it's absolutely beautiful. I had dinner at a tiny vegetarian restaurant in Dubrovnik, which I'll never forget because I hadn't eaten pasta in months and they served sweet potato spaghetti. It was the first time I'd tried pasta made from something other than wheat flour and it tasted divine. Here I've used parsnip, fresh Brazil nut pesto and artichoke hearts in my recipe to create a wonderfully filling, slightly sweet, subtle combination of flavours.

1 sweet potato

2 parsnips

3 tablespoons Brazil Nut Pesto (see page 98)

258g jar artichoke hearts in oil, drained and halved if large

Juice of ½ lemon

Salt and pepper

Basil, to serve (optional)

Use a spiraliser to create sweet potato and parsnip spirals.

Bring a pan of water to the boil, then turn off the heat and gently lower your raw root pasta spirals into the water: they literally need a minute or two in hot water. You don't want them overdone and soggy as they will fall apart, so keep an eye on them to ensure they retain a crunchy texture.

Drain the spirals and gently spin the root pasta in a salad spinner to remove any excess water.

Stir the pesto through the pasta. Carefully stir through the artichoke hearts and squeeze the lemon juice over the dish. Season to taste – I like to add some basil and a twist of black pepper.

♥ *Artichoke extract is frequently used in creams and cosmetics because of its high antioxidant content. Included as part of a healthy diet, artichoke can also improve digestion, lower cholesterol and aid the body's natural immune system.*

Beet Burgers

⟵⟶

Makes 8

These delicious beet burgers were inspired by a vegan black pudding served up at my favourite vegetarian restaurant, Greens, in Manchester. I love the dish so much I asked what it's made with: turns out the key ingredient is beetroot. I figured if it's good enough for black pudding, it's good enough to make a burger... and sure enough it works brilliantly.

2 tablespoons olive oil
1 red onion, chopped
2 celery sticks, chopped
100g quinoa
2 raw beetroot
1 carrot
1 garlic clove, crushed
Juice of ½ lemon
400g can black beans
1 free-range egg
Handful of chopped chives
2 teaspoons dried sage
1 teaspoon dried oregano
1 teaspoon garlic powder
50g sunflower seeds

Heat the olive oil in a frying pan over a medium heat and fry the red onion and celery for 10 minutes to soften.

Put 250ml water in a saucepan and bring to the boil. Add the quinoa and simmer for 15–20 minutes until soft.

Meanwhile, preheat the oven to 170°C/fan 150°C/gas mark 3 and grease a baking tray.

If you have a juicer, juice the beetroot and carrot. Retrieve the pulp from your juicer bucket and add it to your food processor. You won't need the juice for this recipe but it tastes great with some added apple and ginger. If you don't have a juicer, use a grater instead and squeeze the excess moisture from the grated veg before adding them to the food processor.

Add the softened celery and onion, the garlic, lemon juice, cooked quinoa, black beans, egg, herbs, garlic powder and seeds to the food processor bowl. Blitz on pulse – you want to keep some texture and firmness in the mix: it should be soft, sticky and easy to form into little patties.

Use your hands to make 8 patties, place on the prepared baking tray and bake in the oven for 20 minutes. Carefully flip and bake in the oven for a further 10–20 minutes.

I love serving these burgers on a bed of salad topped with Guacamole (see page 100) or sandwiched in a gluten-free bun.

♥ *Beetroot contains lots of nitrate, which has been shown to lower blood pressure and may help to fight heart disease. Beets were particularly popular in Roman times when they were used to treat fever, constipation, skin problems and even used as an aphrodisiac.*

Sweet Potato Shepherd's Pie

Serves 6–8

This is my absolute favourite winter dish. Hearty, filling, comforting and all-round seriously satisfying. It's really simple to make and can even be frozen, so that you've always got a nutritious meal handy on those cold, winter nights.

200g dried red lentils

2 tablespoons olive oil

2 red onions, finely chopped

1 small leek, finely chopped

2 garlic cloves, crushed

2 large carrots, diced

2 celery sticks, chopped

200g frozen peas

150g mushrooms, roughly chopped

1 teaspoon dried rosemary

1 teaspoon dried thyme

Zest of 1 lemon

FOR THE TOPPING

2 large sweet potatoes, cut into chunks

3 tablespoons coconut oil

100ml almond milk

Bring a pan of water to the boil, lower the heat to a simmer, add the lentils and simmer for 10 minutes until they just begin to soften. Drain and set aside.

Heat the olive oil in a pan, add the onions, leek and garlic and sauté for 5–7 minutes until they begin to soften. Add the diced carrots, celery and peas and continue to cook over a low heat for 10–15 minutes until soft.

Add the mushrooms and cook for a further 5 minutes. Stir in the herbs and lemon zest, then add the cooked lentils. Spoon the mixture into a casserole.

Preheat the oven to 190°C/fan 170°C/gas mark 5.

Bring a pan of water to the boil and simmer the sweet potatoes for 15 minutes until soft.

Remove from the heat, drain and add the coconut oil to the warm pan – it will quickly melt. Add the almond milk and mash the sweet potato until it's soft and creamy.

Spoon the sweet potato mash evenly over the vegetables in the casserole and bake in the oven for 25–30 minutes until the top begins to turn golden brown.

♥ *Lentils are a fantastic source of iron and protein, essential for strong, healthy skin and hair. They're brilliant at aiding digestion and their anti-inflammatory properties will keep your blood sugar levels in check.*

Sunday Nut Loaf

← →

Serves 4

I love the simplicity of this recipe. Nut roast is, of course, the perfect vegetarian accompaniment to Sunday dinner. When you've got enough to worry about with your roast potatoes and honeyed parsnips, the last thing you need is the added hassle of a complicated nut loaf recipe. This version is so simple and can even be made in advance and stored in the fridge until you're ready to roast it. Whole cooked chestnuts are now commonly available in most delis and big supermarkets. They usually come peeled and vacuum packed to seal in their delicious, sweet flavour. They are ready to use and I find them perfect for adding to both sweet and savoury dishes.

1 tablespoon olive oil, plus extra
    for greasing
1 large onion, finely chopped
1 small leek, finely chopped
1 garlic clove
1 free-range egg
180g whole cooked, peeled and
    ready-to-use chestnuts
150g mixed nuts (walnuts, pecans,
    hazelnuts and Brazil nuts),
    roughly chopped
200g chestnut mushrooms
1 teaspoon dried thyme
1 teaspoon dried sage
1 teaspoon dried rosemary
Salt and pepper

Preheat the oven to 180°C/fan 160°C/gas mark 4. Grease a sheet of baking paper with olive oil and use it to line a 900g loaf tin.

Heat the olive oil in a saucepan and gently sauté the onion, leek and garlic for about 10 minutes until soft. Set aside to cool.

Add the onion mixture to a food processor along with all the other ingredients and season with salt and pepper.

Use the pulse button to combine everything coarsely. The softness of the chestnuts and the egg should bind it all nicely. I like my nut loaf to have texture, so be careful not to over-blitz.

Spoon the nut loaf mix into the lined loaf tin and compress firmly. Cover with foil.

Bake in the oven for 20 minutes. Remove from the oven and place a baking tray over the loaf tin. Carefully invert the loaf on to the tray and peel away the baking paper. Return to the oven for 10–15 minutes to crisp the outside.

Serve warm, cut in slices.

♥ *Chestnuts are highly alkaline. They are a great source of vitamins B1, B2 and B6 and folic acid, which help produce red blood cells, promote healthy skin and enhance brain function.*

Lentil *and* Mushroom 'Meatballs'

←—————————————————→

Makes 12–16 (Serves 4)

Spaghetti topped with meatballs has got to be one of my favourite comfort-food dishes. Meatballs remind me of my childhood. I played hockey at school and my mum would always feed my sister and me pasta the night before a competition game. The theory was to load me up with lots of carbs for energy. I'm not entirely sure how well this theory worked – I should perhaps have been eating a carb-heavy breakfast, instead of going to bed on a belly full of pasta, but I absolutely loved spaghetti and meatballs so I was never going to complain!

These meatless balls don't, of course, actually taste like meat; I honestly think they taste better! The combination of herbs gives them a lovely Italian flavour, they're really filling and they work brilliantly served on top of rice spaghetti or with a fresh green salad.

100g dried red lentils

100g chestnut mushrooms

70g gluten-free rolled oats

1 tablespoon nutritional yeast

1 teaspoon Vegemite or Marmite

1 teaspoon Dijon mustard

Handful of parsley

1 teaspoon dried oregano

1 teaspoon dried thyme

1 tablespoon melted coconut oil

1 small red onion

2 garlic cloves, chopped

Juice of ½ lemon

100g gluten-free or rice flour, plus extra for dusting

1 tablespoon olive oil, for greasing

Salt and pepper

Preheat the oven to 180°C/fan 160°C/gas mark 4.

Bring a pan of water to the boil. Add the lentils and simmer for 10 minutes – they need to be a little undercooked. Drain and set aside to cool.

Put all the remaining ingredients, except for the flour and olive oil, in a food processor. Add the cooled lentils and pulse until a sticky dough forms. Season with salt and pepper.

Scoop the mixture into a bowl and begin to stir in the flour, a little at a time, until it forms a firm, workable dough.

Flour your worktop, break off a small palmful of the mixture and roll into a ball. Repeat until you have 12 to 16 balls.

Grease a baking tray and place the lentil balls on to it. Bake in the oven for 15 minutes, then remove the tray and give the balls a little shake. Return to the oven for a further 10–15 minutes to ensure they're lightly browned all over.

♥ *Selenium is found in large quantities in mushrooms, and can benefit bone health as well as strengthening our teeth, hair and nails. Selenium is also really good for skin and, like Brazil nuts, mushrooms are a brilliant vegetarian source of this essential mineral.*

Kale *and* Cauli Buddha Bowl

⟵─────────────────⟶

Makes 4 bowls

If you've never come across Buddha bowls before, I guarantee you will fall in love with them. So-called because the bowl has a rounded 'belly' appearance on the top, perfect for cramming full of your favourite combinations of grains, legumes and vegetables to make a deliciously filling winter dish.
I first came across these Buddha bowls being served at a little French hippy market. They're basically super filling bowls of plant-based goodness, which is precisely what this recipe is. Feel free to experiment with the ingredients. A combination of root vegetables, green leaves and a tasty sauce to serve is a good place to start.

1 sweet potato, cut into 8 wedges
½ head of cauliflower, outer green
 leaves removed, broken into
 florets
2 tablespoons olive oil
½ red onion, finely sliced
2 large handfuls of kale, thick
 stems removed
1 tablespoon coconut oil
400g can chickpeas, drained
 and rinsed
1 teaspoon ground cumin
½ teaspoon garam masala
½ teaspoon ground turmeric
Pinch of ground cinnamon
Salt and pepper

**FOR THE MAPLE TAHINI
 DRESSING**
50g tahini
1 tablespoon maple syrup
Juice of 1 lime

TO SERVE
1 teaspoon sesame seeds
Handful of fresh coriander

Preheat the oven to 200°C/fan 180°C/gas mark 6.

Toss the sweet potato wedges and cauliflower florets in olive oil and spread out evenly in a roasting tin. Season with salt and pepper and roast in the oven for 10 minutes.

Remove from the oven and shake the tin to ensure the veg roasts evenly, then roast for a further 5 minutes.

Turn the oven down to 160°C/fan 140°C/gas mark 3. Add the onion and kale to the roasting tin with a touch more oil and season again with a pinch of salt and pepper. Roast for a further 10 minutes, watching to ensure the kale doesn't char, then remove the tin and set aside.

Heat the coconut oil in a heavy-based frying pan. Once it is hot, add the chickpeas and toss in the spices, stirring frequently to coat the chickpeas well. Once the chickpeas are browned and fragrant, remove from the heat and set aside.

Finally combine the dressing ingredients in a bowl and whisk well to combine. You may need to add a little warm water or extra lime juice to make a pourable sauce.

Fill four bowls equally with the roast veg, kale leaves and sautéed chickpeas. Drizzle the dressing over the Buddha bowls and sprinkle with sesame seeds and fresh coriander leaves to serve.

♥ *Cauliflower contains lots of antioxidants that act as an anti-inflammatory agent and help to build a healthy immune system.*

Falafel Balls *with* Coyo Dip

Makes 8–10

I love serving these falafels warm alongside a cool yogurt dip. Coconut yogurt is now available from most health-food and organic stores. With a velvety-smooth texture and the same lovely tang of dairy yogurt, it's wonderfully aromatic, with a unique, subtle sweetness that the flavour of coconut brings. If you have a little patience and a yogurt maker, you can make your own using coconut milk and a good probiotic.

400g can chickpeas, drained and
   rinsed
400g can kidney beans, drained
   and rinsed
2 tablespoons gram flour
1 teaspoon ground cumin
1 teaspoon ground coriander
2 tablespoons garam masala
Handful of fresh coriander
Handful of parsley
1 red onion, roughly chopped
1 garlic clove
Juice of ½ lemon
2 tablespoons coconut oil
Pinch of salt

FOR THE COYO DIP
100g coconut yogurt
Handful of mint
Handful of parsley
1 tablespoon manuka honey
Juice of 1 lime
Pinch of salt

First make the dip. Put the yogurt into a bowl. Strip the mint leaves from their stalks and finely chop the leaves along with the parsley. Stir into the yogurt with the honey, a pinch of salt and the lime juice. Keep in the fridge until ready to serve.

Put the chickpeas and kidney beans in a food processor along with the flour, spices, herbs, onion and garlic. Squeeze in the lemon juice and add a pinch of salt. Blitz until smooth, scraping down the sides of the processor as you go. You may need to add a drop of water to ensure everything blends smoothly together.

Scoop out the mixture and mould into 8 or 10 small falafel balls. Flatten each ball a little.

Heat the oil in a frying pan and use a fish slice to place the falafels carefully into the pan. (Work in batches if need be.) Fry over a medium heat for 5–10 minutes on each side until golden brown.

Serve warm on a bed of salad with the dip.

♥ *Chickpeas are rich in iron, phosphorus, manganese, calcium and other minerals that are essential for a healthy digestive system and glowing skin.*

Curried Chickpeas *with* Baby Spinach

←——————————→

Serves 4

This recipe works perfectly as a side dish or filling meal in itself. The curry is super easy to make and ready in only 20 minutes.

1 tablespoon olive oil
1 medium onion, chopped
2 garlic cloves, crushed
1 teaspoon ground cumin
1 teaspoon garam masala
400g can chickpeas, drained and rinsed
100g raisins
400g can coconut milk
200g fresh or frozen leaf spinach
Juice of ½ lemon
Salt and pepper
Fresh coriander, to serve

Heat the olive oil in a large, heavy-based saucepan over a medium heat and add the onion. Cook, stirring, for about 5 minutes or until tender.

Add the garlic, cumin, garam masala and a little salt and pepper. Continue to cook, stirring, for a minute or two, until fragrant.

Add the chickpeas, raisins and coconut milk. Bring to a simmer, then cover, reduce the heat and simmer for 10 minutes.

Stir in the fresh or frozen spinach, a handful at a time, until each addition has wilted.

Add the lemon juice, with salt and pepper to taste, and simmer, uncovered, stirring often, for 5 minutes.

Serve with fresh coriander.

♥ *Spinach is packed with nutrients needed for healthy skin cells. It is a great source of vitamin K, which is needed to help the blood clot and to strengthen blood-vessel walls.*

Red Lentil Dhal

←——————————→

Serves 2

Hearty, filling dishes like this one are wonderful during the cold autumn/winter months. The combination of spices in this dhal creates a deliciously fragrant dish and makes the kitchen smell amazing.

200g dried red lentils, well rinsed
Chunk of ginger, sliced
2 bay leaves
1 cinnamon stick
2 tablespoons coconut oil
2 teaspoons cumin seeds
1 large onion, finely chopped
2 garlic cloves, crushed
2 teaspoons ground turmeric
1 teaspoon ground coriander
½ teaspoon garam marsala
Juice of 1 lemon
Salt and pepper
Handful of fresh coriander leaves, to serve

Put the lentils, ginger, bay leaves and cinnamon stick in a saucepan with 500ml cold water. Bring to the boil, lower the heat to medium and simmer, stirring occasionally, for 10–15 minutes. Discard the spices. Most of the water should be absorbed, but if not, carefully drain the lentils and set aside.

Heat the coconut oil in a large frying pan over a medium-high heat. Fry the cumin seeds until toasted and fragrant. Add the onion and sauté for 5 minutes. Stir in the garlic and spices and cook for a further minute until fragrant. Stir in the lemon juice and season with salt and pepper to taste. Add the lentils to the pan and mix well. Cook for a further 3 minutes, stirring constantly. Serve with fresh coriander.

♥ *Turmeric is full of curcumin, which displays anti-inflammatory properties and is also a fantastic immune-system regulator, calming an over-active and boosting an under-active immune system.*

Perfect Pad Thai

⟷

Serves 2

I ate pad Thai every single day when I was backpacking around Thailand. It rarely tastes identical because all restaurants and street vendors add their own unique ingredient twist to this quick and healthy meal. I watched the street chefs with intrigue to see how they cooked up the perfect pad Thai with such limited space at the side of a busy road. I wanted to create this vegetarian version using simple ingredients and an easy method of cooking to make it super quick to throw together.

1 tablespoon coconut oil

2 carrots, grated

Chunk of ginger, grated

4 spring onions, finely chopped

1 garlic clove, crushed

150g beansprouts

Juice of 1 lime

2 servings dried flat pad Thai rice noodles

1 heaped tablespoon almond butter

1 tablespoon manuka honey

1 tablespoon tamari (gluten-free soy sauce)

2 free-range eggs

TO SERVE

Handful of fresh coriander

10 almonds, crushed

Lime wedges

Heat the coconut oil in a wok, then lower the heat.

Add the carrots, ginger and spring onions, together with the garlic, beansprouts and lime juice. Stir continuously, keeping the heat low.

Meanwhile, bring a medium pan of water to the boil. Once the water is bubbling, add the rice noodles and lower the heat. Simmer for 5–10 minutes until the noodles are just softening – you want them a little on the firm side as they will continue to cook in the wok. Remove from the heat and drain.

Stir the almond butter, honey and tamari through the ingredients in the wok, then add the drained noodles.

Beat the eggs together, pour over the veg and noodles and mix through.

Once the egg has cooked, serve in bowls topped with some fresh coriander, crushed almonds and a squeeze of lime.

Traditionally Thai street vendors sprinkle peanuts over pad Thai, but I use almonds as they are more alkaline and taste just as delicious.

♥ *Omega-3 fatty acids help regulate blood sugar, reduce blood pressure and body fat, maintain muscle mass, support the immune system, boost energy levels and improve skin radiance. The body cannot make these essential fatty acids, but almonds and almond butter are a fantastic dietary source.*

Roast Squash *and* Pineapple Massaman Curry

Serves 4

I love the sweet, tangy flavours in this curry. The combination of delicious spices, coconut, pineapple and tamarind creates a wonderfully creamy, savoury-sweet Thai taste. It's fantastic served with fresh coriander and accompanied by a bowl of steamed, fragrant brown rice.

1 butternut squash
1 tablespoon olive oil
250g pineapple chunks (from a can) or $^1/_3$ fresh pineapple, skinned and cut into chunks
1 tablespoon coconut oil
1 garlic clove, crushed
1 white onion, chopped
2 x 400ml cans of coconut milk
1 tablespoon tamarind paste
2 star anise
1 teaspoon ground turmeric
1 teaspoon ground coriander
1 teaspoon ground cardamon
Pinch of ground cloves
Pinch of grated nutmeg
Pinch of ground cinnamon
1 tablespoon tamari (gluten-free soy sauce)
1 tablespoon manuka honey
4 spring onions, chopped
100g green beans, trimmed
50g cashew nuts
Juice of 1 lime
Handful of coriander leaves, to garnish
Steamed brown rice, to serve

Preheat the oven to 180°C/fan 160°C/ gas mark 4.

Slice the squash in half and scoop out the seeds. Cut the flesh into rough chunks and add to a large roasting tray with a drizzle of olive oil. Roast in the oven for approximately 30 minutes.

Add the pineapple chunks to the roasting tray and turn up the oven to 220°C/fan 200°C/ gas mark 7. Roast for a further 10 minutes until lightly browned and tender. Meanwhile, heat the coconut oil in a large saucepan. Fry the garlic and onion for 5 minutes until softened. Add the coconut milk and stir in the tamarind paste, spices, tamari and honey. Simmer for 10 minutes until the spices and tamarind are fully absorbed.

Add the roast squash and pineapple, the green beans, spring onions, cashews and half the lime juice to the pan and simmer for a further 5–10 minutes.

Serve warm, sprinkled with fresh coriander leaves and the remaining lime juice, alongside a bowl of steamed brown rice.

♥ *The spices in this dish possess incredible healing potential. Cardamom has immense antioxidant properties and helps to remove toxins from the body; turmeric holds fantastic immune-regulating benefits; whilst coriander helps to reduce inflammation and calm the skin.*

DESSERTS
and SWEETS

Cranberry Cookies

⟷

Makes 15–20

These tasty cranberry biscuits are so easy to bake. The batter can be thrown together in a food processor, but if you don't have one, you can still make them by hand in a regular mixing bowl. I love the tartness of the dried cranberries and the slightly soft, chewy cookie centre. If you prefer your biscuits crunchy, simply pop them in the fridge to cool once they're baked.

125ml melted coconut oil

1 free-range egg

3 tablespoons manuka honey

½ teaspoon vanilla extract

100g rice flour

100g almond flour

50g gluten-free rolled oats

25g desiccated coconut

Pinch of bicarbonate of soda

Pinch of ground cinnamon

75g dried cranberries (try to find ones sweetened with fruit juice as opposed to sugar)

Pinch of salt

Preheat the oven to 180°C/fan 160°C/gas mark 4. Line two baking sheets with greaseproof paper.

Put the coconut oil, egg, honey and vanilla extract in your food processor and blitz together. Scrape down the sides.

In a mixing bowl, combine the rice and almond flours, the oats, coconut, bicarbonate of soda, cinnamon and a pinch of salt and stir to combine. Add half the dry mixture to the wet ingredients in the food processor and blitz. Scrape down the sides, then add the remaining dry mixture. Continue to process until the dough is well combined.

Stir in the cranberries, ensuring they are evenly dispersed throughout the dough.

Spoon tablespoon-sized scoops of cookie dough on to the prepared baking sheets about 5cm apart. Bake in the oven for 10–12 minutes until just golden brown.

These cookies will be very soft when you first take them out of the oven but will firm up once they're cool. Store in an airtight container for up to 1 week.

♥ *The antioxidants present in cranberries can be helpful in reducing skin disorders, keeping skin looking younger and more radiant.*

Cherry Chocolate Bark

←——————————————————————→

Makes 10 large chunks

If you were ever in any doubt as to how easy it is to make your own, healthy alternative to shop-bought chocolate, this is as simple as it gets. If you're transitioning away from a diet high in refined sugar, you may need to add a little more honey to the recipe to begin with. Once your tastebuds adapt, you'll find you crave sugary foods less and less, and bitter, dark chocolate will begin to taste sweeter.

100ml coconut oil
3 tablespoons manuka honey
4 tablespoons raw cacao powder
100g dried cherries
100g chopped nuts

Simply melt the coconut oil in a saucepan over a gentle heat, add the honey and stir until it melts.

Add the cacao powder and stir well until the mixture is perfectly smooth. Allow to cool.

Add 80g of the dried cherries and 80g of the chopped nuts to the pan. Mix well.

Pour the mixture into a shallow, silicone baking tray approx. 15cm square. A silicone tray makes it much easier to freeze and remove the chocolate once set.

Sprinkle the remaining cherries and nuts on top and allow to set in the freezer for a couple of hours.

Store in the freezer and break off chunks to serve.

♥ *Cherries contain 20 types of skin-boosting antioxidants. Antioxidants help in fighting wrinkles and delay the ageing process. Cherries are a great source of vitamins such as A, B, C and E – all of which are needed by the body to give you a healthy and glowing complexion.*

Nut Butter Popcorn

← →

Makes enough for 2

This is a foolproof recipe your kids are going to love! Not only does it taste delicious, but there's also something childishly fun about hearing those corn kernels pop in a pan. If you're a fan of savoury popcorn, simply shake a little salt over the popped kernels. I like a mixture of savoury and sweet. This nut butter version tastes amazing.
It's important to avoid pre-packaged, microwave popcorn, which is often full of butter, salt, glucose syrup and refined sugar. The chemicals in the packaging have also come under some suspicion as they may break down or destroy the healthy parts of the hull of the corn, severely decreasing its beneficial impact on protecting the body against free radicals.

3 tablespoons coconut oil
2 tablespoons almond butter
1 teaspoon maple syrup
100g popping corn
Pinch of salt

Gently heat 2 tablespoons of the coconut oil, the nut butter and maple syrup in a saucepan until everything is melted. Set aside to cool slightly.

In a separate pan, add the remaining coconut oil and gently warm until it melts.

Add the popping corn and put a lid on the pan. Wait... this is the fun part! It will take around 5 minutes of gentle heat to encourage the corn to begin popping.

Once all the corn has popped, transfer it to a big mixing bowl.

Stir in the still-warm nut butter caramel and ensure every piece is well coated. Add a pinch or two of salt and stir through evenly.

♥ *In addition to its role as a high-fibre food that helps promote gastrointestinal health, popcorn has been shown to contain more antioxidants than any other snack food. Studies have shown that whole grains such as popcorn contain as many antioxidants as fruits and vegetables, while in comparison, refined and processed grains contain very few.*

Coconana Nut Chunk Ice Cream

Makes 1 litre

I love ice cream – who doesn't! After quitting dairy I was determined to find a replacement which tasted equally sweet, creamy and delicious. This coconana ice cream is so ridiculously simple to create and makes perfect use of any overripe bananas lurking at the bottom of the fruit bowl.

FOR THE NUT FUDGE
2 tablespoons nut butter
1 tablespoon melted coconut oil
1 tablespoon maple syrup
75g pitted dates, chopped
Pinch of sea salt

FOR THE ICE CREAM
2 very ripe bananas
400ml cans coconut milk
2 teaspoons vanilla paste
2 teaspoons maple syrup (optional)

First make the fudge by whizzing together the nut butter, coconut oil, maple syrup, dates and salt in a food processor, using the pulse button. You're looking to combine everything but keep the mixture chunky.

Spoon the combined nut mixture on to a baking tray lined with baking paper. Flatten it down with the back of a spoon. Place in the freezer to set for at least an hour.

Meanwhile, blitz together the bananas, coconut milk and vanilla paste in the food processor or in a blender until beautifully smooth. You may need to add a teaspoon or so of maple syrup for additional sweetness, depending how ripe your bananas are.

Pour the coconana cream into your ice-cream maker and add three-quarters of the frozen nut fudge chunks (save the rest as a topping). Churn, following your ice-cream maker guidelines. Once your ice cream is ready, spoon it into a tub to freeze. (If you don't have an ice-cream maker, spoon into a tub and cover loosely with foil to help freeze. You can take this out after a couple of hours for a chilled, mousse-like ice cream, or freeze for 3–5 hours for a solid scoop ice cream. Remove from the freezer 20 minutes prior to scooping, and use a scoop warmed under hot water.)

Keep the remainder of the fudge chunks handy in the freezer until ready to serve.

The ice cream will keep in the freezer for up to 1 week, but it's always best when fresh.

♥ *Bananas are rich in potassium, which is a key player in cell integrity. It maintains electrolyte balance and internal fluids, keeping cells hydrated and skin internally moisturised.*

Raw Carrot Cake

←——————————————————→

Makes 9 squares

Carrot cake has to be one of my coffee-shop favourites. The combination of fragrant spices and moist texture, combined with sweet, buttery icing is irresistible! This super-simple raw version, with an added dollop of dairy-free cinnamon cream, recreates that flavour combination perfectly.
As kids, my sister and I always preferred eating raw cake mixture straight from the bowl. I never really understood the point of putting it in the oven to bake when the pre-baked stuff tasted so good! The beauty of raw recipes – aside from ease of preparation – is that you don't have the hassle of baking. Plus you get to do the one thing you always loved as a kid: eating the mixture straight from the bowl.

FOR THE CAKE
100g walnuts, chopped
100g raisins
100ml melted coconut oil
100g ground almonds
5 carrots, grated
3 apples, peeled, cored and finely
    chopped
1 teaspoon ground cinnamon
1 teaspoon ground cloves
1 teaspoon ground allspice
Pinch of ground ginger
Pinch of grated nutmeg
Pinch of salt

FOR THE CINNAMON CASHEW
    CREAM
200g cashew nuts, soaked in
    warm water for 1–2 hours,
    then drained
150ml coconut milk
4 medjool dates, pitted
2 tablespoons coconut oil
2 teaspoons ground cinnamon
1 tablespoon maple syrup

TO DECORATE
Grated carrot
Chopped walnuts

Combine the carrot cake ingredients together well in a large mixing bowl.

Spoon into a 15cm-square silicone baking tray, flatten down using a spatula and place in the freezer for an hour to set.

Meanwhile, blitz all the cinnamon cashew cream ingredients in a blender to create a smooth topping. Use a spatula to smooth the cream over the chilled carrot cake and return to the freezer for an hour.

Use a sharp knife to cut the carrot cake carefully into squares and serve decorated with grated carrot and chopped walnuts.

These carrot cake squares will keep in the fridge for 3–5 days.

♥ *Carrots contain high amounts of beta-carotene and lots of vitamin A. They offer many health benefits and their combination of vitamins and antioxidants is particularly beneficial for the eyes, skin, digestive system and teeth.*

Apple *and* Blackberry Crumble

⟵⟶

Serves 4

This delicious fruit crumble is so simple to make. I love to bake it in a huge ceramic dish and add lots of warming spices, which apart from anything else make the kitchen smell heavenly. If the fruit you use is very ripe, you shouldn't need too much added honey to sweeten the recipe and the crumble topping works brilliantly made with a combination of almond flour, coconut oil and chopped nuts and seeds.

200g apples

100g pears

200g blackberries

Juice of ½ lemon

1 tablespoon manuka honey (more if the fruit isn't too ripe)

1 teaspoon ground mixed spice

FOR THE CRUMBLE

200g almond flour

100g mixed chopped nuts and seeds

3 tablespoons melted coconut oil

1 tablespoon manuka honey

1 teaspoon ground mixed spice

Preheat the oven to 180°C/fan 160°C/gas mark 4.

Peel and core the apples and pears and cut them into 2cm dice. Put them in a mixing bowl with the blackberries. Squeeze over the lemon juice and stir in the honey and spices.

Transfer the fruit to a large ceramic pie dish.

To make the crumble, stir together the almond flour, chopped nuts and seeds, coconut oil, honey and spices in a separate bowl until well combined.

Sprinkle the crumble topping evenly over the fruit. Bake in the oven for 25–35 minutes or until the fruit is cooked and bubbling juices seep through the crumble.

Why not try serving it piping hot with a splodge of thick, dreamy Cinnamon Cashew Cream (see page 158).

♥ *The vitamin C in high-antioxidant foods like apples and pears helps increase the skin's immunity and has anti-ageing effects because it promotes skin cell renewal.*

Rice Cacao Crispy Cakes

←————————————→

Makes 10–15 mini cakes

As a kid I used to love making rice crispy cakes. It was one of those simple recipes made with puffed cereal and melted chocolate that we'd always be allowed as a treat at birthday parties! This version is perfect for children's parties and comes without the downside of sugary cereal and milk chocolate.

2 tablespoons almond butter
4 tablespoons manuka honey
2 tablespoons coconut oil
2 tablespoons raw cacao powder
Pinch of ground cinnamon
150g puffed brown rice crisps (buy natural ones, free from added salt and refined sugar)

Line 1 or 2 silicone muffin trays with cup-cake cases.

Gently melt the almond butter, honey and coconut oil over a low heat.

Mix in the cacao powder and a pinch of cinnamon and keep stirring until everything is smooth and combined.

Allow to cool for 10 minutes, then stir in the puffed rice crisps.

Scoop heaped tablespoons of the chocolate rice crisps into the lined muffin trays.

Place in the freezer for an hour, then transfer to the fridge and leave overnight.

These crispy cakes will keep for a day or so before turning chewy.

♥ *Manuka honey is produced in New Zealand by bees that gather pollen and nectar from the native manuka bush. It is used in both traditional and modern skin medicines for its natural antibacterial properties. It is a potent anti-inflammatory, which soothes inflamed skin while healing blemishes.*

Super-rich Chocolate Truffles

←————————————→

Makes 10

Truffles are traditionally made with thick double cream and sugar. These beauties are equally rich, but they're made using creamy avocado and manuka honey, which makes them so much healthier. Vitamin E is great for the skin, and fantastic when it's obtained from natural sources such as avocados.

1 ripe avocado
4 heaped tablespoons raw cacao powder, plus extra for dusting
2 tablespoons manuka honey
3 Brazil nuts
1 teaspoon melted coconut oil

Blitz all the ingredients together in a high-powered blender until perfectly smooth, then transfer to a bowl. Place in the fridge for a couple of hours to set and firm up a little.

Use a tablespoon to scoop a spoonful of truffle from the bowl, sprinkle liberally with cacao powder and carefully roll into a ball.

Roll the ball in extra cacao powder and place in the fridge to firm up.

Repeat until you have used up all the mixture.

These rich, delicious treats are best kept in the fridge and eaten within a day or two.

♥ *The selenium in Brazil nuts is a powerful antioxidant. It works alongside other antioxidants such as vitamins E and C and is essential for a healthy immune system. Just 4 or 5 Brazil nuts a day cover your recommended daily amount.*

Vegan Blackberry Marble Cheesecake

Makes 6–8 slices

This is such a pretty cake to make. It's gluten-free, dairy-free and requires no baking. And because it's frozen you can make it well in advance. Simply remove the cake from the freezer to thaw and decorate with fresh berries and edible dried flower petals before serving. It makes such a gorgeous summer party centrepiece.

FOR THE BASE
250g pitted dates, chopped
75g almonds
75g Brazil nuts
3 tablespoons melted coconut oil

FOR THE CREAM TOPPING
200g cashew nuts, soaked in
    warm water for 1–2 hours,
    then drained
Juice of ½ lemon
2 tablespoons maple syrup
3 tablespoons melted coconut oil
1 teaspoon vanilla extract
400ml can coconut milk
150g blackberries

TO DECORATE
Blackberries
Edible dried rose petals and/or
    cornflowers

Blitz the base ingredients in a food processor until they resemble sticky breadcrumbs. Press into an 18cm springform round cake tin. Place in the freezer for an hour.

To make the topping, blitz the soaked cashews, lemon juice, maple syrup, coconut oil, vanilla extract and 300ml of the coconut milk together to form a rich, thick cream. Separately blitz the blackberries and remaining coconut milk.

Pour the cashew cream topping on to the frozen cake base and carefully swirl through the blackberry cream to create a beautiful marbled effect. Return to the freezer to set (about 1–2 hours).

Transfer from the freezer to the fridge for a couple of hours, slice and leave to stand at room temperature for 20 minutes to thaw before serving.

Decorate with fresh blackberries and rose petals and/ or cornflowers.

♥ *The vitamins A, C and K in blackberries are excellent for skin rejuvenation. What's more, their seeds are rich in omega-3 and omega-6 fatty acids, vital for healthy skin.*

Innocent Millionaire's Shortbread

←————————————————→

Makes 8–10

These delicious millionaire's shortbread bites are so tasty it's hard to believe they're good for you! Unlike the traditional version, which is full of refined sugar and wheat flour, these are made using nuts, lots of coconut oil and delicious raw cacao. Cacao is one of the world's best sources of antioxidants, so you can eat these bites with your halo firmly in place, assured that they're actually benefiting your skin. These will also keep in the freezer for a month or two, so you always have a delicious sweet snack to hand.

FOR THE SHORTBREAD BASE
150g ground almonds
75g Brazil nuts
50g pitted dates, chopped
3 tablespoons melted coconut oil

FOR THE CARAMEL LAYER
100ml coconut oil
3 heaped tablespoons almond
   butter
Generous pinch of salt
8 medjool dates, pitted
2 tablespoons maple syrup

FOR THE CHOCOLATE LAYER
100ml coconut oil
4 heaped tablespoons raw cacao
   powder
2 tablespoons manuka honey

First make the base by combining all the ingredients in a food processor and blitzing until the mixture forms a chunky paste.

Push the mixture down into the base of a silicone tray, approx. 15cm square, until it's about 1cm thick. Pop in the freezer.

Next make the caramel layer by combining all of the ingredients together in a high-speed blender until you have a smooth, gooey texture.

Spoon the thick caramel mixture over the cooled base and smooth out until even. Place into the freezer for an hour until hard.

For the chocolate layer, heat the coconut oil in a saucepan until melted. Remove from the heat and stir in the raw cacao powder and manuka honey until the mixture is chocolaty and smooth. Pour this over the caramel layer and return to the freezer for 30 minutes. Remove and cut into squares.

Store the bites in the freezer and remove 30 minutes before serving to allow them to soften a little.

♥ *The polyphenol antioxidants in cacao belong to the same group of antioxidants found in green tea. These protect our cells from premature oxidation and destruction and can keep us looking and feeling younger for longer.*

Turmeric *and* Ginger Chia Chocolate Pudding

Makes 2

Turmeric and ginger have so many incredible health properties. The ground versions are great for recipes, but if you're able to use the actual roots they'll often prove even more beneficial. Fresh ginger root, for example, is not only superior in flavour but also contains higher levels of gingerol, its active, beneficial constituent. Added to freshly pressed juices, turmeric and ginger provide a real kick. I also love making turmeric milk, which can be drunk on its own or used to create a delicious chia seed pudding such as this one.

1 ripe pear
Thumb-sized chunk of ginger
Thumb-sized chunk of
    turmeric root
100ml almond milk
1 teaspoon plus 1 tablespoon
    manuka honey
3 tablespoons chia seeds
½ large avocado
2 dates, pitted
1 tablespoon raw cacao powder
1 tablespoon manuka honey
Drop of almond milk (optional)
Pinch of ground black pepper

TO SERVE
10 raspberries
20g flaked almonds

Run the pear, ginger root and turmeric root through a juicer. Add the liquid to a large measuring jug with the almond milk and stir in 1 teaspoon of the honey and the chia seeds.

Leave the chia seeds to absorb the liquid – within 30 minutes they will gradually have expanded and turned into a jelly pudding. Place in the fridge until needed.

Blitz together the avocado, dates, cacao, remaining honey and a pinch of pepper. Depending on how ripe the avocado is, you may need to add a drop of almond milk to blend everything together smoothly. You want the mixture to achieve the consistency of chocolate mousse.

Spoon the set chia pudding equally into two glasses or bowls, top with a spoonful of chocolate mousse and scatter over some raspberries and flaked almonds before serving.

♥ *Ginger and turmeric have so many wonderful skin-healing benefits. Ginger has around 40 antioxidant properties that prevent free-radical damage and protect against ageing. It also evens skin tone and improves elasticity. Adding turmeric to your diet can help counter the harmful effects of sun-damage, ultraviolet radiation and the formation of wrinkles and dark spots.*

Ginger Rhubarb *with* Chia Seed Custard

Makes 4

Rhubarb is the one thing that grows magically in my garden each year without fail. It usually appears in April and lasts a month or two, depending on how quickly I use it. Rhubarb and custard is one of those wonderful, typically English desserts, and I love this version made with dairy-free custard thickened by those super-healthy chia seeds.

½ lemon

3 pears

Thumb-sized chunk of ginger

1 tablespoon manuka honey

4 rhubarb sticks

FOR THE CUSTARD

200ml almond milk

2 tablespoons manuka honey

3 free-range egg yolks

1 teaspoon vanilla extract

5 tablespoons chia seeds

Grate the zest from the lemon half, then run the fruit through a juicer along with the pears and ginger. Pour the juice into a saucepan and add the honey and lemon zest.

Roughly chop the rhubarb sticks and add them to the pan. Bring to the boil, then lower the heat and simmer for 5 minutes until the rhubarb is soft and cooked, but still retains its shape.

Meanwhile, to make the custard, gently warm the almond milk and honey in a separate saucepan.

Turn the heat off and carefully whisk the egg yolks and vanilla extract into the milk. Allow to cool, then stir in the chia seeds. Leave to stand for 5–10 minutes and then stir again (this just helps prevent the seeds clumping).

Divide the rhubarb evenly between four glasses and serve each topped with a large spoonful of chia seed custard.

♥ *Rhubarb contains lots of vitamin A, which is a natural antioxidant. This can neutralise the free radicals in your body, delaying the signs of ageing such as fine lines and wrinkles.*

Tiramisu *in a* Jar

$\longleftrightarrow$

Makes 2

This is such a wonderfully indulgent, rich chocolate dessert. Most definitely one of my dinner-party favourites. The secret to making a delicious caffeine- and alcohol-free tiramisu is raw cacao nibs. You can think of cacao nibs as unprocessed chocolate. They look like a cross between coffee beans and chopped nuts and their flavour is extremely bitter, even more bitter than that of dark chocolate. They taste almost like an alcoholic liquor, even though they contain no alcohol whatsoever. It's this intense, bitter flavour that makes them perfect for making a healthy tiramisu.

2 scoops of ground espresso
  decaffeinated coffee

FOR THE BASE
75g ground almonds
1 teaspoon manuka honey
Drop of vanilla extract
2 teaspoons raw cacao powder

FOR THE MIDDLE LAYER
50g cashew nuts, soaked in
  warm water for 1–2 hours,
  then drained
100ml coconut milk
Drop of manuka honey
Drop of vanilla extract
1 teaspoon coconut oil

FOR THE TOP LAYER
½ large ripe avocado
2 tablespoons raw cacao powder
1 tablespoon raw cacao nibs
1 teaspoon manuka honey
Drop of vanilla extract

TO SERVE
Raw cacao nibs or grated
  dark chocolate

Make 2 small cups of decaf. espresso coffee and set to one side.

Place the ingredients for the base in a mixing bowl, add one of the cups of warm espresso coffee and stir well. Divide the base evenly between two jars and place in the fridge to cool.

Meanwhile, blitz together all the ingredients for the middle layer in a food processor to form a smooth cream. Place in a bowl in the fridge to set.

Finally, blitz together all the ingredients for the top layer, then slowly add the remaining cup of espresso until the mixture forms a rich, smooth chocolate cream (you may only need half a cup, depending on the ripeness of the avocado). Place in the fridge.

Now spoon the middle layer on top of the cooled base layer in the jars, and finish with the top layer. Decorate with raw cacao nibs or grated dark chocolate and return to the fridge until ready to serve.

♥ *Raw cacao has been shown to improve digestion, thanks to the fibre it contains that stimulates the body's digestive enzymes. Enriched with minerals and vitamins including vitamin C, magnesium and omega-6 fatty acids, cacao promotes blood flow and can increase cellular healing to give the skin a beautiful, youthful glow.*

Raw Banoffee Pie

← →

Serves 4

This is one of my most favourite ever dinner-party dessert recipes. Not only is it simple to make with no baking involved, but the three layers complement each other so wonderfully. I find the contrasts of texture, velvety cream, salt and sweetness work beautifully.
This stunning dessert can be made a day in advance and stored in the fridge. Then simply add a freshly chopped banana and some cacao nibs to serve.

FOR THE BASE
100g almonds
100g pecans
100g gluten-free rolled oats
100g pitted dates, chopped
½ teaspoon ground cinnamon
2 tablespoons coconut oil
1 tablespoon maple syrup
1 tablespoon almond butter
Pinch of salt

FOR THE TOFFEE
100g medjool dates, pitted
4 tablespoons almond butter
2 tablespoons maple syrup
1 teaspoon vanilla bean powder
Pinch of salt

FOR THE CREAM
Cream from 400ml can coconut
   milk (chilled overnight in the
   fridge so that the cream sits on top)
100g cashew nuts, soaked in warm
   water for 1–2 hours,
   then drained
2 ripe bananas
1 tablespoon coconut oil
3 medjool dates, pitted

TO SERVE
1 banana, chopped
1 teaspoon raw cacao nibs

First make the base. Put the almonds and pecans in a food processor and process until coarse. Add the oats, dates, cinnamon and salt and pulse until the mixture resembles coarse sand.

Add the coconut oil, maple syrup and almond butter and process until the mixture comes together. The dough should feel sticky when pressed between your fingers. If necessary, add a teaspoon of water and blitz again. Spoon the base mixture into a 20cm round shallow glass pie dish, press down firmly and transfer to the freezer for 15–20 minutes to set.

Next make the toffee. Put the pitted dates in a bowl and pour boiling water over the top to cover. Leave for 5–10 minutes, then drain the dates (discarding the water) and add them to the food processor along with the almond butter, maple syrup, vanilla bean powder and salt. Process until smooth. Remove the chilled base from the freezer and use a spatula to spread the toffee layer evenly on top. Return to the freezer for a further 15 minutes.

For the cream, open the can of chilled coconut milk and carefully scoop the white cream off the top using a spoon.

Add the coconut cream, soaked cashews, ripe bananas, coconut oil and medjool dates to the food processor and blitz until smooth and combined. Spoon the banana cream on to the chilled toffee layer and place in the fridge until ready to serve.

Serve decorated with fresh banana and cacao nibs.

♥ *Thanks to their high levels of vitamin B6, bananas reduce swelling, protect against type 2 diabetes, aid weight loss, strengthen the nervous system and help with the production of white blood cells. In addition, dates contain vitamin A which protects the eyes and maintains healthy skin and mucous membranes.*

Salted Caramel Nut Butter Cake

Makes 10–12 slices

This recipe contains a ton of good fats in the form of coconut oil, nuts and nut butter. In fact it's pretty much made up of all my favourite raw dessert recipe ingredients and I can't even begin to tell you how incredible it tastes. It's super rich, so you really need only a very thin slice, but you can quite easily store it for a month or two in the freezer, so there's plenty of time to get through the lot yourself if you're not in a sharing mood! I love making this for friends' birthdays. It looks so impressive it's hard to believe it's healthy.

FOR THE BASE LAYER
200g pitted dates, chopped
200g mixed nuts
100ml melted coconut oil
2 heaped tablespoons raw cacao
powder

FOR THE CARAMEL LAYER
250g almond butter
100ml coconut oil
2 tablespoons maple syrup
4 pinches of pink Himalayan salt
200g cashew nuts, soaked in
warm water for 1–2 hours,
then drained

FOR THE TOPPING
100ml coconut oil
1 tablespoon maple syrup
3 heaped tablespoons raw cacao
powder
Chopped and whole hazelnuts

TO SERVE
Chopped nuts
Grated lime zest

Blitz together all the base layer ingredients in a powerful food processor until they have a sticky, breadcrumb texture. Press into the bottom of a 20cm springform round cake tin and place in the freezer.

For the caramel, melt the almond butter, coconut oil, syrup and salt in a small saucepan over a low heat. Allow to cool for 10 minutes, then tip into the food processor, add the soaked cashews and blitz. Spoon the mixture on to the base layer, use a spatula to spread it evenly and return the tin to the freezer.

For the topping, melt the coconut oil and maple syrup in a pan over a low heat and stir in the cacao powder until it has dissolved to create a rich chocolate sauce.

Remove the cake tin from the freezer and pour the melted chocolate sauce over the caramel layer. The cake should be so cold from the freezer that the top layer sets quickly.

Store in the freezer and transfer to the fridge for an hour or two before serving to allow the cake to soften a little.

Decorate with chopped nuts and grated lime zest to serve.

♥ *Coconut oil has so many incredible benefits. It strengthens the immune system because it contains antimicrobial lipids, lauric acid, capric acid and caprylic acid, all of which have antifungal, antibacterial and antiviral properties. Candida overgrowth is a problem caused by uncontrolled growth of a yeast –* Candida albicans *– in the gut. Coconut oil provides relief from the inflammation caused by candida, both externally and internally.*

SKIN CARE

Manuka Honey *and* Almond Oil Cleanser

⟵————————————⟶

Makes enough for 1 cleansing

This simple combination is a wonderful, natural facial cleanser, ideal for lifting everyday dirt and grime.

1 teaspoon manuka honey
1 teaspoon almond oil

Place the jar of honey in a bowl of hot water to warm it a little.

Mix a teaspoon of the melted honey with a teaspoon of almond oil.

Use the mixture on a cotton pad to cleanse your skin.

Make the cleanser fresh as needed and use once or twice daily.

Avocado *and* Manuka Honey Face Mask

⟵————————————⟶

Makes 1 mask

Avocado is one of my favourite-ever foods. Blitzed into a fresh guacamole or scooped straight from the skin with a spoon, I just love it! Applied to the skin, avocado offers benefits too. Avocado face masks are amazing for nourishing and revitalising the skin. Packed with skin-friendly minerals such as iron, calcium, potassium, copper and magnesium, vitamins A, E, B and K and unsaturated fats, this homemade mask is perfect for acne-prone and dry or sensitive skin.

1 ripe avocado, halved and stoned
1 tablespoon manuka honey

Scoop the avocado flesh into a bowl and, using the back of a fork, mash it to a creamy pulp.

Add the manuka honey and stir until it becomes a uniform paste.

Apply to the skin and leave on for 10–15 minutes.

Rinse off the mixture with lukewarm water and pat dry your face with a soft, clean towel.

Avocados go off quickly, so this face mask will need to be used within an hour of preparation. I love using this at least once a week.

Banana *and* Soda Face Mask

←——————————————→

Makes 1 mask

This mask is brilliant for combating wrinkles, removing pimples, brightening the complexion and so much more. Bananas protect the skin from free radicals, helping to delay the ageing process. The potassium in bananas combats dry skin by moisturising and hydrating skin cells.

The addition of bicarbonate of soda breaks down grime and dirt, and helps remove excess oil which can clog skin pores and lead to acne breakouts.

1 ripe banana
1 teaspoon bicarbonate of soda

Peel the banana and use a spoon or fork to mash it in a bowl until it forms a smooth, lump-free pulp.

Add the bicarbonate of soda and mix thoroughly. If the mixture seems too thick to apply, add a little water.

Apply to the face and leave on for 10–15 minutes.

Rinse off the mixture with lukewarm water and pat dry your face with a soft, clean towel.

Once peeled, bananas go off quickly, so this face mask will need to be used within an hour of preparation.

This is a fantastic mask to use once a week or whenever skin feels particularly dry.

Manuka Honey *and* Cinnamon Mask

←——————————————→

Makes 1 mask

Honey is so incredible sticky, and cinnamon is all warm and spicy. So you might think these are two things you'd want to avoid getting anywhere near your face! Surprisingly, although it might sound a little odd, manuka honey and cinnamon make a killer duo when it comes to combating acne. Cinnamon has antimicrobial properties, so it can help prevent bacteria from getting out of hand. Manuka honey is a natural antibiotic, and has the remarkable ability to promote fast healing and prevent infections.

It may seem more obvious to apply the mask before you shower, meaning you can wash it straight off. But waiting until using this after your shower will benefit the skin so much more because the steam from a warm shower will have opened up your pores.

2 tablespoons manuka honey
1 teaspoon ground cinnamon

Mix together the honey and cinnamon until they are thoroughly blended and have formed a paste.

This mask is really sticky, so you might want to use a clean soft foundation brush to apply it to your face. Applying with a brush ensures that most of it ends up on your face, not over your fingers, clothes or the floor, and it makes it easier to focus on those real problem areas.

Leave on for 10–15 minutes, then rinse off the mixture with lukewarm water and pat dry your face with a soft, clean towel.

This is a wonderful mask to use once or twice a week.

Scar-reduction Combination

←——————————→

Makes 125ml

Skin conditions such as acne, psoriasis and eczema can leave visible scars even after clearing. I likened my psoriasis scars to little dalmatian spots all over my body. Although not all scars and stretch marks will completely heal, you can certainly make visible improvements by using the right combination of essential oils.

For scar reduction, rosehip oil remains my favourite carrier oil. It can lighten scarring, reduce wrinkles, regenerate skin and help the skin regain its natural tone and colour. Combined with frankincense oil, it not only smells heavenly, but the frankincense also promotes cell regeneration and reduces the appearance of stretch marks and scars. Calendula oil is a common ingredient in skin treatments because it has wound-healing, antifungal, antibacterial and anti-inflammatory properties. In combination with other healing ingredients calendula ointment has been shown to effectively treat and heal scar tissue. I include lavender to lessen pain and itching and promote rapid healing.

125ml rosehip oil
20 drops frankincense oil
10 drops calendula oil
10 drops lavender oil

Combine all the ingredients in a dark glass bottle and store in a cool, dark place for up to 6 months.

Apply to your skin with clean fingers, and blot with a tissue if required to remove excess oil.

Use a few drops of oil gently to massage cleansed face, neck and décolletage or on tummy stretch marks or body scars. Apply morning and night.

Soothing Scalp Solution

←——————————→

Makes enough for 2 applications

An inadequate diet, poor hydration, use of chemical shampoos or underlying conditions such as eczema and psoriasis can all result in irritated, flaky skin on the scalp. Medicated shampoos can sometimes offer a short-term fix, but avoid using them long term because often the problem will come back worse.

If the scalp is a particularly problematic area for you, try this combination of essential oils, which can soothe and calm dry, irritated skin. In fact, jojoba isn't an oil but a mix of liquid wax esters that, structurally and chemically, closely resemble human sebum, which means it doesn't clog pores. It makes a great carrier for the essential oils here.

3 tablespoons jojoba oil
10 drops lavender oil
8 drops tea tree oil
8 drops rosemary oil

FOR THE RINSE
500ml warm water
2 tablespoons apple cider vinegar

Mix together the oils thoroughly.

Take a shower to wet your hair and scalp but don't use shampoo. Using the tips of your fingers, massage the oil into your damp hair and scalp.

Cover with a shower cap or wrap your head in a towel and leave for an hour or two.

Rinse thoroughly with warm water. Shampoo gently. Then, as a final rinse, use a 500ml jug of warm water with the apple cider vinegar stirred in.

Use every other day until the flakes on your scalp begin to reduce. Then switch to using once a week.

Natural All-spice Bronzer

←————————————————→

Makes 1 small pot

This bronzer is so simple to make and it smells divine. I smile every time I apply this to my face, it's so lovely to bronze my cheeks with the sweet scent of spices as opposed to a ton of chemicals. By adjusting the proportions of spice you can tone it to your skin throughout the seasons. Although I've suggested a teaspoon of each spice, the quantity can vary depending upon the shade you're looking to achieve.

Cinnamon is a really skin-friendly spice. It helps to prevent and fight skin infections and improves the overall quality, texture and complexion of skin.

2 tablespoons cornflour
1 teaspoon ground cloves
1 teaspoon grated nutmeg
1 teaspoon ground cinnamon

Scoop the cornflour into a mixing bowl and begin to add the ground spices a little at a time, stirring everything together. It may take a little trial and error to get the combination just right for your complexion, but once you've perfected it the beauty of these ingredients is that you can add and amend throughout the year as your skin tone changes from winter through to summer. Cornflour naturally lightens the powder and nutmeg adds darker tones.

Store in a pot with a screw-on lid and apply using a bronzing brush.

This powder smells absolutely delicious and should feel feather light on your skin. You can use it daily and remove it using my Manuka Honey and Almond Oil Cleanser (see page 178).

Soothing Vanilla Lip Balm

←——————————————→

Makes 4–6 small tins

Beeswax and cocoa butter are essential in any luscious lip balm as they are so naturally nourishing. They soften the skin, forming a protective coating and defend against the elements. Beeswax also has antibacterial properties which aid in healing sore, chapped lips and I love the tasty addition of sweet, soothing vanilla oil.

1 tablespoon beeswax pearls (also called pellets or pastilles)
1 tablespoon pure shea butter
2 tablespoons sweet almond oil
6 drops vanilla oil

Bring a saucepan of water to the boil and gently simmer.

Place a heatproof glass bowl on top of the saucepan over the boiling water.

Melt the beeswax, shea butter and almond oil together in the bowl and gently stir as the mixture melts.

Once the mixture has become liquid, remove from the heat and immediately stir in the vanilla oil.

Quickly transfer the finished liquid into a jug to make it easier to decant. Then carefully pour it into lip-balm tins or tubes.

Let the balms cool completely until solid, about 20–30 minutes. Store in a cool, dry place for up to 1 year, or longer in the fridge.

Shea Butter, Raw Chocolate *and* Peppermint Lip Balm

←——————————————→

Makes 4–6 small tins

I love the delicious, chocolaty, minty taste of this lip balm. Not only is the flavour divine, but the ingredients also have incredibly beneficial moisturising properties. Beeswax has a number of benefits for the skin, including an anti-inflammatory action that helps to calm and soothe. The concentration of natural vitamins and fatty acids in shea butter means it is incredibly nourishing and moisturising. And peppermint oil can aid in oil secretion in skin, which makes it wonderful for healing cracked and chapped lips.

2 tablespoons coconut oil
1 tablespoon shea butter
1 tablespoon sweet almond oil
2 tablespoons beeswax
1 teaspoon raw cacao powder
5 drops peppermint oil

Bring a saucepan of water to the boil and gently simmer.

Place a heatproof glass bowl on top of the saucepan over the boiling water. Add the coconut oil, shea butter, almond oil and beeswax to the bowl and gently stir as the mixture melts.

Once the mixture has become liquid, remove from the heat and stir in the cacao powder and peppermint oil.

Quickly transfer the finished liquid into a jug to make it easier to decant. Then carefully pour it into lip-balm tins or tubes.

Let the balms cool completely until solid, about 20–30 minutes. Store in a cool, dry place for up to 1 year, or longer in the fridge.

Dead Sea Salt, Lemon *and* Rosemary Sports Scrub

←—————————————→

Makes enough for 8–10 baths

This is without doubt one of my favourite natural body scrubs. Not only does it smell clean and fresh, but it also comes with a ton of skin health benefits. The unique combination of minerals found in Dead Sea salt have proved incredibly beneficial for skin conditions such as psoriasis. Here the other ingredients bring their own skin benefits too: lemons are alkaline and full of vitamin C, while almond oil can calm conditions such as dermatitis and eczema and also assist with the skin's elasticity, working to reduce stretch marks and scars. Putting salt and lemon on cut or broken skin is going to sting – literally rubbing salt into the wound! So take it easy if you want to use it for body brushing, or allow it to dissolve in bath water rather than rubbing it directly into your skin's surface.

500g fine Dead Sea salt
5 tablespoons almond oil
Zest of 1 and juice of 2 lemons
3 rosemary sprigs

Add the salt to a bowl and stir in the almond oil and the lemon zest and juice. Stir well and leave to sit while you finely chop the rosemary leaves.

Add the leaves to the bowl and stir well. Spoon the combined ingredients into a sealable glass jar.

Use a handful as a scrub directly on unbroken skin or add a scoop to your bath if you prefer. I like to use this scrub two or three times a week.

Because this scrub is free from chemical preservatives, use within a few weeks or store in the fridge.

Soothing Dead Sea Salt Exfoliant

←—————————————→

Makes 1 large jar

Used for centuries by the Egyptians to promote beautiful and radiant skin, geranium oil can treat acne, reduce inflammation, alleviate anxiety and balance hormones. Similarly, patchouli oil has been shown to assist in the treatment of eczema, dermatitis, psoriasis and sores. Combined with Dead Sea salt, these oils make a sweet-smelling, relaxing body scrub that is a wonderful, calming exfoliant.

300g fine Dead Sea salt
150ml almond oil
6 drops geranium oil
6 drops patchouli oil

Put the Dead Sea salt in a clean, dry bowl, add the almond oil and mix with a wooden spoon.

Mix in the geranium and patchouli oils.

Store in a sterilised glass jar and use once a week as a soothing, relaxing, all-over body exfoliant.

Because this scrub is free from chemical preservatives, use within a few weeks or store in the fridge.

Calming Jojoba Bubble Bath

←——————————————→

Makes enough for 5 baths

The reason commercial foams are so foamy is down to the chemicals they contain – usually sodium laurel sulfate (see page 31). Without it a good 'shop-like' bubble bath is hard to concoct. I'm not going to lie and promise you those big, foaming, chemical bubbles, because homemade bubble bath is nowhere near as bubbly, but it's equally cleansing and I'd much rather soak in this sweet-smelling, natural combination than a bath full of chemicals any day.

Castile soap is a vegetable soap traditionally made from 100 per cent pure olive oil, water and lye. It's believed to have originated from a region in Spain historically called Castile – hence its the name. Available in health-food stores and easy to find online, Castile soap is available in bar or liquid form.

Jojoba oil closely resembles sebum, an oily substance naturally produced by the oil glands just below our skin's surface. It also has anti-inflammatory properties that help in reducing inflammation caused by skin dryness.

250ml Castile soap (liquid form)
80ml vegetable glycerine
15 drops jojoba oil

Stir the ingredients together gently – you don't want to make bubbles just yet.

To use, pour half a cup under running water and agitate the water to create bigger bubbles.

This should keep for 2–3 months in a glass bottle stored in a cool, dark place.

Skin-soothing Sandalwood Bath Oil

←——————————————→

Makes 125ml

Of all the aromatherapy oil combinations I use in the bath, this has to be my absolute favourite. Sandalwood has such a deep, exotic scent – it warms you, lifts your mood and creates a soothing, sensual atmosphere. In addition to its grounding, de-stressing effect on the emotions, sandalwood is also especially good for healing skin, making this aromatherapy bath oil perfect for conditions such as eczema and psoriasis.

Lavender instantly triggers your body to calm the nervous system and relax your muscles, whilst ylang ylang can prove extremely effective in maintaining moisture and the oil balance of the skin to keep it looking hydrated, smooth and young.

25 drops sandalwood oil
10 drops lavender oil
2 drops ylang ylang oil
125ml jojoba or sweet almond oil

Combine all the ingredients in a dark glass bottle and store in a cool, dark place for up to 6 months.

Run the bath, then pour in 1 tablespoon of the oil and relax. Use once or twice a week to help heal problem skin.

Oatmeal *and* Lavender Bath Soak

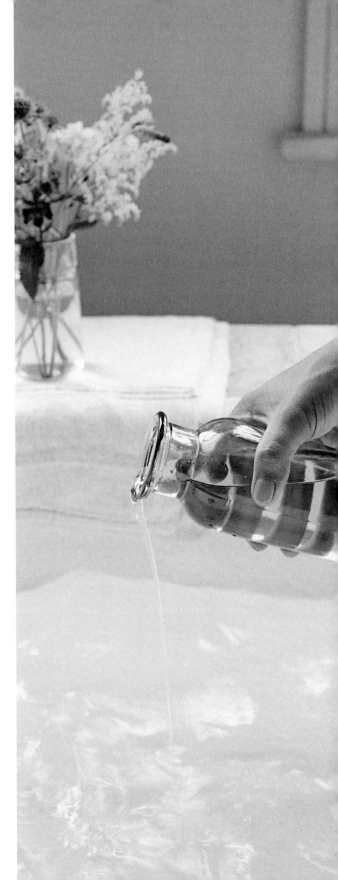

Makes 2 bags

This incredible combination of oats and lavender really helps to soothe itchy, irritated skin and leaves it feeling super-soft. If you struggle with skin irritations such as eczema or psoriasis, this gentle blend is ideal for everyday use. Often used in masks, scrubs and other skincare products, oatmeal soothes dry, irritated, itchy skin while gently cleansing pores. Lavender is beautifully calming and the flowers contain antiseptic properties which can reduce inflammation and aches.

200g rolled oats
50g dried lavender flowers
5–10 drops lavender oil

2 small muslin bags or cheesecloths

Scoop the whole oats into a food processor and pulse to create a fine powder.

Add the oatmeal to a bowl and mix in the dried lavender flowers and lavender oil. Stir together well.

Divide the mixture evenly between two muslin bags or cheesecloths, pull the drawstring tight and tie a double knot. Seal the bags in a glass jar and store in a cool, dark place for up to 3 months.

Submerge a bag in your bath water or rub the wet bag gently over your skin so that it acts as a mild exfoliator to slough away any dead dry skin cells.

Index

⟷

Acknowledgements

There have been so many people involved in my story and transforming it into this beautiful book. If I begin to try and thank everybody individually I am bound to miss someone out. Needless to say, I am enormously grateful to all my family and friends for your continued love, encouragement and taste testing!

A special thank you to Rachel who has been with me on this journey from day one. Rach, I could not ask for a better friend, your support and enthusiasm have been constant and unwavering. I know that seeing my health and skin change through food and juicing inspired you to do the same and I love that this message is instilled in Grace and Freya as they grow up. I've never met anyone who adores those green juices as much as Gracie J!

To my fantastic agent Becky: for completely understanding my story and mission from the moment we met. You helped transform my jumble of words into something clear and concise that I know will change lives. You turned my dream vision for this book into reality and kept me grounded all the way. I hope I am allowed to get excited now?!

To my wonderful publishers: Kyle and Judith, thank you for having such faith in me and enabling me to share my story with the world. Tara, your diplomacy, patience and attention to detail are just brilliant. Thank you for guiding me effortlessly through this process. And to Amberley for doing so alongside you. To the photoshoot team for making my time in London so much fun; Emily and Anna for creating and styling my recipes to look incredible and providing constant entertainment in the kitchen! My photographer Jo for your glowing loveliness and of course incredible photography. To Stephanie for helping me get the words just right. And Tania, thank you for transforming all those words into such beautifully designed, easy to read chapters, which I know will make this mountain of information much easier to take in.

To everyone involved in the health and wellness fraternity, especially the writers, bloggers and magazine editors who have told their stories and helped me to share mine, I'm honoured to be part of this brilliantly supportive collective. A huge thank you to Lucy Bee - I love your products and ethos - your endorsement and kind encouragement mean the absolute world.

To those whose testimonials feature in this book; Warda, from the moment I read your first email I knew you had your healing journey sussed. You approached it with such positivity and enthusiasm and we continue to follow very similar paths. Your words of thanks are so lovely and I have absolute faith that you too will inspire people to get truly well again. Amy, the pictures and messages you sent me on day one were heartbreaking. I absolutely felt your pain. You've come such a long way and those pictures will undoubtedly help others. You are amazing and your skin looks incredible. Alice, I know just how hard you have worked to come this far - on your mind, body and soul. You took time out to heal and followed your heart and passions in life. I'm so proud of you and it's amazing that your wellness journey has led you down a whole new path. I wish you continued success in your exciting venture.

Finally, to everyone who has been kind enough to share stories and photographs with me. The one thing I've learned is that whilst our skin problems and healing patterns may vary slightly, we've experienced many of the same emotional battles along the way. I am incredibly proud and thankful to be a part of such a strong, inspiring little community.